1998

# Leisure and
# Leisure Services
## in the 21st Century

*by*

*Geoffrey Godbey*

# Leisure and
# Leisure Services
## in the 21st Century

*by*

*Geoffrey Godbey*

 **Venture Publishing, Inc.**
State College, PA

Production Manager:  Richard Yocum
Manuscript Editing and Design:  Michele L. Barbin
Additional Editing:  Matthew S. Weaver
Cover Design/Illustration:  Sandra Sikorski, Sikorski Design

Library of Congress Catalogue Card Number 97-61792
ISBN 0-910251-92-4

This book is dedicated to people in recreation, park and leisure services. It has been my great good fortune to know many of them. There is a kind of self-selection that leads people into these services and, while the human race remains both unpredictable and dangerous, those in leisure services seem to possess qualities which make the world safer, kinder and more beautiful. May they flourish.

GCG

# Contents

# *Technology*

# Values

# Demography

# *Economic*

# Health

# Work and Free Time

## Governance

# Section Three
## Rethinking Leisure Services:
## Personal and Organizational Strategies ..... 211

# List of Figures

# List of Tables

# Acknowledgments

Special thanks to Michele Barbin, Karla Henderson, Sandy Little, and Doug Sessoms for reviewing earlier drafts of this manuscript and making many worthwhile suggestions. Also, my gratitude to Tom "The Terrier" Goodale, who suggested many needed changes (and would probably still do so).

# Section One
# Introduction

*The future woke me with its silence.*
*W. S. Merwin*

This book is about change—and some implications of change for leisure and for those who study or work for recreation, park and leisure services. The concern here is for leisure and leisure services interpreted broadly— leisure being what we do more or less voluntarily and pleasurably within our ways of life; leisure services being all those occupations and organizations which deal with leisure behavior from tourism to therapeutic recreation to parks.

For several years I have been obsessed with trying to understand what the future may hold, convinced that the scope and rate of change in the world is so huge that to ignore it consigns one to failure in one's jobs and in one's life. Because leisure is reinvented by succeeding cultures and by the values and preoccupations of each civilization, the ways in which the near future unfolds will reinvent leisure and every organization which provides leisure services. In doing so, such change will reinvent what you are studying or what your job will become.

The reinvention of leisure is happening right now but, just as fish presumably do not see water, it may be hard for those interested in leisure services to see such change. Perhaps these changes can't be seen (or understood) directly, but require that leisure services professionals learn more about what is changing in the environment, the economy, society, in the use of technology, and in values. If, for instance, "classical" music means European music to North Americans, learning that:

1. Most of the growth in the North American population is coming from immigration,

2. Almost none of the new immigrants to North America are from Europe, and

3. Europe will likely represent little more than seven percent of the world's population in another 50 years

may help one understand that the music thought of as classical will become more diverse.

It is a major premise of this book that in the emerging world, leisure will increasingly become the center of life and it will not be possible to provide "leisure" services based merely on good intentions or past models. As G. B. Shaw observed, the road to hell is paved with such intentions. Leisure services are increasingly becoming information-using services and their ability to obtain, to paraphrase T. S. Eliot, information from data, knowledge from information, and wisdom from knowledge will determine the fate of such services.

## A Common Need to Understand Change

The transformation to industrialism is largely at an end in North America, although it is going on in many countries of the world as diverse as Brazil and South Korea. The world is now at the beginning of multiple revolutions that will cause fundamental changes in what leisure is, its qualities and its use. These changes will cause each vocational specialty in leisure services to reinvent itself or perish.

Modern nations are also different from developing ones in terms of their population characteristics. Compared to developing nations, more of the population of modern nations live in suburbs. Modern nations are less and less a youth culture, a mass culture, or a common culture. The privileged get the good jobs in modern nations; not more leisure. The majority of adult women are in the labor force.

Emerging "nations," many of which are not really nation-states at all, are faced with huge problems of population, conflict, and environmental challenges. The fundamental problem they face, as it is for those in modern nations, is ignorance.

Also, while technological change always runs far ahead of the ability of the human race to understand or evaluate it prior to its introduction, today such change defies both our understanding and even our imagination.

Perhaps as a result, leisure is more important, even as much of the world's population feels more rushed and overwhelmed. The American public need not be convinced leisure is important—survey after survey shows that they think it is, even if they do not always understand its consequences for society. While they think it is important, the link between leisure and health may not be realized, so that leisure services may still be thought of as "amenities" rather than critical wellness services. The link between the quality of leisure resources and economic development is only slowly being understood. Our assumptions about what we do in time and space, what we should own and how the world will unfold are further and further from what is actually happening around us. New technologies are transforming our work, our leisure and our very identities.

The first thing to do, if we are really to *imagine* what is happening in the world, is to counteract the tendency of the mind to assume that things are the same each day when we awaken. While the changes that affected our ancient ancestors who lived in caves were often dramatic—the appearance of a carnivorous animal, for instance—and they took immediate, short-term action in relation to that change—fight or flight—today's changes are incremental and often almost hidden from view. These incremental changes, from the introduction of computers in every aspect of our lives, to the build up of toxic nuclear waste, to the shift in the ethnic makeup of the United States—and the world—often seem less dramatic. In combination, however, they represent multiple revolutions which will reshape not only every aspect of leisure services but also our very lives.

## Some Diverse Measures of Change

The dimensions of change in the world are difficult to define or fit into neat categories. The following diverse measures give testimony to how fundamental such change is:

- The world's population of six billion inhabitants is in the process of a huge increase, possibly doubling in the next 50 years. While it took 1,700 years after the birth of Christ for the world's population to double, it has doubled three times since then in increasingly shorter durations. Today, the biomass, or collective weight, of human beings is over 300 million tons, which is probably greater than any other animal species, with the possible exception of cattle, whose explosive population growth has produced increasing desertification and contributed to methane gas throughout the world.

- Ninety-five percent of those who are born into our world during the next 50 years will likely be residents of underdeveloped nations. North America and Europe combined may contain only about 10 percent of the world's population.

- In 1960 nearly 70 percent of the world's people lived at or below subsistence level. Today less than one-third do. The percentage living in fairly satisfactory conditions (as measured by the United Nations Human Development Index) rose from 25 percent to 60 percent between 1960 and 1992.

- The richest one-fifth of the world's population have increased their share of wealth from 70 percent to 85 percent.

- Since most of the world's population explosion is now attributable to poverty and the low status of women, lowering the birth rate will have to deal directly with these issues (UNESCO, 1988).

- Since 1990, there has been little increase in the world grain harvest (Brown, 1995).

- For the first time an adult mammal, a sheep, was successfully cloned using DNA from a six-year-old ewe to create a genetically identical lamb. Whether or not humans can be similarly cloned remains to be seen, but it is a distinct possibility.

- The increase in ultraviolet light due to the thinning of the ozone layer is so severe that, at high altitudes, those who climb glaciers find that their nylon ice-climbing ropes may snap without warning from increased exposure to ultraviolet radiation even though the ropes look brand new.

- The amount of sunlight which has healthy effects on our skin—zero percent. Many Australian and New Zealand children, who live close to a hole in the ozone layer, must now routinely put on sunscreen and a hat with a neck cover when going swimming or even out to recess.

- The amount of information which exists for humans to master is doubling every five years.

- Early in the next decade, the central processing units of 16 Cray YMP super computers, once costing collectively some $320 million, will be manufacturable for under $100 on a single microchip. Such a silicon sliver will contain approximately one billion transistors, compared to some 20 million transistors in the current leading-edge devices.

Meanwhile, the four-kilohertz telephone lines in America's homes and offices will explode into some 25 thousand billion of possible hertz through the use of fiber optics. Twenty-five thousand gigahertz is the intrinsic capacity of every fiber thread: enough communication power to hold all the phone calls in America on the peak moment of Mother's Day (Gilder, 1994).

- One-third of all animal species have become extinct during the last 100 years. Existing animals, which are more sensitive to environmental degradation, such as frogs and birds, are disappearing at rapid rates.

- Cattle take up one-fourth of the landmass of our planet (Rifkin, 1992, p. 17).

- An energy revolution may be underway which will reshape our everyday lives. A solar-hydrogen economy is emerging. Hydrogen, the simplest of chemical fuels, is entirely carbon-free and endlessly available. All the world's current energy needs could be met with one percent of today's fresh water supply. Solar energy is being used increasingly throughout the world. Norway has 50,000 homes powered by photovoltaic cells. Five million buildings in Japan have solar hot-water systems. Wind power will also grow. The cost of wind-generated electricity is now lower than that of new coal plants in many regions. Wind farms in California already provide enough energy for all residential needs in San Francisco.

- The former Soviet Union may be the first "country" to die of "ecocide," a level of environmental pollution and degradation unknown in the history of the world.

- China's increasing industrialization is projected to result in a shortfall in their grain production of 207 million tons per year. Even if consumption per Chinese resident does not increase, this amount is roughly that of the entire world's 1994 grain exports.

- The widespread implementation of tree farming could allow the world to meet its entire demand for industrial wood using only 200 million acres of land—an area equal to only five percent of the world's forest land.

- Per capita consumption of raw materials such as forestry products and metals, measured by weight, declined steadily over the past 20 years (Sagoff, 1997).

- "Nation" may be an obsolete concept. The Soviet Union has disappeared. In its place are numerous poor "countries" divided by ethnic and religious strife, often run by crime syndicates. China, India, Pakistan, Canada and many other "nations" may follow. The Province of Quebec voted to remain a part of Canada by a margin of only 0.5 percent in 1995. The world is tribalizing at an amazing rate, even with computerized communication systems bringing us together. The number of such potential splits is too great to mention. It no longer makes sense to talk about national economies or even regional economies. In the United States, for example, a single state may have a multitude of local economies, some of which are in a boom cycle while others are in depression.

- Sega has marketed a children's game, Saturn, which has more computing power than the 1976 Cray supercomputer, which the United States tried to keep out of the Russian hands.

- India's population growth has led to the loss of two-thirds of all its forests in this century alone. One-fifth of West Africa's forest has disappeared in a ten-year period between 1980 and 1990 with remaining forests being rapidly clear cut.

- India now plants four times the area in trees it harvests commercially.

- The economic status of nations changes with increasing speed. The Japanese, whose country lay in ruins less than 50 years ago, have accumulated the largest economic surplus in the history of the world. Even the Japanese economy, however, is not free from problems. Recently they have sold several of the "trophy" purchases they made in the United States, such as Rockefeller Center. Economic ups

and downs occur much more rapidly among nations. Korea's
domestic national product may surpass England's soon.

- The United States, the world's wealthiest nation by most
  measures, now has the world's largest government deficits.
  Government, meaning the American citizenry, is roughly
  $5 trillion in debt (a trillion is a thousand billion; a billion
  is a thousand million.) By the federal government's estimates in 1996, every American owes about $18,000 to pay
  off the debt but anyone who pays attention to the issue
  knows the real total is much higher, since revenues needed
  to accumulate the needed surplus for Social Security payments a decade from now are being diverted and spent as
  general revenues. U.S. corporations are also badly in debt,
  spending, on average, more than two-thirds of their revenue
  amortizing debt.

- Of all Americans working full time between the ages of 18
  and 25, almost one-half are poor as defined by the federal
  government.

- A new automobile emits only about one-twentieth as much
  pollution as one built in 1950. The majority of the weight
  of these new cars will be recycled. The average value of the
  electronics content of new cars in the United States is over
  $800; more than the value of the steel used to make them.

- One of the biggest "welfare" groups in the country is also
  one of the wealthiest—the elderly, on average, collect all
  the money they have put into social security plus interest in
  less than three years but receive payments for many more
  years—a subsidy of over $132,000 per person.

- In most modern nations, about one household out of four
  has only one person in it.

- Our technical understanding of the human body leaps
  ahead with no clear understanding of where such leaps are
  taking us. The genetic code is increasingly understood,
  making it almost certain that future generations of children
  will be "designed," their intelligence enhanced, their life
  spans dramatically increased. Thousands of microorganisms and several animals have already been patented. Gene

splicing and cell fusion techniques make undreamed of combinations possible. In one experiment, a gene that allows fireflies to emit light was implanted in a tobacco plant—the plant glowed 24 hours a day.

• AIDS devastates millions and is, even now, reconfiguring the age distribution of numerous African and Asian nations. It is a devil which may thrash its tail in unexpected directions. While the World Health Organization predicted 30 to 40 million deaths from AIDS worldwide by the year 2000, a 1992 study by Harvard epidemiologists raised the estimate to 100 million, with more deaths in Asia than Africa. It is estimated that about one out of ten Cambodians may die from AIDS.

• United States air quality is considerably better than ten years ago, the percentage of the country which is forested has increased, and water quality is generally improved.

• About one-quarter of American adults have some form of herpes. Most don't know they have it.

• The largest newspapers in the world are now electronic mail networks which have few rules or precedents to guide how people communicate with each other in leaderless situations; this has no precedent in human history. Such communications require no cutting of trees, transporting of newspapers in trucks, or de-inking of scrap newsprint.

• One-third of North American topsoil, which took a millennia to produce, is gone.

• In 1992, temporary jobs accounted for two out of every three new private sector jobs in the United States.

• One percent of the population owns 50 percent of the net financial assets of the United States.

• A 48-by-22 mile chunk of the Larsen Ice Shelf in Antarctica broke off recently, exposing rocks that had been buried for 20,000 years. Experts had predicted it would break off in ten years but it broke two months after their prediction. If the Larsen Shelf is any indication, our atmosphere is warming at unprecedented rates.

- Seventy-five percent of the labor force in most industrialized nations are involved in simple, repetitive tasks which can almost all be done by increasingly sophisticated robots, machines and computers (Rifkin, 1995).

- In just one industry, banking, downsizing will lead to an estimated loss of 30 to 40 percent of all jobs in the next seven years, a loss of 700,000 jobs.

- In Britain, 40 percent of all workers are part time; 33 percent are part time in Spain and the Netherlands.

- The United States, with little more than four percent of the world's population, consumes 50 percent of the world's cocaine supply.

- The sperm count of males is dropping dramatically worldwide, making infertility a rapidly growing problem (or, perhaps, blessing, given the huge increase in population).

- Inhabitants of emerging megacities in developing nations, such as Lagos (Nigeria) and Djakarta (Indonesia) already have population densities per square mile which are more than ten times that of New York City. In Teheran (Iran), the population has increased from five to ten million in only 15 years. The percentage of Turks living in cities is increasing from 44 percent in 1980 to 67 percent in 2000.

This litany of changes is difficult to make any sense of but it may help us understand why things will never be the same. Leisure, and the rest of life, will be rapidly changed in ways which are both predictable and unknown.

## Leisure Services: An Unrecognized Common History

Given these huge and diverse changes, it would seem leisure will be changed for those in both the modern and developing worlds. It would follow that the organizations which serve people providing a broad array of recreation, park, sport, cultural, therapeutic, tourism and other "leisure services" will be, themselves, in a process of change, reinvention, reconceptualization and adjustment.

Before a case can be made that various forms of leisure services have a common need to change, however, it may be helpful to understand that diverse leisure services emerged from a common set of historic circumstances. Many related leisure services dealing with hospitality, parks, play, tourism, sport, outdoor recreation, therapeutic recreation, military recreation, youth services, and others have a common heritage, although it is not often realized. They also have many common goals. *All such leisure services find their beginnings and reach their highest potential in the desire to improve the everyday lives of human beings, and in the ability to be entrepreneurial and informed when they do so.* Those who are interested in government-sponsored leisure services sometimes forget the *entrepreneurial heritage* and those interested in commercial forms of recreation sometimes forget the *helping and reform heritage.*

Diverse leisure services also have in common the fact that, *all such leisure services were developed in reaction to the emergence of urbanization and an economy based largely on the manufacture of material goods.* As work became more ordered under industrialization, and time became the ordering device, the rest of life, for many, became "free time;" an empty container which could no longer be filled with the old forms of play or the holy days which characterized peasant life. New work patterns, the emergence of capitalism and the unplanned urban environment which accompanied the factory system, made former ways of life and leisure obsolete.

If the factory system was a catastrophe for peasant culture—peasant culture was initially a catastrophe for the factory system. Peasants often preferred idleness, drink, working when the mood struck them and the pleasures of the body over the pleasures of the mind. In both Europe and North America, gambling and drinking either accompanied or had been the source of most leisure activity of adult males and some females. Such preferences led to a series of attempts to reform the leisure of the peasants, not only because employers and managers believed that it was necessary to change such habits for industrialism to succeed but also because many, including Charles Dickens, recognized that leisure time was the only arena for the "re-creation" of the physical and psychological capacity to work.

Much of the effort in the rational recreation and other reform movements was to counter such situations, both from altruistic motivations as well as self-interest. At the heart of much reform of leisure in the early nineteenth century was fear of the urban working poor. (Much as it is today.) Evangelists on both sides of the Atlantic sought to "Christianize" leisure through developments such as Sunday School, the Sabbatarian Movement that sought to ban many forms of leisure expression on Sunday, and the female-led temperance movement that sought to ban all use of alcohol. There were also movements against prostitution, sometimes called Social Purity Movements.

Reformers wanted not just to suppress various leisure behaviors, they also wanted to transform leisure behavior, replacing play which was public, inconclusive and improvised with play which was more highly ordered, planned and safer. In doing so, the intent was to make the working class more respectable, more predictable, less dangerous to others, and more amenable to industrial working conditions. In all such change, the ability to treat time as a scarce resource was critical.

Modern leisure was not only the product of attempts to reform the way of life which had developed under industrialization, it was also, and to a greater degree, the "invention" of entrepreneurs who found things people wanted to do during their free time and for which they were willing to pay.

> Beginning in the eighteenth century with magazines, coffeehouses, and music rooms, and continuing throughout the nineteenth century, with professional sports and holiday travel, the modern idea of personal leisure emerged at the same time as the business of leisure. The first could not have happened without the second. (Rybczynski, 1991, p. 121)

*Modern leisure, then, was largely invented by those in "commercial" recreation and such services, at their best, reflected the same ethic of caring about others as did the best of the recreation reform movements.* (At their worst, those in the commercial leisure sector cared only about removing money from their patrons, and those in the reform movements cared only about imposing their beliefs on those thought to be inferior).

Caring about others can be exemplified in the history of any form of commercial recreation. In tourism, for instance, a pivotal event was the development of organized railroad tours. Thomas Cook, an English minister and Secretary of the South Midlands Temperance Association, organized an excursion for his members from Leister to Loughborough for the modest price of one shilling. This success led to more organized tours, "package tours" and traveler's checks, all of which helped facilitate travel.

> The success of [Cook's] operations was due to the care he took in organizing his programs to minimize problems; he had close contacts with hotels, shipping companies and railroads throughout the world, ensuring that he obtained the best possible service as well as cheap prices for the services he sold. By escorting his clients throughout their journeys abroad he took the worry out of travel for the first-time travelers. He also facilitated the administration of travel by introducing, in 1867, the hotel voucher; and by removing the worry of travel for the Victorian population, he changed their attitudes to travel and opened up the market. The coincidental development of photography acted as a further stimulus for overseas travel, both for prestige and curiosity reasons. (Holloway, 1983)

In this example, we see three factors which shape all forms of leisure and hospitality services at their best, over and over again. *The desire to help people, entrepreneurial spirit, and changes in technology which facilitated (or necessitated) such intentions.*

Some of this combination may be found in the social reform movements which brought about many recreation, park, sport, adult education, outdoor recreation, museums and botanical gardens, and other leisure services in the early twentieth century. They evolved, as did commercial recreation, due to changes in how people did work which was driven by advances in technology—the Industrial Revolution. It resulted in the migration from countryside to city, transforming the peasant into the working class, often doing great environmental damage in the process. From serving as partners in agricultural work, most women were constricted to limited work roles or homemaking and childrearing as primary tasks. From work being interspersed with leisure elements, industrialism put work at the center of social arrangements; free time becoming what was left over. Children had no place to play.

In all of these early endeavors, success in contributing to the betterment of humans was not so much dependent upon whether the organization which ultimately provided the service was "for profit," "private-non-profit," or "governmental," but rather on the dedication and vision of the individuals involved. Dorothy Enderis, who served as the Director of Milwaukee's Department of Recreation and Adult Education Department from 1920 to 1948, typified such an individual. Reflecting on her German heritage, Ms. Enderis summarized what may distinguish the truly superior leisure service worker from the others.

> *Leut* is the German word for people, and *selig* is holy, and to me, the finest attribute with which you could credit a recreation worker is to say he is *leutselig*, meaning that people are holy to him. (Butler, 1965, p. 145)

This quote puts into perspective where the dividing line is between those who succeed at the highest level and those who do not. While this is a book about change, the truth of Dorothy Enderis' observation will not change.

Hospitality, which today has often come to mean hotel, restaurants and resorts, also shares a history of thinking that people were holy. Historically, hospitality meant "opening up one's home to total strangers, giving a meal to anyone who chose to come, allowing them to stay the night, indeed imploring them to stay, though one knew nothing about them" (Zeldin, 1994, p. 437). This "free" hospitality began to decline as more and more people traveled, and was gradually replaced by the hospitality industry. The eminent historian Theodore Zeldin saw that, from the roots of this simple hospitality, a new hospitality might spring:

> A new phase of history begins when this ancient and simple hospitality is succeeded by a deeper hospitality, which alters the direction of human ambition. That happens when people become hospitable to strange ideas, to opinions they have never heard before, to traditions that seem totally alien to them, and when encounters with the unknown modify their view of themselves. When foreign travel becomes a necessity, and no longer an exception, when television news is about distant parts more than about one's own city, when one's emotions are roused by the misfortunes of total strangers, what goes on elsewhere becomes a crucial ingredient in the shaping of one's life. It becomes impossible to decide what to do unless one knows about everyone else's experience. This is a deeper

hospitality because it is not just politeness, but involves
admitting new ideas and emotions temporarily into one's
mind. (1994, p. 439)

Thus, in hospitality we see a model which may be extended into a changing world. The tradition of caring about strangers is the common heritage of the *best* of those in all of the leisure services, and this heritage will serve them well in the future. So, too, will the entrepreneurial spirit which the best of those in leisure service exemplified.

While there are many ways to define what entrepreneurship means, what the best of those who have worked in leisure services share is a kind of entrepreneurial spirit which operates on the following assumption:

> *A good idea may result in a good product or service which
> will benefit both those who use the product or service and
> its developer.*

By this definition, the divisions between many forms of leisure services disappear. Entrepreneurs in leisure services bring about a change which benefits others and themselves simultaneously. Thus, a good bowling program for teenagers with mental retardation, a good swimming pool operation at a Florida resort, a good botanical garden in the middle of a big city, a good tour of Amsterdam's "Red Light" District, a good volleyball league for senior women, a good country bed and breakfast, a good arts program for elementary school kids in tough areas of a city, a good restaurant with an imaginative menu, and a good trail walk with some interpretation of the plant and animal life seen by the hikers, all have a common core—the entrepreneurial spirit.

The entrepreneurial spirit, which has been the core of those who excelled at leisure services, will become even more important in the coming era; an era in which things will never be the same.

# Section Two
# Things Will Never Be the Same:
## Get Used To It

*I come back to where I have never been.*
*W. S. Merwin*

If leisure and leisure services have historically been shaped by change then the explosive changes going on in the world will surely transform them in fundamental ways. Let's first review these changes under the categories of:

1. Environment,

2. Technology,

3. Values,

4. Demography,

5. Economy,

6. Health,

7. Work and Free Time, and

8. Governance.

These categories are not only arbitrary, but each issue overlaps, affecting every other. Nevertheless, let's examine these changes in more detail. *(In reading the following material, imagine what such trends mean for leisure and leisure services. While the author has tried to identify some ways in which these changes will affect leisure and leisure services, these observations are meant only to be a basis for discussion, reflection, and debate.)*

# The Environment

# 1

## *The Population Explosion and Its Causes*

The most important trend in the world and the fundamental environmental issue is population increase. The number of people in the world is increasing at an historically unprecedented rate (see Figure 1). The possible doubling of the world's population is occurring almost exclusively in

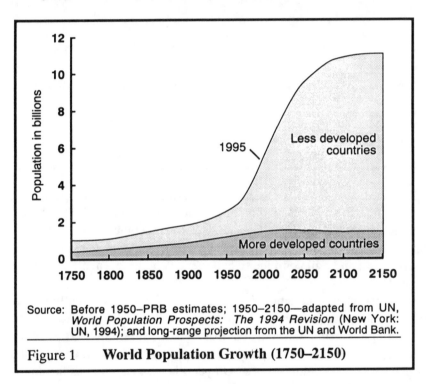

Source: Before 1950–PRB estimates; 1950–2150—adapted from UN, *World Population Prospects: The 1994 Revision* (New York: UN, 1994); and long-range projection from the UN and World Bank.

Figure 1    **World Population Growth (1750–2150)**

"underdeveloped" nations. As may be seen in Figure 2 (page 18), most developed nations are projected to show no population growth from the year 2000 forward.

Most nations in the prosperous industrialized world have reached demographic saturation. These include parts of the Far East, such as Japan, almost all of Europe and, to a lesser extent, North America. In Germany, for instance, if the present birth rate persists, without immigration the population would fall from the present 82 million people to 58 million

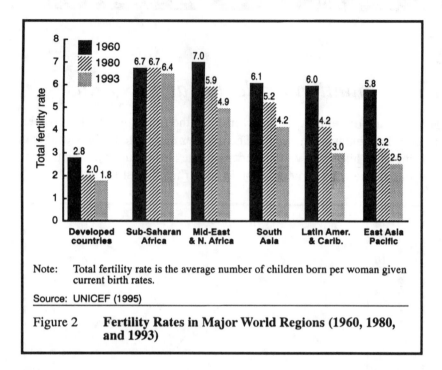

Note:    Total fertility rate is the average number of children born per woman given current birth rates.

Source: UNICEF (1995)

Figure 2      **Fertility Rates in Major World Regions (1960, 1980, and 1993)**

in 2050 and continue to decline. The birth rates of many European countries are significantly below replacement level (Chesnais, 1997). A similar condition exists in Japan, Canada and several countries in economic transition such as South Korea. Less developed nations, conversely, are experiencing and will continue to experience an unprecedented population explosion.

On many environmental issues, developed nations currently produce far more harm than do developing ones, since they consume much more resources per person. On some environmental issues, however, such as increases in methane, developing nations produce just as much a problem per person as do developed ones. On yet other issues, such as the destruction of rainforests, poor people may do more damage.

If the new half of the world's population goes through the cycles of development of their predecessors, environmental disasters are a certainty. Additionally, the potential for both environmental and military catastrophe will increase in a world in which people with little education or food have access to technologically sophisticated weapons. Such population increases make it highly unlikely that democracy will be a prevalent form of government or that the assumptions made about life by middle-class

Americans will be typical. Figure 3 and Figure 4 (page 20) show a number of demographic and consumption/pollution indicators about various regions of the world.

North America has the highest gross national product per person of any country in the world by far. The United States is by far the biggest consumer of material goods and, on most measures, the biggest polluter. (The United States is also becoming one of the biggest recyclers.)

As a United Nations report concluded, the unprecedented increase in human beings in the world is largely associated with poverty, ignorance, and the inferior status of women. Doing something about the population bomb will therefore require doing something about these situations. Put another way, it is in the economic and political interest of those in modern nations to improve the economic well-being and the freedom and power of women in developing nations, since not to do so will produce a world overrun by humans with few

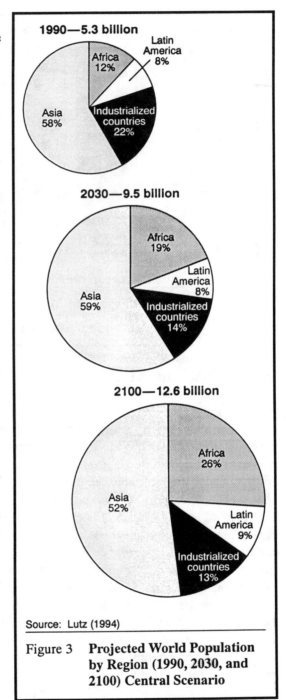

Source: Lutz (1994)

Figure 3    **Projected World Population by Region (1990, 2030, and 2100) Central Scenario**

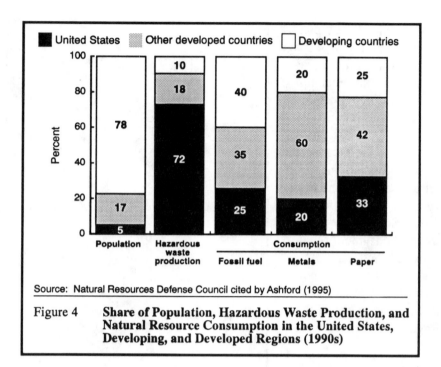

Source: Natural Resources Defense Council cited by Ashford (1995)

Figure 4    **Share of Population, Hazardous Waste Production, and Natural Resource Consumption in the United States, Developing, and Developed Regions (1990s)**

prospects for a satisfying life. The actions of these billions of people will have a negative affect the way of life of those in modern nations.

Women's access to power and education levels are directly linked to family size. As Figure 5 shows, women with higher levels of education have fewer children. In many countries, however, women are denied access to education. Table 1 shows differences in men's and women's literacy and education rates in selected countries. Women also lack political power. The extent to which women are involved in national legislatures is shown in Figure 6 (page 22). Because of these situations, the women's movement in less developed countries is a critical variable in population control. Poverty and ignorance also contribute to the population explosion, so finding ways to minimize poverty and increase education is critical to slowing the population increase. While it would seem to be in the interest of modern nations such as the United States to assist this process, the United States is no longer a leader in foreign aid and, in terms of percentage of gross domestic product given in foreign aid, is now among the lowest in modern nations. Less than one percent of the U.S. federal budget went for foreign aid in 1997.

A primary consequence of huge population growth in less developed countries combined with birth rates which are less than replacement rates

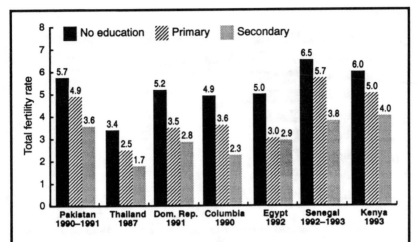

Note: Total fertility rate is the average number of children born per woman given current birth rates. Not all education categories are shown.

Source: Demographic and Health Surveys cited by Riley (1997)

Figure 5    **Women's Education and Family Size in Selected Countries**

Table 1    **Gender Differences in Literacy and Education in Selected Countries (1980s and 1990s)**

| Country | Adult literacy rate 1990 | | Primary school gross enrollment ratio* 1986–92 | |
|---|---|---|---|---|
| | Male | Female | Male | Female |
| Bangladesh | 47 | 22 | 83 | 71 |
| Brazil | 82 | 81 | 101 | 97 |
| China | 87 | 68 | 127 | 118 |
| Columbia | 87 | 86 | 110 | 112 |
| Egypt | 63 | 34 | 109 | 93 |
| India | 62 | 34 | 112 | 84 |
| Indonesia | 88 | 75 | 119 | 114 |
| Kenya | 80 | 59 | 97 | 93 |
| Mali | 41 | 24 | 32 | 19 |
| Nigeria | 62 | 40 | 79 | 62 |
| Pakistan | 47 | 21 | 54 | 30 |
| Phillipines | 94 | 93 | 113 | 111 |
| Spain | 97 | 93 | 109 | 106 |
| Thailand | 95 | 91 | 92 | 88 |
| Turkey | 90 | 69 | 115 | 110 |
| Zimbabwe | 74 | 60 | 120 | 118 |

* Gross enrollment ratio is the number of children enrolled in primary school as a percentage of the number of children of primary school age (6–12 yrs.). Ratios above 100 include children in school who fall outside this age group.

Source: UNICEF (1995)

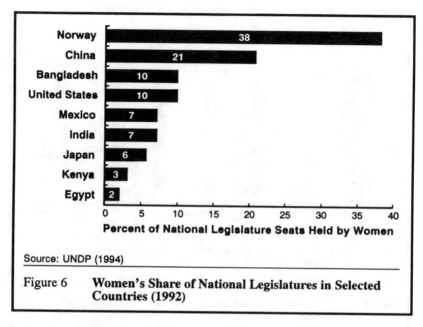

Source: UNDP (1994)

Figure 6     **Women's Share of National Legislatures in Selected Countries (1992)**

in Europe and elsewhere and a rapid aging of the population in all modern nations is that there will likely be a need for the immigration of young people from less developed countries to modern nations. Thus, while immigration may become increasingly controversial, there is every reason to believe that the vastly older population in modern nations will need young people from other countries both to "repopulate" their countries (many of whom have birth rates of 1.4 per marriage or lower) as well as tend to their needs.

## Issue Questions

1. Does women's use of leisure have any role to play in slowing the population explosion in developing nations?

2. How will the population changes described change sport in modern nations? How might sport be changed in developing nations?

3. What negative consequences might this huge population increase have on international tourism?

# Possible Implications for Leisure

Certainly the huge population explosion has consequences for every form of leisure service, from "wilderness recreation" to the need for limits on forms of leisure which consume large quantities of material goods. If twice the number of people in the world want to go shopping for pleasure, the environmental consequences of their consumption will cause huge additional strain on the environment. If double the number of people want to see the Grand Canyon, the canyon may be made into a city to accommodate them. In our lifetime, the population explosion may redefine leisure and leisure services, in all countries, more than any other factor.

Among the many issues are changes in the type and extent of tourism. Many countries with huge growth in their population, such as China, have an emerging middle class (whose number may equal the population of the United States) and such people want to travel for leisure experiences in other countries which have more opportunities for contact with the natural environment, different histories, and unique tourist attractions. It is not surprising, then, that there are now more tourists from other countries coming to North America than North Americans traveling to other countries. Mainland Chinese tourists, for example, can already be found in Las Vegas, on tours organized by Taiwanese entrepreneurs. This has many implications.

For a popular national park like Yellowstone, it means that the area is managed more to accommodate the needs and desires of Japanese, Taiwanese, Chinese and visitors from many other countries. The park gift shop becomes more important, since the tradition of taking small presents back to friends after a trip is strong in many Asian countries. Learning some Japanese or Chinese phrases is critical for park staff. Dealing with people who have had little experience with wild animals or wilderness means changes in standard operating procedures.

The population densities of the world are so diverse that many people who can afford it will travel elsewhere for their leisure. Australia, the United States and China, for instance, are about the same size geographically, yet Australia has less than 20 million people while the United States has about 270 million and China has 1.25 billion. Thus, in the same size landmass, there are more than 100 times as many Chinese as Australians. China currently has the second largest economy in the world so many of the people from its crowded country are financially able to go elsewhere for recreation. India, which will have more than a billion people in the near future, is also developing a bigger middle class, thanks in part to its booming computer industry. Thus, there will likely be more tourism from "developing" nations to "developed" nations—a reversal of historical trends. Since many leisure services in developed nations are increasingly entrepreneurial, they are likely to cater to whomever can and will pay for their services.

There is also the simple issue of crowding at recreation sites. Take a given site—a ski resort, a playground, a gym used for a wheelchair basketball league—and double the number of participants. Crowding produces the need for more organization of activities, changes and often diminishes the quality of the experience, increases the need for privacy, and in many other ways shapes the experience. For people with financial means, there may be new ways developed to avoid crowding by paying more money for privacy. Being alone in nature is likely to cost more—with the result that only those with financial means experience it.

More people is also likely to mean that leisure, particularly for the have-not portion of the world, will consist more and more of entertainment and the "interpretation" of various leisure services rather than active participation. It is far cheaper to use televised entertainment and other passive forms of leisure than most forms of active leisure which involve travel, specialized equipment and other expenses. Instead of active involvement in leisure, many will be left with computer-television forms of entertainment, drugs, and other vicarious experiences. In many recreation facilities, people's access will be limited in order to avoid ruining it from the sheer crush of people. Instead, the facility will be "interpreted" to them, using high-tech methods of presentation from virtual reality to museum-type displays of the area. The ability to actually move around in the recreation facility will be increasingly restricted.

There is also likely to be a variety of recreation, park and leisure services introduced to those in developing nations. Within many nations, as diverse as Brazil, Taiwan, South Africa and South Korea, which are in the process of "developing," there is a common progression of interest in providing leisure services by those whose background is physical education. This progression seems to go as follows:

1. Interest in elite athletes and helping their country do well in international sport competition. This involves sponsoring youth programs for athletes who show potential, identifying those who are gifted and coaching and training them.

2. Promoting "sport for all" type programs in an attempt to bring sport to a larger segment of the population, often at low cost. Such programs attempt to increase the fitness of the population, but usually concentrate on youth and, often, on males.

3. Interest in the population's use of free time. This step represents an extension of interest in sport to an interest in leisure and the provision and facilitation of a variety of types of leisure services to people of all ages, sometimes with emphasis on urban residents or those who are poor. It is this step which requires that those involved receive educational training in leisure and leisure services rather than physical education. Sport is a relatively small use of free time and a relatively small part of the leisure lives of urban residents or the leisure services which will need to be offered.

Often, those trained in physical education are resistant to dealing with the issue of the free time of an urban population in any comprehensive way. Thus, in South Korea, Australia, Brazil, Taiwan, New Zealand, South Africa and in many industrializing countries, we see a change in the education of leisure service workers from physical education to a more diverse curriculum of study.

Among the many other issues that surface from the population explosion will be the need for anyone interested in environmental interpretation, nature centers, outdoor recreation, forest recreation and related areas to understand that the doubling of the world's population will mean huge declines in habitat for most forms of animal (and plant) life. Planning for environmental interpretation programs without including the central issue of population control and the steps which must be undertaken in an attempt to control it, will mean such programs are simply comforting entertainment which ignores the relation between the huge increase in humans and the loss of habitat of other animals.

# 2

# *The Environmental Problems Caused by Poverty and the Gap Between Haves and Have-Nots*

The gap between poor people and people who are not poor is increasingly the cause of numerous environmental problems. The economic haves and have-nots are splitting further apart in most nations, particularly in the United States, where one percent of the population owns 40 to 50 percent of the real financial assets. The U.S. federal government contributes to this gap since it redistributes much more money to wealthy people than to poor ones. Perhaps the single most stunning statistic in terms of economic change is that the wealthiest 400 people in the world have about the same financial wealth as the lower 40 percent all the people in the world (Rifkin, 1995). This truly obscene situation may become even worse.

Overall, economic conditions have actually improved greatly in the world since 1960, when 70 percent of the world's population lived at or below the subsistence level, as measured by the United Nations Human Development Index (Sagoff, 1997). Less than a third live at or below the subsistence level today and the percentage enjoying fairly satisfactory conditions rose from 25 percent to 60 percent. During this period, however, the gap between rich and poor has increased dramatically:

> Although world income measured in real terms has increased by 700 percent since the Second World War, the wealthiest people have absorbed most of the gains. Since 1960 the richest fifth of the world's people have seen their share of the world's income increase from 70 to 85 percent. Thus, one-fifth of the world's population possesses much more than four-fifths of the world's wealth, while the share held by all others has correspondingly fallen; that of the world's poorest 20 percent has declined from 2.3 to 1.4 percent. (Sagoff, 1997, p. 94)

This huge imbalance in resources forces poor people into ways of behaving which are environmentally harmful. As Alan Hammond of the World

Resources Institute pointed out, "if poor nations cannot export anything else, they will export their misery—in the form of drugs, diseases, terrorism, migration, and environmental degradation" (quoted by Sagoff, 1997, p. 93). Indeed, the overexploitation of natural resources by the poorest of the poor, such as cutting all the trees from tropical forests, often for fuel, slash-and-burn farming by displaced peasants, and other desperate practices may be causing as much natural resource depletion as the other three billion people in the developing world put together (Sagoff, 1997).

If the United States is to be a leader in minimizing environmental damage, attention will have to be paid to the expanding have–have-not gap. The gap between rich and poor is resulting in differing definitions of not only political and cultural issues, but also differing constructions of reality. Such disparity eliminates the possibility of "common" sense arriving at answers. (Such common sense is at the heart of "common" law, which could serve as the basis of reforming the hopeless U.S. legal system). There has, as of yet, been precious little political response to the fact that the young are dramatically poorer than other age groups. It is not surprising that young people are considerably more conservative than their parents. They may correctly suspect that the federal government redistributes far more money to wealthy people than to poor ones, and far more money to old people than to young ones.

# Issue Questions

1. What steps could be taken to close the gap between haves and have-nots in the United States and other modern nations? (Or can it be closed?)

2. Should public recreation and park services provide different services for the haves and have-nots? How can the integration of rich and poor be encouraged within public parks, museums, sport facilities, environmental centers, and other places where recreation occurs?

3. Should the highest priority of government leisure services be to serve the have-nots?

4. Can tourism be managed in ways which improve the environment of poor countries or poor sections of a country? If so, how?

## Possible Implications for Leisure

The have–have-not world will need to be changed if massive environmental damage is to be avoided. If it is not avoided, we can expect very diverse forms of recreation and leisure for the two factions. Public agencies charged with the provision of recreation, park, cultural, sport and other leisure-related services would increasingly have to take a two tier approach to what they provide—one set of strategies for the have segment of society and another for the have-nots. Parks in the midst of pollution and squalor in one area for the have-nots, but in pristine natural areas in another for the haves. In the commercial sector, there would be tourism for the haves, and drugs and TV for the have-nots.

For public and private, nonprofit leisure services, helping to bridge the have–have-not split will likely mean that different strategies need to be taken in the provision of services. The task for the have-nots may be "educating for leisure."

# Global Warming

The Earth appears to be warming with large-scale consequences for every aspect of life. Almost all scientists agree our planet is warming, and such warming is likely related to increased amounts of carbon dioxide and other gases and particulate matter emitted into the atmosphere. This polluting of the atmosphere comes from numerous forms of human activity; with automobiles being a particularly important contributor. While there is disagreement about how much the atmosphere is warming due to trapped gases and other pollution, a rise of only 3°C (or 5.4°F ) would change all aspects of our life. Conversely, a drop of three degrees would be responsible for starting a new ice age (Weiner, 1990). As the atmosphere warms, low-lying countries such as Holland or Bangladesh will suffer flooding, since water expands when heated and the volume of water in the oceans will increase due to the melting of glaciers. Coastal cities where the shoreline is nearly flat are already in this process. The east coast of the United States, as we know it, will not survive another 50 years. Crops that previously grew in one part of the country may no longer do so (although they might in another part). Trees will try to "migrate" north, or south below the equator, but may not be able to spread their seeds in the appropriate direction fast enough to compensate.

While there is always some doubt about any issue, the Intergovernmental Panel on Climate Change (IPCC), consisting of 2,500 climate scientists, recently issued a statement on climatic change which declared bluntly that the earth was entering a period of climatic instability which was likely to cause "widespread economic, social, and environmental dislocation over the next century" (IPCC quoted by Gelbspan, 1995). The continued emission of greenhouse gases would create protracted, crop-destroying droughts in continental interiors, a host of new and recurring diseases, hurricanes of extraordinary malevolence, and rising sea levels that could inundate island nations and low-lying coastal rims on the continent (Gelbspan, 1995, p. 32).

To understand why there is massive denial of this issue, consider the following. The energy industries are the single largest enterprise known to humankind. They are also linked directly to the well-being of other industries, including automobiles, farming, shipping, air freight, banking interests, tourism, and governments dependent upon oil revenues for their existence. The oil industry has annual sales of more than one trillion dollars, and, essentially by itself, supports the economies of the Middle East, and large segments of the Russian, Mexican, Venezuelan, Nigerian, Indonesian, Norwegian, and British economies.

> Begin to enforce restriction on the consumption of oil and coal, and the effects on the global economy—unemployment, depression, social breakdown and war—might lay waste to what we have come to call civilization. (Gelbspan, 1995, p. 32)

Thus, the warming of the planet is as much a political issue as an environmental one.

In the United States, there was a massive rise in the use of fossil fuels after World War II. When the smoke and pollution became obvious from such practices, the response, in the 1950s, was to build smoke stacks hundreds of feet tall, to dilute the pollution, allowing sulfurous pollution to travel 1,000 miles or more where it formed acid rain across the mountains of New York, New England and southern Canada. In Vermont, the rain has an acidity factor (pH) of 3.8 to 4.0. The pH factor is "logarithmic" so a change from normal (5.6) down to 4.6 means the rain has gotten ten times as acidic as normal; at 3.6 the rain is 100 times as acidic as normal (Montague, 1996). This means, quite simply, that trees are dying.

Under the Reagan and Bush administrations, the U.S. Forest Service simply lied about this issue. When Jack Ward Thomas became director of the U.S. Forest Service in 1992, he issued the following message to his employees: (1) Obey the law, (2) Tell the truth, (3) Implement ecosystem management. It was only then that a Forest Service report admitted that timber mortality had increased 24 percent between 1986 and 1991 "in all regions, on all ownerships, and for hardwoods and softwoods" (Little, 1995). Hardwoods are particularly affected in the southern United States, where the mortality increase is 37 percent. "If we don't take these lessons to heart, and soon, the trees will survive but probably we won't" (Montague, 1996).

Another lesser known aspect of global warming is the increasing rain and snow it is producing. A warming climate doesn't mean there aren't any winters since warmer air can hold more moisture and warmer temperatures mean moisture on the ground evaporates more rapidly. In combination, this means more water cycles between the earth and the sky evaporating more quickly and coming down as rain or snow in greater volume. "This more vigorous hydrological cycle is one of the most certain characteristics of the greenhouse-altered climate" (Mathews, 1996).

The weather has become more extreme, based upon century old records, with an index of extreme weather 40 percent higher than natural fluctuation would produce. Heavy rain and snow has been the greatest single change—the proportion of two inches of rain or more falling at one time. In 1995, Midwesterners coped with two "100-year" floods and Texans got hailstones the size of baseballs. "Think of the blizzard of '96 as a glimpse of the likely greenhouse future" says Jessica Mathews (1996), a senior fellow at the Council on Foreign Relations. At the National Climate Center in Asheville, North Carolina, scientists have developed a "climate extreme index" which demonstrates that the frequency of extreme weather events has been 1.5 times more frequent since the mid-1970s than in the 65 preceding years.

The warming of the earth's atmosphere means that fossil fuels, principally oil and coal, must be replaced by solar, geothermal, wind and other renewable forms of energy or we may all suffer the consequences. (As we will see later, there is reason to believe this can be done).

Lest we think that global warming is the only environmental issue which will reshape our future, consider the following list:

1. Loss of crop and grazing land use due to desertification, erosion, conversion of land to nonfarm uses, and other factors;

2. Depletion of the world's rain forests, leading to loss of forest resources, serious watershed damage, and other adverse consequences;

3. Mass extinction of species, principally from the global loss of habitat and the associated loss of genetic resources;

4. Rapid population growth, burgeoning third-world cities, and ecological refugees;

5. Mismanagement and shortages of freshwater resources;

6. Over fishing, habitat destruction, and pollution in the marine environment;

7. Threats to human health from mismanagement of pesticides and hazardous substances, and from waterborne pathogens;

8. Climate change caused by the increase in the "greenhouse gases" in the atmosphere;

9. Acid rain and, more generally, the effects of a complex mix of air pollutants on fisheries and crops; and

10. Mismanagement of energy fuels and pressures on energy resources, including the shortage of "fuel wood," the poor person's oil.

These massive problems, in combination, will change how we live both by choice and necessity.

# Issue Questions

1. What impact do various uses of leisure have on global warming?

2. How can recreation, park and leisure services contribute to a lessening in global warming?

3. How are people's uses of leisure likely to change due to increased global warming?

# Possible Implications for Leisure

Outdoor recreation, tourism and other forms of leisure expression will increasingly be reshaped by environmental change. Global warming, in particular, will reshape almost all forms of leisure expression. Outdoor recreation will become more dangerous if it involves being in the full sun, particularly during late morning and early afternoon. There will be changes in dress, activity, and the location of outdoor recreation.

Tourism will also be directly affected. Beach erosion from rising tides will decimate many tourist destination areas, particularly where the slope of the land back from the ocean is gradual, such as much of the east coast of the United States. Climatic change which will take place may also create new tourist spots as it decimates old ones. Even a few degrees of warming will melt snow at ski resorts but, perhaps, make areas further north (or south below the equator) more viable. Flooding and severe storms may also make problems for many tourist destination areas.

Global warming will produce different attitudes toward the sun. The notion of a "healthy" tan or "bathing" in sunlight will be negative. Tourism sites which stress the sun, such as Spain's Costa del Sol, may rename themselves.

The depletion of the ozone layer will also affect design of recreation facilities such as swimming pools, golf courses, tennis courts, and other traditionally outdoor sites. There will need to be more shade, perhaps roofs over the spots where people tee off on golf courses. The temperature will need to be made cooler in many leisure locations, combining more intelligent design of buildings with increases in trees and other foliage. Some leisure facilities will be developed underground.

Tourism and most forms of outdoor recreation are highly dependent upon people being able to travel freely and at reasonable expense. Global warming may produce limitations on travel, particularly forms of travel which further global warming. As this is being written, in 1997, one jumbo jet drops over a ton of particulate matter into the environment from a single transcontinental flight. Many U.S. and German made cars get less than 20 miles per gallon of gas. Additionally, the most highly polluting automobiles, which are almost always very old ones, are allowed to continue running. Such polluting means of travel may be increasingly restricted, taxed or otherwise discouraged. In particular, travel for leisure purposes using such means may be discouraged or eliminated.

The depletion of the ozone layer may affect hunting and fishing in numerous ways. First, some forms of wildlife may disappear as the temperature rises, either due to extinction or migration to cooler climates. Additionally, hunting and fishing may be prohibited in attempts to save dwindling numbers of migrating animals. In other areas it may be encouraged, as animal populations suddenly increase.

The warming of the earth's atmosphere will affect style of participation in leisure almost everywhere. It will limit our freedom in ways which legislation could not. At tennis tournaments such as the Australian Open, many spectators and lines people for the tournament who have become aware of the increasingly carcinogenic nature of sunlight are wearing hats with neck and ear covers. Officials for the tournament wear long pants and warmup jackets, even in the hot sun, and hats which cover their entire head and neck. Those who are not yet aware of the changes in the environment continue to sit frying their skin in shorts and T-shirts. As they become aware of the risk of sunlight, perhaps they too will dress more like our rural ancestors used to do in the hot sun or like people do in Saudi Arabia. If they do not, there will be increased amounts of skin cancer and suffering in later life.

# Global Urbanization

The world will become increasingly urbanized in almost every region. People stream into cities from rural areas in almost every country in the world, hoping for a better future. Part of this migration to cities is due to the fact that agriculture is being mechanized and there is no longer a need for many people to be farmers. This situation is true in countries as diverse as Turkey, where 44 percent of the people lived in cities in 1980, 59 percent did in 1990, and 67 percent are predicted to in the year 2000, to Canada, where the agricultural province of Manitoba may soon find the majority of residents have migrated from small towns where grain production was the basis of the economy, to a single city—Winnipeg. In Africa, the percentage of the population living in urban areas has grown to 25 percent and will likely reach 50 percent in the year 2000 (Oliver, 1991).

The quality of urban life will be a critical variable in world peace and prosperity. As may be seen in Figure 7, there are predictions of huge increases in urban areas of 20 million or more emerging in many less developed nations, as people come in from the countryside in the transition from labor intensive farming to industrialized farming. There will also

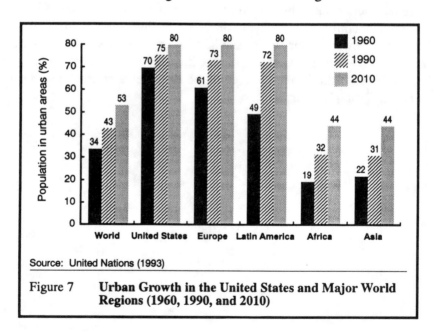

Source: United Nations (1993)

Figure 7    **Urban Growth in the United States and Major World Regions (1960, 1990, and 2010)**

be growth in the size of urban areas in developed nations. The fate of the world may have to do with the conditions of life these people experience.

In an increasingly urbanized world, people will live in more highly interdependent configurations. One of the difficulties of migration to these large urban areas is that those who move there are likely to have, on average, almost two children more per couple than those who already reside there. This is likely to contribute to the newcomers being poor and likely to drive many of those who resided for a long time in the city into the suburbs. Urban planning will become critical and will require increasing sophisticated demographic understandings.

To stop the huge migration from rural villages to cities will require that there be as many opportunities in the village as the city. In writing about this process in Iran, Kapuscinski (1982) stated that the key to modernizing was the ability to make village life so attractive that peasants would stop the ceaseless migration to the urban areas. Kaplan (1996), after personally traveling from West Africa all the way to Cambodia, stated he saw precious little evidence of villages being made more attractive. Instead, cities were growing uncontrollably and, in the process, being turned into huge villages.

## Issue Questions

1. What role can tourism play in keeping rural residents from moving to urban areas?

2. How might the higher population densities of emerging urban areas change people's use of leisure?

3. What roles will leisure services need to play in the emerging high density urban areas?

4. How can contact with nature be assured for such residents?

## Possible Implications for Leisure

As urban planning becomes more critical, planning for people's use of leisure (e.g., the arts, culture, sport, theater, museums, libraries, parks, nature conservatories, dining out, socializing, and other diversions) will become central. Leisure services will become more essential to everyday life, rather than less.

Different models of leisure services provision are emerging in developing nations all over the world. While, in many cases, these models may imitate North America, such imitation may be increasingly dysfunctional. Just as biodiversity is important to protect the world's plant and animal life, so the diversity of cultures is important to protect the social life of humans. The North American model of leisure services, whether market sector, private, nonprofit or governmental, will not serve as appropriate models of leisure provision for numerous reasons. North Americans have been far wealthier on a per capita basis than those in most developing nations. The United States has a higher percentage of arable (farmable) land than most of these countries, a lower population density (except for Australia and New Zealand) and a natural resource base which is abundant. Developing nations are creating their own notions of what "parks" mean and how they should be created and administered. It will make little sense for, as an example, Seoul (South Korea) or Jakarta (Indonesia) to imitate the model of park provision found in a North America city. Population densities in such cities are up to ten times higher, government has less financial resources and the cultural traditions of the people are different.

The inappropriate importation of North American or European culture has had negative consequences historically, ranging from the desertification in parts of Africa where cattle were introduced by Europeans to changing attitudes toward and access to handguns promoted in part by North America mass media to high-fat "fast food" imported by North American corporations. One even sees youth in some warm weather countries wearing U.S.-style baseball caps, although such caps are not very helpful in combating the major problem of skin cancer (nor are they in the United States). This is not to indict all North American culture as evil, only to say that because much of it is unsustainable in North America in spite of its great wealth. Other models which reflect different cultures, demographic and economic circumstances must be developed.

For this to happen, many nations must either find a way to limit exposure to North American mass media, which dominates television almost everywhere, or develop their own programming to the extent that such domination is neutralized.

Leisure services in all sectors are likely to grow since they are associated with the growth of urban areas and the United States, like almost all other regions of the world, continues to have an increasingly higher percentage of its population in urban areas. As we saw in Figure 7 (page 34), the United States, like most of the world, continues to have a higher and higher percentage of its population in urban areas, with estimates that 80 percent of Americans will live in urban areas by 2010. This increasing urbanization has historically been associated with increased need for a variety of leisure services within the public, private, nonprofit and market sectors. Basically, urbanization created leisure services and the increasing level of urbanization will likely make leisure services more critical to quality of life in emerging urban areas.

# 5

# The Transition From a Fossil Fuel Economy

The necessary transition to a world energy supply based on nonfossil fuel sources is primarily a political problem rather than a technological one. Such a transition, as it comes about, will reorder daily life. The evidence that the world cannot stand the environmental damage being done to it through a combination of the burning of fossil fuels, primarily coal and oil (or wood), while the population is in the process of both doubling and industrializing, is overwhelming. There is a kind of mass denial at work in the world because our way of life, our economic and our political orders are all dependent upon the current energy system. Increasingly, however, it is becoming apparent that the problems of transforming our energy use to solar, wind, hydrogen and other nonfossil energy forms are mainly political. While the Reagan administration cut funding for solar energy

| Table 2 | Cost of Power Generation in the United States (1985, 1994, and 2000) | | |
|---|---|---|---|
| **Technology** | **1985** | **1994** | **2000** |
| | (1993 cents per kilowatt hours) | | |
| Natural Gas | 10–13 | 4–5 | 3–4 |
| Coal | 8–13 | 5–6 | 4–5 |
| Wind | 10–13 | 5–7 | 4–5 |
| Solar Thermal[1] | 13–26 | 8–10 | 5–6 |
| Nuclear | 10–21 | 10–21 | *[2] |

1 With natural gas as a backup fuel
2 No plant ordered since 1978; all orders since 1973 subsequently cancelled.

Source: Flavin and Lenssen (1994)

research, its use in the world increases. Five million buildings in Japan, for example, already have solar hot water systems. Electricity generated from wind-driven turbines is already less expensive than electricity coming from that of new coal-powered electric plants in many regions.

> Within the next decade, it is projected to fall to three to four cents per kilowatt-hour, making wind the least expensive power source that can be developed on a large scale worldwide. (Flavin and Tunali, 1996)

China's Inner Mongolia region alone has enough wind power to provide power to the whole nation.

Part of this change from fossil fuels is occurring because large utility systems are being broken up in Brazil, India, Poland, Great Britain, Japan, the United States and elsewhere and sold to private investors. This has led to huge innovation, as independent energy producers must become more efficient and build less expensive plants to survive. Most of the more recently built plants in the United States use natural gas (the cleanest burning fossil fuel) rather than coal or nuclear energy.

Perhaps the greatest energy change will be to hydrogen.

> Scientists have foreseen the possibility of a transition to hydrogen for more than a century, and today it is seen as the logical "third wave" fuel—hydrogen gas following liquid oil, just as oil replaced coal decades ago. The required technology—using electricity to split water molecules through electrolysis—is already being used commercially. (All the world's current energy needs could be met with less than one percent of today's fresh water supply, and hydrogen can also be produced from sea water.) Although many people worry that hydrogen is dangerous, if properly handled, it will probably be safer than fuels like gasoline that are widely used today. (Flavin and Tunali, 1996, p. 19)

(Keep in mind, of course, that the same was said about nuclear energy.) In combination, these nonfossil fuel sources may overcome some of the problems that each one may have individually. While wind and solar energy are sometimes found at the wrong place or the wrong time to provide energy in a given area, they can be used to provide power to the electric grid when demand is high and produce storable hydrogen when it is not. While hydrogen power may not enter the market for a decade or two, several companies already have experimental cars powered by hydrogen.

One of the chief advantages of a hydrogen-solar power energy system is that it will take up much less space than hydroelectricity, which results in the flooding of large areas, often prime farmland. The solar-hydrogen system will be largely invisible. Fuel cells and flywheels will be hidden in the basement; solar rooftops will look much like regular roofs. Many of the larger wind and solar plants will be in remote areas such as deserts.

The transition to these energy sources will produce many changes. It is, of course, not possible to know what they will be, but it does seem that the potential for individualized energy sources, not dependent upon any large corporation, will increase dramatically. Much of the massive transportation of fossil fuels from one area to another, often in noisy trucks and spill-prone oil tankers, will decline. Past that, there is the possibility that our lives will be more leisurely. The new energy forms will intrude less on our lives, allow forests to survive, both because of less acid rain and less need for fuel wood, and otherwise make our lives more leisurely.

What could prevent this transition is the vested interests of the coal, oil and nuclear energy companies. These companies not only are huge political forces themselves, but also they will be joined by those which manufacture automobiles, sell gasoline, and a host of other financial interests. In the short run, large corporations may be able to stop this transition; in the long run it will be more difficult as the damage to the environment becomes painfully obvious, as the cost of solar and wind energy declines and as governments begin to tax those who sell and use fossil fuels more in line with the amount of environmental damage produced. Even now the insurance industries are sufficiently concerned about global warming that they are beginning to support environmental legislation.

# Issue Questions

1. Should the recreational use of fossil fuels be more highly taxed than fuels used for "essential" purposes such as manufacturing and commerce? Why?

2. Imagine a society whose fuel source was limitless solar and wind energy? How would people's use of leisure be changed by such a situation? Would a society of leisure evolve?

3. What problems and opportunities would low-cost, non-polluting energy sources make for the tourism industry?

# Possible Implications for Leisure

The implications for leisure during this transition are difficult to predict. (As are all the others.) Aesthetically, the environment will provide for a higher quality of leisure experience if the air is clearer, fewer trees are cut down for fuel, automobiles and trucks make less noise and smoke, and the environment is otherwise less changed by humans consuming energy. There are also issues of whether leisure services organizations will become more centrally involved in designing bicycle trails for both leisure and work purposes, whether they will be leaders or followers in the use of solar and wind energy, and whether solar and wind generating "energy farms" will be placed on land currently managed by recreation and park agencies.

Beyond these possibilities, use your imagination. If energy is almost nonpolluting, will people travel more? Will it cost less to travel? If it does, will the skies and road fill up with travelers, creating all-time traffic jams?

Renewable energy sources could further limit the need for work, since such energy supplies seem limitless. Regardless, a nonfossil fuel economy would make life more quiet, tranquil and take us a giant step toward a society of leisure. Energy from the sun, wind, and other renewable sources generally doesn't produce noise when energy is generated, doesn't involve much human activity to supply them compared to coal, oil, wood and other nonrenewable sources which must be mined, transported in trucks, stored in tanks, and otherwise prepared for use much more than the renewable sources.

# The Shift to Sustainable Industries—The Potential to Decouple Economic Growth From Materials, Energy and Work Time

As we have seen and will see in other identified trends, the potential exists for economic growth to be "decoupled" from the use of raw materials, from the consumption of energy and from the amount of time spent working. Such claims are only partially justifiable at this point but, suffice it to say, the evidence is that almost all materials humans use can be recycled. There is also abundant evidence that the amount of energy needed for our society to prosper can decline and change in ways which are sustainable. Finally, there is evidence that the amount of time spent working is declining, even as economic growth continues. Many of these issues will be examined in more detail later.

In terms of use of material goods, massive changes are beginning to occur in the ways products are manufactured in many regions of the world. The movement toward "sustainable" industries is a movement about which there is little choice:

> The world's economy is temporarily upsetting the balances that occur in nature. It is putting carbon into the atmosphere faster than the flora can remove it. Under its management, the rate of extinction of species far exceeds the rate of their evolution. The balances long established in the world's forests, prairies, and oceans are being undone. This cannot continue indefinitely. Just as the water in a well can be drawn down faster than it replenishes itself only for a short time before the well runs dry; so all these balances must eventually be restored. (Brown, 1996, p. 152)

Industry will have to mimic nature, reusing and recycling every chemical and material used in a cyclic process rather than an open-ended one. Recycling will become "normal" and those industries which do not use recycled products will be more heavily regulated and limited. This does not necessarily mean that we will buy inferior products. It means instead that we will do things differently and ultimately get rid of words such as "trash" and "garbage," as it becomes apparent that everything can be re-used. In terms of scrap paper, for instance, the Taiwanese already use 97 percent "scrap" in their paper production, with Denmark, Mexico and Thailand close behind. The American Forest and Paper Association hopes to reach a goal of 50 percent by the year 2000. Automobiles are being designed so that almost every part of the car can be recycled. The United States already reuses 75 percent of the weight of every automobile, and automobile manufacturers such as BMW have cars in the design process which can have almost all of their weight recycled.

In terms of the use of material goods, some environmentalists have raised the question of whether "dematerialization" is underway. Broadly speaking, dematerialization refers to the relative reduction of the quantity of materials required to serve economic functions (Wernick, Herman, Govind and Ausubel, 1996). This issue is particularly important in the United States, which consumes more material goods and generates more solid waste than any other country (see Figure 8). The carbon content of

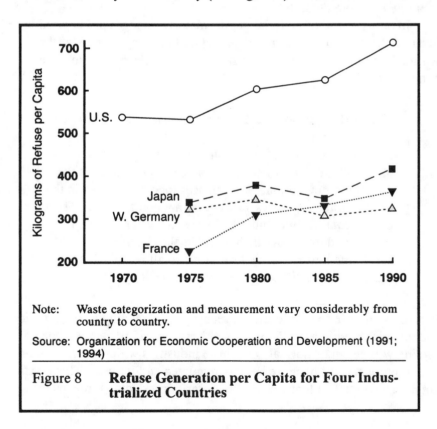

Note:    Waste categorization and measurement vary considerably from country to country.

Source:  Organization for Economic Cooperation and Development (1991; 1994)

Figure 8    **Refuse Generation per Capita for Four Industrialized Countries**

the materials humans use and "throw away" is a particular problem, posing threats such as global warming, oil spills, water and air pollution, and other environmental and health problems. It appears that the amount of carbon in relation to gross national product and the production of energy is occurring steadily but absolute carbon consumption by weight in the United States grew at a compound rate of 1.8 percent per year between 1950 and 1993.

The issue seems to be one of how quickly less material can be used and how quickly more toxic materials, such as lead, can be replaced with less toxic ones. There is hope that this will occur. So far, it has not. "Individual items in the American economy may be getting lighter, but the economy as a whole is physically expanding" (Wernick, Herman, Govind and Ausubel, 1996, p. 179). Put another way, North Americans continue to use more stuff, and there are more of us. On some issues, there is progress, recycled aluminum cans require only five to ten percent of the energy used to make the original can and more and more aluminum is recycled. Cans and other products are being "light weighted," requiring less materials.

The substitution of recyclable plastic for metal and other more energy intensive products is another positive sign. The use of electronic mail to send messages increases by about ten percent per month. Batteries, paper, and pasteboard are increasingly recycled. While the potential exists for economic growth which is less materials consumptive, this is not yet happening.

A related trend is occurring in regard to agriculture, where, even though U.S. cropland shrunk by one percent between 1975 and 1992, the U.S. population grew by one-fifth. Farmers are producing more on less land. Farmers raised yields of feed grain, lessening the area of land per unit of feed grain produced by 2.4 percent annually. This is critical, since animal feed (corn, oats, barley, and sorghum) is grown on one-third of U.S. cropland. As more Americans move toward a vegetarian diet, less of this cropland will be needed for livestock feed. As may be seen in Table 3 (page 44), 25 percent of the total landmass of the United States is used for pasture. Thus, eating a vegetarian diet would open up a huge amount of land for growing food for humans.

Finally, as we will see later, people are spending a shorter portion of their life working and are, on average, working less hours per week. *In information economies, it is cooperation and the application of intelligence rather than hours of work which are the key determinants of economic well-being.*

Table 3      **Land Use in the United States (1992)**

| Use | Thousand Hectares | Percent |
|---|---|---|
| Crop | 187,776 | 19.6 |
| Pasture | 239,172 | 25.0 |
| Forest | 286,200 | 29.9 |
| Other* | 244,163 | 25.5 |
| Total | 957,311 | 100.0 |

\* Includes built-up (e.g., urban) and barren land

Source: Food and Agricultural Organization (1994)

As the world's population doubles, the decoupling of economic growth from materials, energy and work time must occur at least as quickly as the population increases for humans to maintain their standards of living. Some optimistic environmentalists think it can occur more quickly.

## Issue Questions

1. What implications could more mandatory recycling have on people's use of leisure in modern nations?

2. How can tourism become a "sustainable industry?"

3. If economic growth is decoupled from materials use, energy, and work time faster than the world population increases, what implications might there be for leisure?

## Possible Implications for Leisure

Such efforts will have many positive effects on a variety of recreation environments, much as will the transition from a fossil fuel economy. Fewer forests will be cut down. The ocean and rivers will be used less as industrial toilets. Wildlife will have a better chance of surviving. As this happens, being in the "natural environment" will become an increasingly pleasant use of leisure. Some urbanized areas may become wild again.

# 7

# *Decreasing Biodiversity*

While biodiversity may be a difficult concept to understand, it is a critical one in shaping the well-being of those species which survive on earth.

> Biodiversity is commonly analyzed at three levels: the variety of ecosystems within which organisms live and evolve, the variety of species, and the genetic variety within these species themselves. (Ryan, 1992, p. 7)

Measuring the ecosystems, species and genes which make up the living world is difficult but it is clear that the diversity is collapsing at rates which are alarming. Harvard biologist Edward O. Wilson estimates that, in tropic rain forests alone, which are rich in diverse life forms, 50,000 species per year are either condemned to becoming extinct or become extinct.

> Entire ecosystems and genetic varieties within species (including both wildlife and domesticated crops) are also disappearing, likely at rates greater than the extinction of species themselves. (Ryan, 1992, p. 6)

While the disappearance of species is nothing new, all species eventually disappear, but the length of time at which individual species survived was generally from one to ten million years, with only one to ten species disappearing per year. This process has been sped up several thousand times due to habitat loss, pollution, overexploitation, and other human activities. Table 4 (page 46) makes it clear that the rate at which animals are disappearing must change or we may soon live (or be unable to live) in a world in which we are the only animal, perhaps with the exception of a few species which adapt to a degraded environment: rats, flies, pigeons.

Biological diversity is critical not only in protecting species which have evolved over millions of years but also is worth doing for its own sake. The beauty of the world is in its diversity for there can be no beauty apart from difference. Every living thing is beautiful, as the song goes, in its own way.

Table 4        **Selected Animal Species in Jeopardy (Early 1990s)**

| Species Type | Observation |
|---|---|
| Amphibians[1] | Worldwide decline observed in recent years. Wetland drainage and invading species have extinguished nearly half of New Zealand's unique frog fauna. Biologists cite European demand for frogs' legs as a cause of the rapid nationwide decline of India's two most common bullfrogs. |
| Birds | Three-fourths of the world's bird species are declining in population or threatened with extinction.[2] |
| Fish | One-third of North America's freshwater fish are rare,[3] threatened, or endangered; one-third of U.S. coastal fish have declined in population since 1975. Introduction of the Nile perch has helped drive half of the 400 species of Lake Victoria, Africa's largest lake, to or near extinction. |
| Invertebrates | On the order of 100 species lost to deforestation each day. Western Germany reports one-fourth of its 40,000 known invertebrates to be threatened. Roughly half the freshwater snails of the southeastern United States are extinct or nearly so. |
| Mammals | Almost half of Australia's surviving mammals are threatened with extinction. France, western Germany, the Netherlands, and Portugal all report more than 40 percent of their mammals as threatened. All cetaceans (whales and dolphins) are treated by the *Convention on International Trade in Endangered Species* as threatened or likely to become so. |
| Carnivores | Virtually all species of wild cats and most bears are declining seriously in number. |
| Primates[4] | One hundred sixteen of the world's roughly 200 species are threatened with extinction. |
| Reptiles | Of the world's 270 turtle species, 42 percent are rare or threatened with extinction. |

1  Class that includes frogs, toads, and salamanders.
2  Definitions of "threatened" and "endangered" vary, but generally "endangered" means in imminent danger of extinction, and "threatened" includes species imperilled to a lesser degree.
3  Many species are naturally rare; others have been made rare due to human activities. Rare species are vulnerable to endangerment in any case.
4  Order that includes monkeys, lemurs, and humans.

Source: Ryan (1992)

There are also practical reasons for protecting biodiversity. Time after time in human history, plants and animals thought to be of no value turn out to be crucial to our well-being. Predator animals driven to extinction no longer keep populations of pests in check. Mangroves cut for firewood no longer protect coastlines from erosion by the ocean; earthworms killed by pesticides and mechanized tilling and planting equipment no longer aerate soil. Additionally, the huge variety of plants disappearing from tropic forests that are being converted to cow pastures mean that future medicines to treat a variety of diseases will not be discovered.

## Issue Questions

1. What can recreation, park and leisure services do to promote biodiversity? How?

2. What role can environmental centers play in interpreting the importance of biodiversity? How would they go about undertaking this role?

3. What can zoos do to promote and protect biodiversity?

## Possible Implications for Leisure

Since any meaningful strategy to protect biological diversity will mean protection of wild lands, not only in remote areas of the planet, but also in those we live in, protecting biodiversity has many implications for parks, conservation areas and outdoor recreation.

Today, there are just under 7,000 nationally protected areas in the world, covering…4.9 percent of the earth's surface, or 1.3 percent of the earth as a whole. (Ryan, 1992)

While "parks" represent a large part of this area, many are "park" in name only. Most of the acreage in parks which potentially have environmental value exist in name only. They have little or no staff, are politically weak, often subject to corruption, and are managed in ways which do not protect them from damage (Ryan, 1992).

Additionally, many parks encourage profitable activities which are destructive, such as logging and mining. Many such parks place recreational activity ahead of protecting biodiversity:

And in Europe, Canada, and many of the world's marine areas, parks are oriented primarily toward recreation, with biological conservation a secondary or nonexistent concern. Because tourists part with their money more readily than cash-strapped governments, many parks rely on them [tourists] to pay the bills, often at the price of serious crowding, pollution, and harmful degradation. (Ryan, 1992, p. 20)

Parks, in other words, are not necessarily a good thing in terms of protecting biological diversity. If they are exploited like the rest of the earth, no habitat may be sustained for the plants and animals which might otherwise flourish there. Parks which have flourished have typically had a buffer zone established around them where limited exploitation of natural resources by local inhabitants is permitted.

The huge boom in tourism which may emerge as hundreds of millions of Chinese and those from other developing nations increase their economic standard of living will provide a huge challenge to the management of such areas. Personal freedom of humans to visit such areas will have to be limited or simply stopped if such parks are to contribute to the critical issue of biological diversity.

Past that, there are issues of whether local and state parks can contribute by planting and protecting a diversity of plant life rather than depending upon nurseries which grow common varieties of trees, shrubs and other plants. In some countries, particularly those of the former British Empire, it was assumed that a local recreation and park director was first and foremost a "horticulturist." Today, those who direct recreation and park services at the local level in many countries need more education about plant and animal life and what can be done in local, county and state parks to enhance biological diversity.

Optimists think that recreation and conservation are compatible ideas. "Ecotourism," in which people's visits to various recreation areas are designed to have minimum impact on the environment, will be a technique of protecting parks. Pessimists say that you must simply keep people out of areas you wish to conserve. At this point, it is difficult to tell who is correct.

# 8

# Water Scarcity

The delicate balance between water resources and population may be lost; making water a more precious fluid than oil. The amount of water we have is not endless. The renewal rate of water is fixed and extremely slow. There are no untapped reserves of water, but there may be unused flows that could be developed (Falkenmark and Widstrand, 1992). Due to a combination of poor water use practices and an exploding population, by 2025 over one billion people worldwide will be living in areas subject to extreme water scarcity. The arid and semiarid areas of Africa are already living on the hydrological margin. Agriculture, where irrigation is increasingly common, accounts for nearly 70 percent of the world's water use. Industry accounts for about 23 percent and household use the remainder. The solutions to water shortages include slowing population growth, conservation, appropriate agricultural policies, and increased storage facilities. Such solutions, of course, are easier said than done.

One emerging problem between both water-scarce countries and within countries is water rights. In the Middle East, for instance, the building of dams by one country may significantly affect the water resources of a neighbor. In the United States, areas with little rainfall, such as the southwestern states, are currently dependent on water diverted from other areas. Cities such as Phoenix, Arizona, have already used all the ground water within the area and will be increasingly dependent on water "imported" from other areas. In the United States, the overpumping of ground water has led to the depletion of the huge Ogallala aquifer and some experts believe it may be emptied during the next 25 years (Falkenmark and Widstrand, 1992). In India's Tamil Nadu region, excessive pumping of ground water has lowered the local water table by 30 meters in just a few decades.

The increased building of dams and the diversion of rivers to accommodate urban growth in areas which get insufficient water to support the population presents numerous problem of both a political and environmental nature. "Alteration of ground water systems and river deltas is an unavoidable outcome of building a dam" (Falkenmark and Widstrand, 1992, p. 13). Other problems, however, such as salinization, water logging of soil downstream, the spread of waterborne diseases and the rapid silting of reservoirs can be avoided with proper planning. Political problems are another matter.

# Issue Questions

1. What forms of leisure behavior would water scarcity or rationing of water affect? How?

2. Can the use of bodies of water for recreational purposes be compatible with the conservation of water? If so, how?

3. Do you think people will be able to swim safely in "natural" bodies of water, such as lakes, streams and oceans in this country in 50 years?

# Possible Implications for Leisure

The consequences of water shortages or scarcity are likely to have different consequences in different areas. The damming of water has great consequences for recreation.

> With proper foresight, dam reservoirs can provide desirable habitats. Fisheries, boating, flood control, and recreational activities can be developed in conjunction with the building of a dam and hydropower plant, counterbalancing the unavoidable side-effects of this form of human intervention. (Falkenmark and Widstrand, 1992, p. 13)

Where there are outright attempts to limit water use, facilities such as golf courses, which are "water intensive," may need to be managed in different ways, limited to the use of waste water for keeping the course green, or even banned. Private swimming pools may also be restricted in terms of water use, putting an even bigger burden on public swimming pools in hot weather.

In countries where population migration is increasingly moving toward semiarid or desert areas, such as Australia and the United States, there will be greater demand for those who manage recreation and park services to fight for "appropriate" landscapes. This means, for instance, that parks in Phoenix, Arizona, or Brisbane, Australia, must fight for landscaping which reflects the low rainfall in the area. Keeping grass alive with irrigated water "borrowed" from somewhere else in the world makes no ecological sense and only demonstrates the colonial mentality of the population. In many cases, Arizona's landscape has been irrigated to look like the east coast of the United States which in turn was landscaped to look like Britain.

# Increasing Vegetarianism

Vegetarianism will be increasingly promoted for environmental, spiritual and health reasons. Consumption of food will increasingly take on environmental, political and lifestyle overtones, as people become more aware that meat-based diets waste millions of tons of grain which could be used to feed other people and that cattle do huge environmental damage. Additionally, increased medical costs associated with high-fat diets and increased health and longevity associated with many vegetarian diets will encourage people to eat less meat.

A number of environmental dilemmas are linked to what we eat. Eating cattle, pigs, sheep, horses, dogs, fish, and other animals is linked to numerous environmental and health problems. In the United States, 70 percent of all grain is fed to cattle and other livestock. Animal feed (corn, oats, barley, and sorghum) is grown on one-third of U.S. cropland (Waggoner, Ausubel and Wernick, 1996, p. 538). In the world, one-third of the grain supply goes to this purpose, even though a billion people suffer from malnutrition or starvation. It should not be surprising, therefore, that the amount of energy it takes to produce one gram of protein from animal sources is six to eight times greater than what it takes to produce a gram of protein from vegetable sources. In particular, cattle are a major source of numerous environmental problems, from the desertification of Africa, where cattle have been inappropriately introduced in semiarid and arid climates, to the production of methane, to simply taking up space. Cows take up 24 percent of the landmass of our planet through designated pasture land (Rifkin, 1992). The collective weight of cattle exceeds that of the human beings who eat them. There are 100 million cattle in the United States, most of which will be slaughtered. Vegetarianism, which can produce a perfectly healthy diet if one receives a little education about what to eat, can help eliminate not only the environmental problems associated with methane production, global warming and other problems, it can help reduce both malnutrition and the diseases of affluence—heart attacks, diabetes, and cancer.

There is some indication that a switch from eating animals is underway. In the United States, for instance, not only are Americans eating more poultry and less beef, but the percentage of consumer spending on meat is declining. These incremental changes may be just the beginning. As those who prepare food become more skilled at preparing vegetarian meals, and as the palates of younger people, who are much more likely to be vegetarian, start to exert their influence in restaurants and supermarkets, the movement toward vegetarianism will likely increase.

## Issue Questions

1. How might increasing vegetarianism affect the use of publicly-owned lands in the western part of the United States and in many other countries which allow cattle to graze on them at subsidized rates?

2. What role can public recreation and park services play in promoting gardening in urban areas? What have they done in the past?

3. How might increasing vegetarianism affect the hospitality industry, particularly restaurants?

## Possible Implications for Leisure

Interest in vegetarianism may reshape some leisure experiences. Restaurant menus will increasingly feature vegetarian choices. Learning to grow vegetables and to make pasta, bread, rice-based dishes and a variety of other vegetarian foods will increase.

For those in the hospitality industry, menu planning in restaurants and convention centers will increasingly be subject to environmental and political considerations. Customers will want to know more about what they are eating, not only in nutritional terms but also where the food came from, whether or not it is organic, and whether it contains animal products. It may be necessary to have more diverse menus to accommodate older people who were raised on a heavy meat diet while also satisfying younger people, who are more likely to be lacto-ovum (egg and dairy product) or vegan (nothing from the animal) vegetarians, as well as others who are semivegetarian.

Vegetarianism also produces more interest in gardening and cooking as a leisure pursuit. More people may grow their own vegetables, bake their own bread and otherwise supply some part of their own food supply. In combination with the aging of the population, increased vegetarianism should make gardening a growth activity for several decades.

# 10

# Intelligence and Access to Information as the Source of Power

The information highway is in the beginning stages of transforming everyday life. Intelligence and access to information have become the new basis for power in the world. The fiberoptic revolution is quickly reshaping how people communicate, the volume of information they have access to, the location of their work sites, shopping, banking, and their leisure. As the millions of miles of braided copper wire hung from poles or buried underground are replaced with fiberoptic cables in our offices and homes (or made user friendly to new communication technologies), life will change. Television and telephones as we now know them will be rendered obsolete—entertainment and access to information will be more diversified and accessible. The mass culture which developed in the 1950s will wither away. The decisions people make will be made from a larger information base. The ability to use this system will represent entrée into the middle class just as the ability to read did thirty years ago. Branch campuses of universities will become virtual; branch banks—ATMs.

Access to knowledge has been historically "privatized." In most organizations, only a few people at the top of the pyramid knew what was necessary for the organization to function. Our whole notion of "profession" is built upon privatized knowledge—so is our notion of "professor." In particular, the education "profession" has been built around the idea of specialized knowledge which only a few people can possess. These ideas are going to simply be discarded as information becomes accessible to huge segments of the population. The ante, to paraphrase T. S. Eliot, may be raised from information to knowledge to wisdom for a professional who wants to avoid being replaced by software. People's need of experts in many areas of their life will decline except for the expert who is truly wise.

Ray Lane, Oracle's president and chief operating officer, says that when computers eventually become as cheap, easy-to-use, and commonplace as telephones and television, the organizational consequences will be vast. The classic balance sheet will become obsolete, because patents and intellectual property will have greater value than real estate or plants and equipment, and companies will become networks of projects "bound together by strategic intention instead of a set structure and hierarchy."

Potential competitors will be everywhere, because they don't have to build the same infrastructure that established companies have, and can grow faster and move more quickly. There will also be dramatic changes in business processes, to emphasize self-service, reducing costs while at the same time empowering and satisfying the customer. Business attitudes and culture will change. English, aided by its omnipresence on the Internet, will be the standard of law and commerce, and global communications and work teams will be the most important factors in the new work world:

> And this will be a threat to everything in the middle—the nation-state as well as any kind of departmental or vertically integrated companies that try to get in the way. (Lane, 1997)

While the bases of economies are never absolute, the transition of economies in the world may be going from hunting and gathering food, to agriculture, to trade and merchant systems, to manufacturing, to the provision of services, to an information or knowledge economy and, perhaps, eventually to an economy which has creativity as the main generator of wealth. Our own economy is currently in a transition from one in which "services" may be thought of as the primary basis of employment and wealth to an "information" or "knowledge" economy. The value of products and services in the world is no longer determined by the amount of labor necessary to produce them, but rather by the amount of intelligence. A computer may have less than $100 worth of silicon, plastic and glass but its worth is unrelated to such materials. The economic impact of an advertising campaign has less to do with how many hours it took a company to design the campaign, but rather its designers' understanding of the consumer they wish to reach. It is information and "information about information" or "knowledge about knowledge" that is separating economic winners from losers. For employees, increasing the productivity of knowledge is the critical variable to success in most enterprises.

Acquiring information will increasingly serve as an important form of leisure expression for those in the "have" segment of the emerging have-and-have-not society.

# Issue Questions

1. As intelligence and access to information become the basis of many economies, how will concepts of "disability" change? What implications will this have for therapeutic recreation?

2. If people use more knowledge in their work, will their leisure behavior be reshaped so that they are also more interested in acquiring and using knowledge during their free time?

3. In an era in which information is critical to economic success, will many leisure services become primarily providers of information rather than direct services?

# Possible Implications for Leisure

A learning component will be built into many leisure experiences for those in the have part of society. Many tourist experiences will be culturally or historically "interpreted" for such groups. For the have-nots, attempts will be made to use leisure as a device for learning functional skills. Thus, youth soccer may be combined with language lessons; recreation programs for inner-city kids may stress use of numbers.

The information revolution may mean that many leisure activities are undertaken with a much better understanding of what is involved and what the outcomes will be. People with a disability who undertake a given leisure activity may have a better information base about what they will encounter and the likelihood that they will succeed. Tourists may see the area they plan to visit via video camera, virtual reality, interactive television or other means. Athletic teams may have sophisticated computer printouts (many already do) about the tendencies of the other teams and the likely effect of various strategies.

Conversely, there may also be a conscious movement away from such information rich experiences by people who want to get away from the world of statistical probabilities and experience the unknown.

Certainly leisure service organizations will be primarily information driven. In many cases, what they supply to their clients, customers or publics will be information about the opportunities for leisure experience rather than the opportunity itself. Those involved in recreation programming may find that potential participants want more sophisticated information before deciding whether or not to participate. People with a disability may want to know about how accessible the park is—by seeing it on their computer.

# 11

# Computer-Assisted Communication

Perhaps the major factor expected to change everyday life in the twenty-first century is the personal computer. The rapidity of that change is reflected in the recent spurt in the diffusion of computers into the home, from less than ten percent of homes having a computer as the United States entered the 1990s to nearly 40 percent by the end of 1995. One of the major factors behind that growth has been the increased popularity and diffusion of on-line information services, whose reach more than doubled from 1994 to 1995 to include almost one in ten Americans according to a 1995 Times Mirror national survey (Robinson and Godbey, 1997).

Past that, pagers, pocket organizers, "smart" houses, cars and appliances communicate more things to humans. As television becomes interactive or more precisely, as television and telephones as we know them are replaced by computers, there will be a huge increase in our ability to communicate. Where a person is will be increasingly irrelevant in terms of communication and, at some point, so will the language they speak. In the future, you will be able to put on your earphones while a person from China does the same and you will talk to each other. The tiny microphone you speak English into will translate through the earphones of the Chinese-speaking person as Chinese. He or she will speak Chinese into his or her microphone and you will hear what he or she says translated into English.

Computer-assisted communication is changing every aspect of life. We communicate more easily with a greater number of people or information sources. Individuals have a better information base available for almost any decision they have to make—although they may not use it.

The vastly increasing ability of humans to communicate through computer-assisted means may further widen the have–have-not society. The author of *The Virtual Community*, Howard Reinhold (1993) raises the following question:

Will the future see an increasing gap between the information-rich and the information-poor? Access to the Net and access to college are going to be the gateways, everywhere, to a world of communications and information access far beyond what is accessible by traditional means.

A major study of the use of personal computers found that this gap is already beginning.

Rather than decreasing use of other media, new technologies are associated with their increased use. The pattern is particularly evident for the print media of newspapers, magazines and books. In other words, *the more one uses new computer technologies on a given day or in general, the more one uses these old print media.* (*Times-Mirror* survey cited by Robinson and Godbey, 1997)

Thus, those who are more likely to have and use a personal computer and otherwise use computers for information are also more likely to spend more time reading.

## Issue Questions

1. Will use of the computer become the primary form of leisure activity in modern nations? Why?

2. How will the widespread use of computers in everyday life reshape how people plan recreational trips?

3. How will computers reshape the lives and forms of recreation of people with physical disabilities?

4. How will the widespread use of computers affect the management of state parks?

## Possible Implications for Leisure

Rapid changes in computer-assisted means of communication will change our leisure in ways which are not yet understood. It is difficult to predict just how leisure will be reshaped by changes in computer technology. Television, itself, is being rapidly changed and, since television viewing is our most time-consuming use of leisure, changes to television have enormous consequences for leisure.

In terms of commercial leisure services, these changes may be fundamental, depending upon the reactions of customers to them. In regard to theme parks, for instance, theme rides such as King Kong at Universal Studios already use an artificial world with animated characters and special effects such as fire, ice, and artificial aromas. In the planning stages are even more high-tech experiences which are headed toward virtual reality. While housed in an enclosed area, participants sit in seats and are bounced and swayed by hydraulics. About twenty feet from the customer is a large screen which provides visual cues synchronized to the physical movement. Such rides may be a precursor to virtual reality experiences. Computer communication also paves the way for both government and private, nonprofit organizations providing leisure services to reach their customers or potential customers in their homes and to have continuing dialogue with them.

The computer revolution will decentralize television and make it interactive.

> Rather than a system whereby a few "stations" spray images at millions of dumb terminals in real time, computer networks put the customer in control, not settling passively for what is on the "air" but actively seeking and even shaping the customer's first choices. Television will die because it affronts human nature; the drive to self-improvement and autonomy that lifted the race from the muck and offers the only promise for triumph in our current adversities. (Gilder, 1994, p. 16)

A critical question here, in terms of future time use, is the extent to which people want endless choice that computers provide or whether they prefer to have their networks decide for them what to watch.

Part of the allure of television is its *freedom from choice.* It is a respite from a complex world. Interactive television, with its capacity to shape what is seen and heard may actually be less appealing to people who may use future televisions less if they must invest more energy and imagination. There is also the possibility, in an increasingly have-and-have-not world, that television will evolve into two different forms. First, it can become a computational instrument of learning and personal growth for a have culture, and second, an instrument of diversion and control of the have-nots.

Perhaps we need to remember that, even though television may be temporarily overwhelming our use of time, there is historic evidence that discrimination can be learned. As historian Theodore Zeldin (1994) observed:

> It needs to be remembered that at the same time as the British invented the consumer society, they also took to drink as never before, and the USA followed suit, but over the last generation there has been a radical change in attitudes to alcohol, with a move to moderate drinking of high-quality wines rather than mass consumption of anything fermented. Watching television may become addictive but gradually discrimination is learned.

For tourism, the implications of increased ability to communicate are fundamental. Potential tourists will have the opportunity to know much more about the site they plan to visit prior to travel. The ability to see where one will stay, speak to people in their own language using computer-assisted "Walkmans," and otherwise communicate about the visit prior to and after it will change the meaning of tourism for many.

Beyond these issues is the bigger question of whether leisure will be an area of life dominated by technology or nature. To the extent that computer-based technology is viewed as a necessary (or unnecessary) evil, leisure may be the realm of escape to the natural environment. The trick, for humans, may be to find ways to intelligently integrate the new technologies into their leisure without losing appreciation for and contact with the other living organisms in our environment, of which we must surely be only a part.

# 12

# *The Genetic Revolution*

The most important technological revolution going on may be the understanding of our genetic makeup. The Human Genome Project is literally mapping the structure of our genes. As the genetic code is increasingly understood, intelligence may be artificially enhanced, longevity extended, many heritable diseases and dysfunctions detected in utero, and, in fundamental senses, new humans designed. Such understandings may also lead to revolutions in agriculture, food grown indoors, and new varieties of plants and animals developed. (Several new animals have already been patented along with thousands of microorganisms.) Such possibilities will lead to legal and political battles of sizable magnitude.

DNA defines our species. Changing it changes humankind in fundamental ways:

> ...the new kind of progress brings a new paradigm.
> People are becoming the subjects rather than the instruments of change. The coming round of progress will alter what people are rather than just what they do or how they live. This raises issues of an altogether different order, and efforts to force them into the old mold offer only confusion. (Paepke, 1993, p. 319)

Genetic engineering may reshape the balance of economic power if one country chooses to begin widespread enhancement of intelligence. In an internationalized economy, other countries would be forced to follow or lose their hope for economic well-being.

Much of the research in genetic engineering goes on outside the awareness of the public. But geneticists are planning a future which will involve us all. Consider the following from Leroy Hood, a leader in human genetic engineering:

> It's important to make a distinction between the two kinds of genetic engineering. When we correct the mistakes in the book of life (i.e., defective chromosomes), the corrections will only be done in the cells that carry out that

particular function you're interested in.... This is...in distinction to rewriting the book of life in sex cells, or the germ cells that create new individuals. If we rewrite anything there, then you pass those traits on to your children and you've permanently altered the gene pool of humanity, and that is a ban that I can't imagine being lifted again into the indefinite future. In man, we will not do sex cell genetic engineering. (Hood, 1989)

If you are a bit worried about geneticists who might go about correcting changes in the book of life, consider that Professor Hood's views have now changed and he believes that parents may employ "homemade eugenics" to produce more intelligent babies (Paepke, 1993).

Such changes will produce genetic winners and losers as genetic screening from a variety of organizations, from insurance companies to the owners of professional sport, may change the life chances of everyone.

## Issue Questions

1. How might the genetic revolution change forms of leisure activity such as sport, chess, or creative writing?

2. How might genetic enhancement change the entertainment industry?

## Possible Implications for Leisure

The genetic revolution has the potential to reshape many forms of leisure expression, particularly "serious" or "specialized" leisure activities which demand skill and talent on the part of the participant. Children (or potential parents) may be screened to find the most likely future Olympic gymnast, international chess champion, or poet laureate. There may also be more genetic manipulation of those involved in some form of serious leisure to further enhance their ability. Such undertakings may mean that many competitions involving sport or other forms of leisure expression will have a "natural" and "genetically enhanced" division, much like some weightlifting competitions are beginning to identify themselves as "drug-free" competitions.

Past this, the ability of genetic manipulation to contribute to the creative ability of humans remains to be seen. To the extent that it can, artistic expression which is now considered unique may become commonplace.

Genetic manipulation may also have considerable impact upon therapeutic recreation, since gene splicing and other genetic techniques may be used to change the genetic makeup of people likely to have a chronic disability such as multiple sclerosis. In many ways, the genetic revolution may change the number and the characteristics of people with disabilities.

# 13

# Reinventing the Automobile and Other Transportation

On average, people make three to four trips per day, rich or poor, with the main round-trip taking 40–50 minutes. They also average three to four trips per year outside their basic territory (Ofreuil and Salomon, 1993). Transportation is of fundamental importance to human environments. Its performance characteristics shape human settlement patterns. The landscape is shaped by its needs. Such transportation consumes about one-third of all energy in a country such as the United States. People in almost all societies, developed and developing, average about one hour traveling per day (Ausubel, Marchetti and Meyer, 1997). Of American travel time, about 30 percent is to work and back, 30 percent to shopping and childcare, 30 percent to free-time activities, and the remainder for meals out and personal care (Robinson and Godbey, 1997).

In terms of how we travel, the automobile rules in modern nations; particularly in North America. While Americans used to walk an average of five kilometers per day, they no longer do.

Automobile travel will be revolutionized in the next decade (Ausubel, Marchetti and Meyer, 1997). Since most travel done by residents of modern nations is done by automobile, the advent of a car which has almost no fuel costs and emits almost no pollution would turn our way of life on its ear: both increasing the desire to travel more extensively and, at the same time, jamming highways and parking lots. Leisure destinations could be profoundly affected in a variety of ways. The hypercar, which is powered by small motors above either front wheel, thus avoiding the huge energy loss from engine to drive train to wheels, may be so fuel efficient as to provide further disincentives for the development of public transportation.

It is the fuel cell, however, which may ultimately revolutionize the automobile. According to many researchers, the obvious answer to needed changes in the automobile "...is the zero-emission fuel cell, where compressed hydrogen gas mixes with oxygen from the air to give off electric current in a low-temperature chemical reaction that also makes water" (Ausubel, Marchetti and Meyer, 1997, p. 14). Daimler-Benz, Ford and other automobile manufacturers are already building prototypes and will likely begin marketing such cars within ten years.

Such improvements in automobile fuel efficiency are critical to the world's well-being. China, home of one-fifth of the world's population, has recently made policy decisions which favor an automobile and highway system of transportation rather than a bicycle to train system, which has been used in India with success. This decision may mean that, as the Chinese economy grows, the number of automobiles in the world will increase dramatically. Figure 9 shows the projected growth of the Chinese automobile fleet from 1990 through the year 2010. If the Chinese model

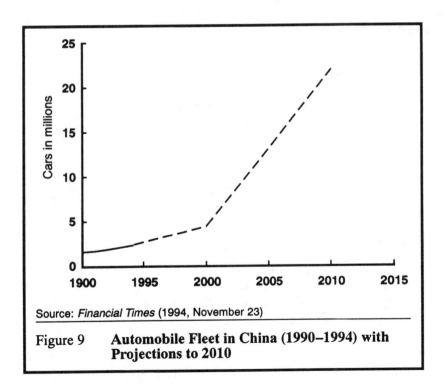

Source: *Financial Times* (1994, November 23)

Figure 9     **Automobile Fleet in China (1990–1994) with Projections to 2010**

their travel patterns after the United States, the automobile will have to be even more radically reinvented than government.

The automobile does not have the potential to serve the densely populated urban areas of the world very well. It will be increasingly regulated, even banned, from many parts of urban areas in attempts to maintain the quality of life for areas where population densities are greater than ever. The magnetic levitation (Maglev) train may be used extensively in such areas. These trains, which have already run up to 600 kilometers per hour, have other advantages such as precision of control, rapid acceleration and absence of noise and vibration. In terms of inter-city travel or across smaller continents, magnetic levitation trains could provide supersonic speed where supersonic airplanes can't fly.

Since transportation consumes about one-third of all energy used in the United States, more efficient transportation systems have the potential to make our environment dramatically cleaner. Since 80 percent of all travel takes place within 50 kilometers of home, these changes could make cities much cleaner and healthier. In terms of transportation, "The future looks clean, fast and green" (Ausubel, Marchetti and Meyer, 1997, p. 26).

## Issue Questions

1. How would an automobile which needed almost no fuel change your personal leisure patterns, if at all?

2. Should automobiles be largely banned from large urban areas? If they were, would the quality of life and leisure be improved? Why?

3. Will magnetic levitation trains make it possible to ban automobiles in large portions of or all of national parks?

## Possible Implications for Leisure

Other than home uses of leisure such as television viewing, almost all leisure activity in North America and, increasingly, in other modern nations, begins by getting into an automobile. People go bicycling after driving their bicycles somewhere in a car, take a walk after driving to the site, go to the theater, museum or art gallery by car and otherwise use the car to get there. Any changes in the automobile will change uses of leisure in direct ways. In the United States, a kind of denial is at work concerning the price of gasoline. The federal government subsidizes automobile travel to an extraordinary extent but the public doesn't think of it in those terms. A drastically more fuel efficient automobile may make many forms of leisure more accessible to poor people (the majority of whom have a car in North America) but at the same time result in such traffic jams at many popular leisure sites which will make them inaccessible. Ironically, a vastly more fuel efficient car may lead to its being banned in some recreational areas where it is currently allowed.

Magnetic levitation trains, traveling at the speed now traveled by jet airplanes, will make it possible for people to travel to tourist destinations in shorter periods of time up to a range that may exceed 1,000 miles. Thus, travelers might spend a smaller portion of their vacation traveling. Thus, "day trips" might increase, whereby a tourist in London went by Maglev train to Edinburgh, Scotland, for the day, returning that evening to sleep in his or her own bed.

These changes may mean that the chief role of the large commercial airliner is for trips of thousands of miles. For shorter trips, people will travel on the ground, seeing the area they travel through and thus understanding more about it.

# 14

# New Forms of War

Conventional ideas about war are largely obsolete. Terrorism and low-intensity wars will become the ways of fighting for the have-nots against the haves. The by-products of nuclear energy increasingly provide the means for terrorists to make nuclear bombs or other powerful bombs with ingredients as common as fertilizer.

The so-called "super powers" have lost recent wars, one in Vietnam and one in Afghanistan. The line between crime and war is disappearing and, as that happens, low-intensity conflicts will replace wars fought from traditional strategies. According to military expert Martin Van Crevald:

'The spread of sporadic small-scale war will cause regular armed forces themselves to change form, shrink in size, and wither away. As they do, much of the day-to-day burden of defending society against the threat of low-intensity

conflict will be transferred to the booming security business; and indeed the time will come,' he predicted, 'when
the organizations that comprise that business will...take
over the state.' (Van Crevald, 1991)

Terrorism may become a significant factor in shaping everyday life for
those who live in our increasingly urbanizing world.

The continued reliance of many modern nations on inherently dangerous nuclear energy provides the means for terrorists to obtain the materials for a nuclear bomb. Nuclear technology has two parts, A-bombs
and civilian nuclear energy power plants. Both use nuclear "fission," the
splitting of atoms of uranium 235 or plutonium 239 to produce energy.
When the fission reaction is controlled it can make steam which in turn
generates electricity. Bomb-grade uranium 235 can be made from natural
uranium using 50-year-old technology (Environmental Research Foundation, 1995). The other A-bomb material, plutonium 239, is created inside
nuclear power reactors but must be purified or "reprocessed" before it
can be used. The United States has abandoned reprocessing but many
other countries continue the practice. Furthermore, a kind of reactor
called a "breeder" creates more plutonium than the nuclear fuel it consumes. While the United States has abandoned breeder technology,
France, Germany, Britain, Russia and other countries continue to use it.

The Russians, after the breakup of the Soviet Union, have no way to
safeguard their nuclear inventories. One need steal only about 2.2 pounds
of plutonium or 6.6 pounds of enriched uranium to make a bomb the
equivalent of 1,000 pounds of TNT. Even in the United States, the unsafe
practices associated with this deadly technology are evident. The U.S.
Army has mistakenly shipped a kilogram of plutonium by Federal Ex-
press which delivered it by airplane. A Department of Energy report in
1994 characterized the nationwide network of weapons complexes as di-
lapidated, some containing plutonium containers which were unmarked,
ruptured, and subject to leaks. Such conditions mean terrorists have the
potential to obtain the materials needed for bombs far more deadly than
those used in Oklahoma in 1995.

# Issue Questions

1. How would increases in low-intensity wars or terrorism change people's use of leisure?

2. What could be done to minimize such problems?

3. Could terrorism ultimately have a greater impact on tourism than other industries? Why?

# Possible Implications for Leisure

Low-intensity war has numerous implications for leisure. First, tourism sites will be more directly affected, since such low-intensity war will drive away tourists, much as Lebanon lost most of its tourism as a result of such conflict. The threat of bombs on planes has already been shown to change the behavior of potential tourists in drastic ways. Tourism-dependent countries such as Britain experienced a summer decline in tourists by almost half as a result of a single explosion on a commercial airliner.

All forms of leisure will suffer, from soccer matches to visits to museums, when people fear terrorist acts. Casual entrance into many recreation areas and facilities will be a thing of the past if there is a fear of terrorist acts. Metal detectors and personal searches could become more common. In all forms of leisure experience which takes place out of the home, the threat of terrorist attack will be a factor. It may take longer periods of time to travel due to security checks.

Those recreation programmers who plan special events in urban areas, particularly those which receive lots of media attention, will be faced with security issues to an increasing extent. They will have to interact with security personnel who understand the technology used by terrorists in bombing attempts as well as develop contingency plans for what to do if a bomb is detonated or a kidnapping or hijacking takes place.

*15*

# Humans Changing Humans—The New Definition of Progress

While "progress" has historically meant humans changing nature, it will increasingly mean humans changing humans. Nature, in modern nations, has been increasingly controlled. Progress is now coming to mean changing humans in ways which increase our likelihood of survival and of happiness. Such control includes our ability to control the world's exponentially increasing population, reshape ways of living until sustainable patterns are developed (or again utilized), and controlling the aggressive impulses of humans which, as technology expands, may devastate our planet.

Humans will also have to be taught or retaught about how fragile our planet is (or how fragile our lives are on this planet). The excesses of the individualism of the Western world will probably have to be tempered if we are to survive. Leisure skills will have to be taught which provide alternatives to mindless consumption. This is not to argue consumption is evil—only that humans must have a better understanding of the consequences of their actions.

## Issue Questions

1. Do you believe it is necessary to try and change the "nature" of human beings for the world to survive?

2. Should public recreation and park services use recreation and leisure activity as a means of changing people's habits? Why?

3. Does television try to change people's habits? How? Does government?

## Possible Implications for Leisure

There seems little doubt that leisure will be the arena in which many of the changes in human beings take place. Such changes may include improving physical condition in order to reduce healthcare costs, social activities designed to produce more understanding of people from diverse cultures, tourism designed to enhance international understanding and awareness of environmental issues, intellectual activity to help both young and old enhance or maintain their intellectual functioning, and many other uses of leisure to change people in ways which are presumed to improve them.

Additionally, there will likely be some attempt to lessen the extent of individual freedom in modern nations, which will affect many forms of leisure. People may not be able to go into sensitive environmental areas when and wherever they want, vehicles which make lots of noise and tear up the ground they run over may be banned or more tightly regulated, and the travel of tourists which pollutes the environment may be more highly taxed, restricted or simply outlawed.

Ironically, it is likely that, in some cases, it will be increasingly documented that leisure activities, which people do for their own sake, particularly in cases where such behavior produces the "flow" state, produce positive health results. Thus, people may be encouraged by government to undertake leisure activities for their own sake since doing so reduces healthcare costs.

These changes may make it more difficult for individuals to assert their right to do nothing, be lazy, or otherwise use leisure for idleness. The thrust of both government and the corporate sector may be to promote leisure activities as a means of changing humans.

# 16

# *The Rise of Efficiency—The Desire for Tranquillity*

Efficiency has become the most important value in American culture, and is an increasingly powerful value in other nations. No other value today can even compete with efficiency, doing more with less, as the country's overarching value. Our desire for efficiency reflects not only massive debt, but also our open-ended aspirations toward the consumption of both things and experiences. The modern world is becoming one in which all acts are means to ends; rendering traditional concepts of leisure almost irrelevant. While a dangerous minority of "crazies" is obsessed with absolute ideologies, everyday life in most modern nations is lived with concern for efficiency more than any other value. This value shapes much of leisure as well as work. It should be noted, of course, that efficiency in isolation from advancing technology does not always improve economic competitiveness—if you become the most efficient at using a bamboo rake to rake leaves and I use a leaf-blowing machine to do the same job, I will "rake" more leaves than you regardless of how efficient you become.

Today, in many areas of our life, we have reached a stage at which increases in efficiency produce diminishing returns. Two hundred years ago it would have taken several months to go from Pennsylvania to California. Now it takes five or six hours. Thus, increases in efficiency can save only a few hours; not months.

It remains to be seen if the value of efficiency can be made to serve the values of leisure rather than the other way around. In almost all historic conceptions of "leisure," it has meant the state of having nothing to do; doing things for their own sake; living outside the pressures of time; slow-paced contemplation, tranquillity, celebration apart from any rational notion of life. Our age, even if it has more time removed from work, has no room for leisure; no imagination to let it happen. This may change.

If efficiency is the most pervasive value in our culture, it may well be challenged for supremacy during the next decade by "tranquillity." Desire for calm, peace, quiet, serenity and simplicity will become more important for a variety of reasons. First and foremost, the population of modern nations is aging rapidly and there seems to be a greater desire for these qualities in later life. Physiologically, for instance, we react differently to loud noise as we age. There is also more desire for tranquillity because of the impact of the multiple revolutions going on in our society, which are reordering every aspect of our lives. As mentioned previously, we feel increasingly rushed and many Americans are willing to sacrifice to slow down this feeling. Tranquillity, which Thomas Jefferson equated with the good life, is also tied to the spiritual life, and our desire for spiritual expression. As desire for tranquillity grows, older notions of leisure and living leisurely may reassert themselves. Graceful living may be desired more than the ownership of expensive possessions for those whose material needs are largely meet.

Tranquillity may come partly from attempts to simplify, but simplifying in today's world will be a difficult task indeed. The important truths of the past were often simple while today they are often hopelessly complex. Certainly, the hope for tranquillity is likely to reshape leisure expression, in particular the desire to experience forms of leisure to which one can either give oneself totally, thus blocking out the complexity of

modern life, or ones which require no effort or thought, such as a sauna
bath or lying on a couch half-conscious of the ghost images of television,
dancing in another world.

## Issue Questions

1. Why is efficiency such an important value in modern
   nations?

2. How can resorts and tourism sites contribute to people's
   tranquillity?

3. What could employees of a municipal recreation and park
   department do to make the town or city they serve more
   tranquil?

4. Does increased contact with the natural environment
   make people more tranquil? Why or why not?

## Possible Implications for Leisure

Leisure may have more to do with the qualities of environment and with
tranquillity and less to do with a standardized cluster of activities. It will
mean increasingly different things to the haves and have-nots. If "leisure"
is shaped by the values of efficiency, it may become no different from
work. While leisure expression is likely to become more diverse, in the
emerging sped-up, postmodern world where massive change is normal,
leisure will be concerned more with contact with the natural environment
(if "natural environment" is a term which continues to have any meaning)
and with tranquillity; a slowing down and opening up to life. Part of this
change will simply reflect the fact that the population of every modern
and some developing nations is getting older. Part will also have to do
with increased urbanization.

Because the world continues to urbanize, ways of relating to the
natural environment will have to be continuously rethought. In particular,
architects, urban planners and public administrators will have to find new
ways to establish "zoning" regulations which promote more contact with
nature: walking to school through woods, minimizing the intrusion of
"development" into the natural environment, promoting learning about
the ecosystem and how it works, and in other ways using creativity to
reimagine how life could be. Our ability to imagine is the critical variable

in determining whether or not we will find ways to change leisure in ways that compliment the continuous changes of the rest of the planet.

Parks and other natural areas will be an important part of this, not just because they have many significant environmental impacts, but because they serve as a symbol of the world of nature. Integrating parks with the everyday lives of people will be a perpetual challenge. Parks will be less a sealed off space and more an approach toward planning human environments.

# 17

# The Tribalization of Culture

An extraordinary dialectic process is at work in the world such that, even as our economies and communication systems have become increasingly internationalized and interdependent, the more significant trend may be the tribalization, or Balkanization, of cultures.

Although national economies are increasingly tied to the fate of other nations, and the Internet and other means of communication pull us toward increased international communication, culturally, the stronger tendency is toward tribalism or Balkanization. This is evident not only in dramatic events such as the splitting apart of the Soviet Union (and the possibility of countries such as China, Pakistan, India, Canada and numerous African nations splitting apart the same way), but also within the United States. In the United States, numerous groups, as diverse as militia groups, cults, and single issue political groups that support everything from Cuban-Americans to the Nation of Islam to gay and lesbian groups to "special interest lobbies" which seek to promote their specific issues and causes are growing in importance while groups which seek to represent everyone are declining. Thus, we have the American Association of Retired Persons, perhaps the strongest group in Washington, DC, the National Rifle Association representing those who manufacture and use guns, the representative of unions, those with specific disabilities, and a variety of other special interest groups. There are very few organizations representing "the public."

Many of the political boundaries which define nations mean less and less as those of different religions, tribes, ethnic groups, clans and other affiliations put the interests of their group ahead of those of the state. In Africa, many parts of the former Soviet Union and huge countries such as India, the state may play a smaller role in determining how people live.

The notion of commonweal is dying as people split apart into special interest groups, based on ethnicity, entitlement status, addiction, region, religion, gender, occupation, age, political affiliation, leisure interests, victimization, lifestyle, or numerous other statuses. Even within such groups there is a splitting apart. While Islam is the fastest growing religion among African Americans, for instance, the fastest growing political movement among them is the Republican right.

Corresponding to this phenomenon of Balkanization is the growing insignificance of the "national" economy in the everyday lives of people. Within states, there are numerous economies, side by side, which have little relation to each other. Economic depression and economic boom exist within close proximity—a few exits difference on an interstate highway or a few blocks in a major city.

Social movements are also experiencing this splitting apart. The women's movement has become a variety of diverse movements with agendas which are as different as simply enforcing laws already on the books against gender discrimination to planning for a society without males.

## Issue Questions

1. In what ways is the tribalization of societies a good thing? A bad thing?

2. How will the splitting apart of our mass culture into smaller groups with special interest affect various forms of leisure services?

3. Should public recreation and park departments attempt to "reunite" such diverse groups in community-wide leisure activities? Why or why not?

## Possible Implications for Leisure

The splitting apart of our mass culture will mean that leisure is increasingly defined within smaller and smaller subgroups of people. Not only will such groups define what is and is not acceptable behavior during leisure, but they will increasingly dictate the style of participation for those within the group.

Such a situation may make it more difficult to find a sense of community in leisure activities. In the United States, this may mean that those involved in programming community recreation will have to be more creative in finding ways to bring divergent (and sometimes antagonistic) segments of the community together—the Christian right and organizations of gay people; Korean Americans with African Americans; prom queens and their courts with radical feminists; rich, old people with the young poor (and the reverse); Mormons, Roman Catholics and agnostics. In many other countries, the issue is much more critical, as Armenians and Turks, Serbs and Croats, Hindus and Moslems, Hutus and Tutsis, and other groups in bitter opposition are brought together in the emerging megacities. It may also mean that many activities undertaken during leisure will be targeted or even confined to a subgroup, rather than the community as a whole.

Conversely, leisure activities may sometimes offer the opportunity to bring diverse groups together to share common events and celebrations. In sharing a festival, park, or girls' soccer match, diverse factions may find they have things in common and opportunities to share. Leisure may ultimately become the tool used to reestablish the sense of community which is so lacking in our everyday life.

# 18

# *The Emerging Postmodern Culture*

In spite of massive increases in available information (or more likely, because of it) the emerging postmodern society is one in which truth is anything people can be made to believe. All problems of organizations will therefore have a public relations and image component.

The postmodern era pits not so much those with one set of beliefs against another but believers against nonbelievers. The collapse of belief is all around us. The concept of relative truth and multiple truths mean that many who live in modern nations are very different from their ancestors and many of those in developing nations who willingly killed each other over absolute beliefs about god(s) and the universe.

> Amidst the chaos, there is progress toward a future in
> which people will live free of belief as we have known it,
> at home in the symbolic universe. We can see, if we look
> closely, at the ideas and events of the postmodern world, a
> new sensibility emerging—a way of being that puts the
> continual creation of reality at the heart of every person's

life, at the heart of politics, and at the heart of human evolution. (Anderson, 1990, p. xiii)

The modern world has brought us into an awareness of multiple and con-
flicting belief systems. It has heightened our concern with what is real.
There is a growing suspicion that all belief systems are social constructions. The nature of truth is multiple or simply a social construction. This
has led us to a kind of freedom which can hardly be thought of as leisure:

> Today we are all "forced to be free" in a way that
> Rousseau could not have imagined when he coined that
> famous phrase. We have to make choices from a range of
> different stories—stories about what the universe is like,
> about who the good guys and the bad guys are, about who
> *we* are—and also have to make choices about how to
> make choices. The only thing we lack is the option of not
> having to make choices—although many of us try hard,
> and with some success, to conceal that from ourselves.
> (Anderson, 1990, p. 8)

Thus, some scientists and religious fundamentalists may find themselves
on the same side—both may have absolute views of what is true. For the
majority, a number of things may be true and the bases for deciding what
is true cannot be attributed to any single method, belief system or variable.
(Historically, the various rationale recreation movements, of course, were
based on absolute belief in what was and was not worthwhile in terms of
leisure).

In the postmodern world, creating image will become critical for organizations in both the public and market sectors. We are entering the
postscientific era. No wonder almost all large organizations treat public
relations as a critical part of their mission.

The postmodern era corresponds to the "saturated self." As psychologist Kenneth Gergen (1991) observed, new technologies have made
it possible to sustain relationships—either directly or indirectly—with an
ever-expanding range of other persons. This has led to a state of "social
saturation" in which the very ways in which we perceive and characterize
ourselves are changed.

> Emerging technologies saturate us with the voices of hu-
> man kind—both harmonious and alien. As we absorb
> their varied rhythms and reasons, they become part of us
> and we of them. Social saturation furnishes us with a mul-
> tiplicity of incoherent and unrelated languages of the self.
> For everything we "know to be true" about ourselves,
> other voices within respond with doubt and even derision.
> The fragmentation of self-conception corresponds to a
> multiplicity of incoherent and disconnected relationships.
> These relationships pull us in myriad directions, inviting
> us to play such a variety of roles that the very concept of
> an "authentic self" with knowable characteristics recedes
> from view. The fully saturated self becomes no self at all.
> (Gergen, 1991)

Thus, the fax machine, call waiting, e-mail, the Web, improved air travel and other technological changes not only complicate our lives but also put our very identity at risk. In such a situation, as others are incorporated into self-concept, their desires become ours. "...[T]here is an expansion of goals—of 'musts,' 'wants,' and 'needs'" (Gergen, 1991). While our use of time may not be changed by this condition, our sense of the necessary is, with the attendant result of making time psychologically more scarce.

# Issue Questions

1. In postmodern culture, is it possible to assume in advance that a given activity is "work" or "leisure?"

2. How will the advertising of commercial recreation and tourism opportunities be changed by the postmodern era?

# Possible Implications for Leisure

In the postmodern world, advance judgments about what is work and what is leisure are more difficult to make. One person is forced to lift heavy objects at his or her job and the next one does so voluntarily and calls it "body building." Hunting may be murder or a wonderful rite of passage between father and son; professional sport decadent or religious experience.

Postmodernism is likely to make leisure even more different than will the splitting apart of our mass culture. That is, leisure will not only mean different things to different people, it will mean different things to the same person at different points in his or her life. Such diversity will make planning for leisure more difficult and increase the need for those in leisure services to maintain a constant dialogue with those they serve or could serve.

It may be argued that leisure has always meant different things to different people but, in the mass society which emerged after World War II, such diversity was either denied or it disappeared. Terms like "basic recreation program" emerged in the public sector. Such "basic" programs no longer exist, if they ever did. What people want to do for recreation and why and how they want to do it will require an ongoing dialogue with all segments of the community; even those who don't want to talk.

# 19

# New Values

New values are replacing old ones for many in modern nations. Many residents of modern nations are in the midst of a paradigm shift that is changing how they see the world. While such changes have not been realized across all segments of our population, there is evidence of shifts in values as can be seen in Table 5.

Such values, of course, don't apply to everyone. The new values are more likely to be held by those who have more education and have led privileged lives. They are also more likely to be held by younger people. Therefore, these new values are in conflict with those of others. Nevertheless, they are becoming more prevalent.

## Issue Questions

1. Will the new values discussed above mean that consumers of leisure services will be more demanding and have higher expectations concerning leisure services?

2. Name some specific ways that these value changes will affect therapeutic recreation, leisure services to the elderly, local parks, tourism, and environmental centers.

| Table 5 | Changing Values |
| --- | --- |
| **Traditional Values** | **New Values** |
| Self-denial ethic | Self-fulfillment ethic |
| Higher standard of living | Better quality of life |
| Traditional sex roles | Blurring of sex roles |
| Accepted definitions of success | Individualized definitions of success |
| Traditional family life | Alternative families |
| Faith in industry, institutions | Self-reliance |
| Live to work | Work to live |
| Hero worship | Love of ideas |
| Expansionism | Pluralism |
| Patriotism | Less nationalistic |
| Unparalleled growth | Growing sense of limits |
| Industrial growth | Information/service growth |
| Receptivity to technology | Technological orientation |

Source: Plummer (1989)

3. Do you think these value changes will make leisure services more or less important? Why or why not?

## Possible Implications for Leisure

These changes are likely to mean that leisure will become a more valued part or perhaps "quality" of life for many. It should be noted, however, that people may be increasingly likely to desire self-directed leisure rather than the regimented, uniform leisure experiences and products which characterized the mass culture we formerly shared. A report from Stanford Research International (1997), which identified the most important status symbols for the next ten years, found the following:

- Self-directed free time;

- Unity of work and play;

- Recognition of one's creativity;

- Nonmonetary rewards; and

- Social commitment.

These desired status symbols will mean both challenges and opportunities for leisure services. Quality of experience will be increasingly important. The ability to find ways in which recreation and leisure enable one to compose a satisfying life will be critical.

# 20

# *The Gay and Lesbian Revolution*

One of the more fundamental civil rights struggles going on today concerns the rights of men and women who are homosexual. The Gay and Lesbian Rights Movement, along with similar movements of women, ethnic minorities, the elderly, people with disabilities, and others who have suffered institutionalized prejudice, is gaining momentum for numerous reasons.

To understand the future of homosexuality, its past must be understood. Sexual desire has, historically, not been a fixed commodity, but rather has varied in what and how it was in evidence. Sexual desire:

> ...is not just an irresistible hurricane, nor a snake responding to the piping of only certain kinds of snake charmers. It is too simple to say that each individual has to discover, helplessly, by what he or she is "turned on." ...Over the centuries, it has been extraordinarily flexible and versatile, serving opposing causes, playing many different roles in history, like an actor, both comic and tragic, sometimes simple roles, reproducing hackneyed stereotypes and sometimes experimental, complex ones, deliberately mysterious. This suggests that other alliances, other excitements, are also possible. (Zeldin, 1994, p. 128)

History tells us, in short, that sexual desire is complex, changing, and subject to further change. The stimuli which evoke desire also change. The female ankle may be thought of as sexually arousing at one time, or the breast, or a full figure or a very skinny one. Males may be considered sexy if they are slender or have huge biceps or long hair (or no hair).

Male and female homosexuality have been historically different based upon differing circumstances of males and females. Lesbian relations and deep friendships between women were historically treated differently from those of men. Since marriage, for many women, has historically meant literally "taking a master," close friendships between women, often with open displays of physical affection, were not only tolerated but sometimes encouraged. Part of this was due to the male notion that women could not satisfy each other sexually or that sexual relations between women were merely a prelude to relations with men.

There were in several eras and places many instances of women who were known to engage in lesbian sex, and they did so with impunity. As long as they appeared feminine, their sexual behavior would be viewed as an activity in which women indulged when men were unavailable or as an apprenticeship or appetite-whetter to heterosexual sex. (Faderman, 1985)

Many deep friendships between women, even women who live together, however, are not primarily sexual in nature. While the male imagination has produced a pornographic literature depicting lesbianism as completely sexual in nature, "...even the sexologists' evidence seemed to suggest that homosexuality was generally no more appropriate a term to describe lesbianism than it was to describe romantic friendship" (Faderman, 1985). What characterized such relations, in which sexual relations might be a part or might not, is that two women's strongest emotions and affections were directed toward each other.

Today, while evidence is inconclusive, it has been argued by many researchers that sexual orientation is to some extent genetically determined. Sex researcher Alfred Kinsey was startled that he could not find one homosexual whose sexual orientation had been changed by any medical procedure. Not only did homosexual orientation not change as a result of the efforts of the medical profession, it was also not possible to document that homosexuals were mentally ill. The administration of various psychological tests showed time and again that homosexuals and heterosexuals could not be told apart by their personality or psychological make-up.

Homosexuality may be said to have gone through four stages but, throughout human history, it has generally not been severely persecuted.

Homosexuality has been more or less accepted in about two-thirds of human societies at some time or another, and it has occasionally concerned large sections of the population. (Zeldin, 1994, p. 122)

The first stage was one in which homosexuality was more or less accepted. It was thought of as a conservative force, strengthening established institutions, an integral part of pagan religions, whose gods enjoyed sex of all forms. It was tolerated even by the Catholic church. In a second stage, homosexuality was punished. In twelfth century Europe, as part of a campaign against heresies of all sorts, which led to the Inquisition, homosexuals were persecuted. In the third stage in Western homosexual history, it came to be thought of as a disease, a sign of defective upbringing, or the result of a genetic disposition. In a fourth stage, being gay or lesbian became a matter of civil rights. But it also became clear that homosexuality did not mean one way of living or behaving sexually. (Any more than being female, African American, an older adult, or Jewish means a single way of living.)

The gay and lesbian revolution is thus ultimately about the right to be different. It would appear that this revolution is gaining ground. Homosexuals are generally of higher income and education level than heterosexuals in modern nations and they increasingly exercise political power. Additionally, there is considerable evidence that younger people are much more accepting of homosexuality than older people.

One important issue in the future of homosexual people is same-sex marriage. To a great extent, marriage legitimizes relationships which have a sexual element. The state of Hawaii has now made same-sex marriages legitimate and other states may follow. Many companies are being pushed to allow insurance benefits for the "spouse" of an employee who is of the same sex. At the writing of this book, United Airlines, Walt Disney Corporation and others have agreed to provide benefits to the partners of employees who live with them, even if they are of the same sex.

Three circumstances make it likely that gay and lesbian people will suffer less discrimination in the coming years. The increasing power of education will make it more likely that homosexuals will be able to gain power and to protect themselves. Second, as mass society pulls apart into smaller enclaves, those who sell goods and services will ignore the gay and lesbian "community" at their peril. The economic power of such groups will be increasingly critical in a world in which products and services must be sold in different ways to different groups for different reasons. As many marketing experts point out, for a company to be antagonistic toward or to ignore the one-tenth (or one-fifth) of the population which is homosexual is to put one's company at risk.

The third circumstance is a simple one—gay and lesbian people generally do not have children. Since control of the world's population is the critical variable in determining our chances for survival and/or the quality of our lives, gay and lesbian people are currently a useful prototype.

## Issue Questions

1. What problems do you think gay and lesbian people have in terms of their use of leisure? What could be done to minimize such problems?

2. How might commercial leisure services profit from the increasing acceptance of gay and lesbian people in modern societies?

## Possible Implications for Leisure

Use of leisure is greatly shaped by sexual orientation. Even in childhood, play may signal sexual orientation. Some research concludes that play which is not gender typical in young boys prior to puberty, such as dressing in women's clothing or playing with dolls, or taking the role of the mother in playing house, indicates a homosexual orientation in 75 percent of the cases. This demonstrates how deeply rooted sexual orientation is. As boys and girls with homosexual orientations go to school, it quickly becomes apparent that most of society has been designed in ways which don't meet their needs, particularly their leisure needs. School dances assume heterosexuality. School sports assume males should be aggressive and females the admirers of that aggression. The explorations of sexuality which teenagers often brag about to each other can be cause for severe persecution if such explorations are with a member of the same sex. The romantic poems read in English class are almost always about the romances of heterosexual ("straight") people. No wonder gay and lesbian teenagers have far higher rates of suicide and emotional problems. No wonder, too, that they sometimes seek to form separate groups or institutions which allow them to be themselves during their free time. In adulthood, gay and lesbian subcultures are often formed in urban areas which are largely segregated from the rest of society. The decision of whether or not to acknowledge one's homosexuality has implications not only for one's work life but also for leisure pursuits, since much of leisure activity revolves around close social relationships. In some cases, those in various gay and lesbian communities develop their own recreation and leisure institutions. In other cases, they attempt to use the resources available to the general public, with mixed success. To an extraordinary extent, gays and lesbians contribute to theater, art, music, literature and other forms of leisure expression enjoyed by the public. The constraints on their use of leisure, however, remain massive.

The portion of the homosexual population which lives "in the closet" is likely to decline in modern nations during the next decade. While there will likely be a backlash among a minority of the population, the gay and lesbian revolution will achieve many goals in the coming years.

Gay and lesbian groups will be increasingly catered to by a wide variety of leisure service organizations. In the commercial sector, this segment of the population offers the opportunity for great profit. In the private, nonprofit sector, it represents a subgroup with special needs and interests, from tourism to social dance. In the public sector, gay and lesbian groups will increasingly request that leisure services recognize their needs for recreation along with everyone else's.

# 21

# *Desire for the Spiritual*

The desire for the spiritual will be an increasingly important factor shaping everyday life during the next few decades, although the ways in which such desire takes shape are uncertain. The necessity of believing in something, having faith, seems a critical need of humans which is reasserting itself in a postmodern era. As the poet Marianne Moore observed, it is wise to have faith in faith. The ultimate truths remain unknowable and the big bang theory of the creation of the universe is no less an article of faith than a world created in six days by a God who needed to rest after he had done it.

Our spiritual needs are also a matter of our failures, such as the failures of democracy. One of the great hopes for democracy was that it would produce respect for everyone. That, it has not done. As eminent historian Theodore Zeldin (1994) observed: "Democracies have not found a way to eliminate the gradations of disrespect created by money, education and appearance" (p. 142). Thus now, as in the past, humans turn to religion for the respect they yearn for. "And when religion did not suffice, other creeds, like stoicism, socialism, liberalism and feminism, reinforced the defenses of human dignity" (p. 142). This search for respect has historically resulted not so much in people overthrowing those in charge as simply ignoring them. Surely one can see this ignoring of political authority in present-day America.

> The prophecy that the twenty-first century will be a religious one is not a prophecy, but an acknowledgment of what has happened quite regularly in the past. It does not mean that politicians are replaced by priests, but that people switch off from the vast mundane pressures which they cannot control. Instead, they turn their energy to their private lives: sometimes that leads them to be selfish, but sometimes they react to the animosities of the big world by seeking more nurture, more generosity, more mutual respect. (Zeldin, 1994, p. 143)

Many of the movements today, concerned with human rights, the environment, women's rights or the rights of ethnic minorities "spring from the same sort of yearnings which the great religions tried to satisfy between twenty-five and thirteen centuries ago" (Zeldin, 1994, p. 143). That is, such movements provide a basis for belief and for the establishment of personal meaning.

## Issue Questions

1. How can parks and outdoor recreation areas contribute to the spiritual life of people? What policies might make such areas contribute more than they do?

2. Are some leisure activities more likely to serve as spiritual expression than others? Which ones? Why?

## Possible Implications for Leisure

The development of spiritual life will become more central to leisure expression. The common denominator of spirituality is the attempt to reduce entropy in consciousness. Historian Theodore Zeldin commented:

> The United States, in the midst of unprecedented material affluence, is suffering from symptoms of increasing

individual and societal entropy: rising rates of suicide, violent crime, sexually transmitted disease, unwanted pregnancy—not to mention a growing economic stability fueled by the irresponsibly selfish behavior of many politicians and businessmen. (1994, p. 25)

Spiritual skills which would help one use leisure well require disciplined habits acquired slowly—order must be imposed on inner processes. Three of four hours of teenagers use of leisure does not do this (Csikszentmihalyi, 1991a). That is, the majority of free time among teenagers is used for purposes such as watching television or listening to music rather than playing it. Such activity does not have rules or provide challenges against which the teenager can develop skill and discipline.

The search for spiritual meaning has huge implication for leisure and its use. Leisure has always been an arena for spiritual expression, whether in the gathering of kindred spirits at holidays, belief in some leisure activity or athletic team, or simply being in the natural environment. As the search for the spiritual intensifies, leisure activity may be based less around consumption and more around affirmation—affirming that life is good. The ritual which is part of many leisure experiences may become even more central to the activity.

## 22

# *The Lessening Sense of Place and of Privacy*

In many modern nations, loss of personal privacy and sense of place are occurring together. Personal privacy has declined for many reasons, including the willingness of both government and corporations to violate constitutionally-based rights to privacy and the increasing technological means to do so. Many fast-food restaurants, banks, gambling casinos and other corporate entities monitor their employees by a number of devices, including television cameras. Electronic mail messages and other communication are routinely monitored.

Law enforcement agencies and private security forces also use a variety of monitoring devices to observe public streets, apartment lobbies, and parking lots. Increasingly sophisticated technology allows the compressing of numerous data sets about individuals, producing a highly detailed record of the individual's financial situation, personal habits and interests. Such information is sometimes sold to interested third parties.

A number of new technologies which identify individuals by their voice, fingerprint, DNA, the iris of their eye or other personal features will make privacy or anonymity even more difficult for the individual.

While people in modern nations seem concerned about the lessening of privacy and the potential for all kinds of surveillance of behavior, they willingly reveal more about their private lives in their conversation, to researchers, and particularly to the media. Not only celebrities but also ordinary people talk freely about their drug addictions, sexual behavior, financial situation and their innermost feelings to almost anyone. While one's politics often remain private, almost everything else is made public.

Sense of place is related to privacy and, like privacy, it is being endangered by technology. First, the ability of people to travel from where they live has increased dramatically. While Pascal thought that all human troubles arise from an unwillingness to stay where they were born, today people routinely travel thousands of miles from their home, many on a regular basis. Higher levels of technology have affected travel, communication and the conduct of business in numerous ways, producing what President of the European Bank of Reconstruction, Jacques Attali, called a "nomadic elite," a class of people who conduct their business from anywhere in the world and owe no allegiance to any country or territory (Attali, 1991).

Travel and tourism has been made into a process in which much of the uniqueness of tourist destinations are sacrificed to masses of tourists. As tourism scholar Dean MacCannell (1976) observed, countries become variations on a theme, with a little difference in their hotels, food, or museums but, for the mass tourist, they are essentially variations on a theme rather than unique places. The "front regions" of a tourism destination, which are created tourism sites, rarely let the tourist get a glimpse of real life in the area. Instead, they present a pretend version which has been manufactured by corporations from outside the area.

Sense of place is also declining due to the franchising of restaurants, hotels, housing developments, swimming pools, air conditioning suppliers an ? ATM machines. Towns, particularly suburban areas, begin to look more and more alike in every modern nation. The string of fast-food shops, convenience stores and strip malls looks very much the same in Orlando, Florida; Eugene, Oregon; or Englewood Cliffs, New Jersey. The loss of sense of place is even creeping into English villages, where "convenience" stores, with a standard design and operating procedure, are beginning to operate almost all night long.

According to Batty (1994):

> The inauthentic is the homogenized, the standardized—the poorly imitated. Inauthenticity emerges out of our very attempts to find and imitate a lost authenticity, a lost world of meaning. The more things become standardized, the more they become interchangeable, and the more they become interchangeable the more we have imitation—and the less we have leisure. Activity free of diversity and difference, free of the possibility of the individual experience of the divine may pass as recreation but does not approach leisure. We desire these imitated activities or places because they are safe and predictable—we know that we can return to our work and our lives (even though they may not be "real").

It is the unique and unreplicatable place, then, that ultimately defines leisure experience. If such places are lost; so is leisure.

## Issue Questions

1. How is privacy an important issue in leisure experience?

2. Do managers of local, state and national parks take sufficient steps to protect the privacy of those who use the parks?

3. In what ways is client privacy an issue in therapeutic recreation?

4. How can tourism be managed to protect the unique sense of place of a given tourist destination?

## Possible Implications for Leisure

Certainly privacy or lack of it is an issue for most profit-making leisure enterprises. In some theme parks, for instance, such as Disney World, managers pride themselves on knowing where their customers are every minute, what they are doing and what they are buying. Some managers of public parks use helicopters for surveillance purposes. Past that, the selling of names and addresses of customers, doing extensive on-site research in which visitors are asked questions about their income, education and other personal matters.

Protecting the privacy of visitors to leisure sites, of course, may cause problems. If you do not monitor visitors to national parks, it may be difficult or impossible to rescue them if they get into a dangerous situation.

Protecting the uniqueness of a tourist or recreation site is also difficult. If such a site becomes popular, people want to be able to visit conveniently, with provision of food, lodging, parking and shopping at about the same level as back home. There is also profit to be made in doing so. Thus, whenever a recreation site is looked at primarily as a resource to be economically exploited, its uniqueness begins to disappear.

23

# A Rapidly Aging Population

The most important demographic change shaping the United States and every other modern nation continues to be the aging of the population. Table 6 shows how rapidly the population is aging. The proportion of older adults in the United States has steadily increased over this century and this graying of America is projected to continue well into the next century. Hagestad (1987) has called this revolutionary demographic change a "watershed period" in American history—an unprecedented time that requires both American invention and ingenuity to meet the demands of the shifting population structure.

Many developing countries also have an aging population although their populations are much younger, on average. China and India have different aging issues. In China, where government policy on birth control has made some progress in slowing the rate of population growth, in

| Table 6 | U.S. Population and Population Age 65 and Older (1900–2050) | | | | |
|---|---|---|---|---|---|
| | Population in thousands | | Percent | Percent increase from preceding decade | |
| Year | Total | Age 65+ | Age 65+ | Total | Age 65+ |
| 1900 | 75,994 | 3,099 | 4.1 | — | — |
| 1910 | 91,972 | 3,986 | 4.3 | 21.0 | 28.6 |
| 1920 | 105,711 | 4,929 | 4.7 | 14.9 | 23.7 |
| 1930 | 122,755 | 6,705 | 5.5 | 16.1 | 36.0 |
| 1940 | 131,669 | 9,031 | 6.9 | 7.3 | 34.7 |
| 1950 | 152,271 | 12,397 | 8.1 | 15.6 | 37.3 |
| 1960 | 180,671 | 16,675 | 9.2 | 18.7 | 34.5 |
| 1970 | 205,502 | 20,107 | 9.8 | 13.5 | 20.6 |
| 1980 | 227,225 | 25,707 | 11.3 | 10.6 | 27.9 |
| 1990 | 249,415 | 31,224 | 12.5 | 9.8 | 21.5 |
| **Projections** | | | | | |
| 1995 | 263,434 | 33,649 | 12.8 | — | — |
| 2000 | 276,241 | 35,322 | 12.8 | 10.8 | 13.1 |
| 2010 | 300,431 | 40,104 | 13.3 | 8.8 | 13.5 |
| 2020 | 325,942 | 53,348 | 16.4 | 8.5 | 33.0 |
| 2030 | 349,993 | 70,175 | 20.1 | 7.4 | 31.5 |
| 2040 | 371,505 | 77,014 | 20.7 | 6.1 | 9.7 |
| 2050 | 392,031 | 80,109 | 20.4 | 5.5 | 4.0 |

Source: U.S. Bureau of the Census (1975, 1993a)

combination with living longer, is producing a hugely increasing aging population. The one child per couple policy means that a young couple is sandwiched between four aging parents and one young offspring, creating a 4:2:1 population pyramid. It also means that the single child will someday have sole responsibility for both parents.

In India, where the population will very soon reach one billion, the population remains younger. The median age of a person in India was 23 in 1995, compared to 27 in China and 34 in the United States. Over one-third of all people in India are age 14 or younger (Visaria and Visaria, 1995).

In the United States and other developed countries, not only is the percentage of people age 65 and over increasing, but also the baby-boom generation is also aging. As this cohort, comprising almost three out of ten residents of the United States who are between the ages of 50 and 32, moves toward later life, every segment of our culture and economy will be changed. Yet, these changes signal only the beginning of a trend. The current number of older adults will continue to increase from the current 12 percent to almost 25 percent by the year 2025 and these changes will have impacts at every level of government and for each type of service provider. The older population is currently the fastest growing portion of the population due to low birth rates, increased life expectancy, and the aging of the baby-boom generation. Yet, unheralded within this segment of the population, the numbers of people over 84 are growing even faster. As for people over 100 years of age, there are already 100,000 of them in the United States.

Elderly people are, by many measures, the wealthiest group in North American society, the most politically powerful, and the biggest recipients of "welfare." About two-thirds of retired Americans own their homes outright. While they will receive Social Security payments, on average, between one and two decades, they will be paid back all the money they paid into it with interest in less than three years. The elderly are no more likely to live in poverty than average and, in terms of net financial assets, are the wealthiest or second wealthiest age group. Their rates of foreign travel, dining in upscale restaurants and otherwise leading the good life represent a completely unsustainable model which almost no politician dares confront. Over 22 million Americans, for instance, belong to the American Association of Retired Persons (AARP), the most powerful lobby in Washington, DC. There is no counterpart for young people. Thus, elderly people today enjoy political power to an extent unknown in our history. Table 7 (pages 95–96) shows the characteristics of future older adults in North America, based upon numerous sources.

Table 7    Social Forecasts Re Characteristics of Future Older Adults

**The Numbers**
- More of them.
- Larger percentage of the general population.
- Increased older (75+) part of the population, reaching almost 50% of the population.

**Dependency**
- Expanded decision-making involvement and influence on society.
- Reduction in the dependency ratio of the nonworking-age population (primarily retirees) to the working-age population. Older persons seen as being less burdensome.

**Life Expectancy and Health**
- Increased longevity and life expectancy.
- Improved levels of health throughout the later years of life.
- Growth/increase in public and private sector health costs as a proportion of overall health costs.

**Socioeconomic Status**
- Better educated—both formally and informally.
- Higher occupational status resulting in greater income.

**Cultural Aspects of Aging**
- Higher proportion of older population born and raised in Canada due to decline in European-born older adults.
- Increased percentages of Asian and Third World older adults.

**Residential Living**
- Continued concentration of residences of older adults primarily in larger urban centres, with some movement to living in smaller communities and/or the suburbs.
- Greater prevalence of planned retirement communities.
- Continued migration to warmer climates for at least part of the year during the later life stages by more and more people.
- Continued living in personally owned, older, single family independent households.
- Increased numbers of people living alone.

Source: Heywood (1993)    Continued on page 96...

**Impacts of Aging on Our Society.** Aging will reshape our society in many ways. Older people, on average, commit less crime, appreciate nature more, move more slowly through space, make significantly greater demands on our healthcare "system," have a stronger sense of place, and are more politically active. Although aging has historically been associated with dependency and loss, the next generation of elderly may challenge such associations. Our ways of dealing with elderly people in arenas such as healthcare are hopelessly archaic, expensive, and suffer from cultural lag.

The elderly, despite often being stereotyped, are not an undifferentiated lump of humanity. Aging is a multidimensional process that occurs at biological, psychological, and sociological levels (Maddox, 1987; Soldo, 1984) and changes at these levels are manifested at different rates

---

Table 7     **Social Forecasts Re Characteristics of Future Older Adults** (continued)

**Political Power and Activism**

- Political power growth in federal, provincial, and local government decision-making.
- Greater political activism among future older adults.
- Declining status as a deprived minority limiting effectiveness and extent of political activism.

**Retirement**

- Growth in percentages of the labour force moving into retirement, including larger numbers of those opting for early retirement before age 65.
- Less attachment to work giving rise to seeing retirement much more as a time of opportunity.
- Emergence and expansion of various work opportunities other than full-time employment as retirement activities.

**Leisure and Recreation**

- Greater involvement in educational and community organizations.
- Increased cultural interests throughout the spectrum of high culture, mass culture, and pop culture.
- Greater interests for women outside the home.
- More travelling and more wide-spread travel.
- Greater variety of leisure lifestyles.
- Greater emphasis on service roles and voluntarism as a part of leisure pursuit.
- Attainment of a stronger leisure literacy leading to being better able to cope with leisure in retirement.
- Increased societal respect for old age and expanded awareness of valued leisure lifestyles in retirement.

Source: Heywood (1993)

---

within and between people. No universal timetable exists for aging. Genetic disposition toward aging combined with the events of life, lifestyles, and the personality of the person to deal with the changes (e.g., widowhood, harsh lifestyle) produce a wide array of aging paths and individual differences in aging.

Because of increasing longevity and the escalating numbers of oldest old, those defined as elderly include people aged 60–65 up to those aged 95 or more, a 30-year span. In no other period of life would we consider people separated by 30 years to be at the same point of development and possessing the same needs. Comparing a 20-year-old college student with a 50-year-old businesswoman would be ludicrous, yet 65-year-olds have often been grouped with 95-year-olds. Distinctions such as the terms young-old and old-old attempt to address this issue, but policy decisions and service delivery often remain based on a mass definition of the elderly.

Different birth cohorts age with different experiences of medical care, educational attainment, exposure to information and world events, and life styles. One must look to the current middle-aged population to learn the characteristics of the old of tomorrow.

**A New View of Aging.** Life-span developmental psychologists have also theorized about the process of aging and argue that development occurs throughout the life span in both continuous and discontinuous ways and in a multidimensional manner. Although aging has been associated largely with decreases in functioning, development is characterized by both gains and losses throughout life and the potential for change and new learning in old age. This concept has been called "plasticity," the malleability of people to contexts and interventions (Baltes, 1987).

These approaches stress the various pathways aging can take and the possibilities for prolonging involvement in life, and recognize the plasticity and the room for growth that remains even in later life. Service providers must first recognize the diversity of the population and provide opportunities that promote successful aging, the maintenance of lifestyles and lifelong interests as well as promoting the development of new interests.

## Issue Questions

1. Identify some ways in which the aging of the population will change the management practices of local parks.

2. What will happen to theme parks as society ages?

3. What leisure activities do you think will decline or increase in popularity as the baby-boom generation approaches old age?

4. Do you think intergenerational activities will increase as a use of leisure as the population ages? Why?

## Possible Implications for Leisure

A rapidly aging society has great implication for leisure and leisure services from theme parks to the Professional Golf Association of America. In making the massive changes which will need to be made to meet the leisure needs of an older population, new concepts of aging must be made operational, particularly "plasticity."

If it is assumed that human beings are characterized by intraindividual differences and the potential for different behaviors and development (Baltes, 1987), then individuals are not constrained to a single developmental trajectory. Rather, the interplay of various biological, psychological, social, and environmental contexts are responsible for differential development of individuals. While limits to plasticity exist and the potential for plasticity decreases with age, particularly at the molecular level, the limits of plasticity are unknown and are, themselves, subject to change or plasticity.

There is reason to believe that the elderly, particularly those in good health and with adequate incomes, will be at differing levels of specialization with regard to many leisure activities, and that there will be a higher level of specialization with succeeding generations due to greater socialization into various leisure activities during their youth and much higher levels of formal education.

In spite of this, recreation, park, and leisure services for the elderly are often still based upon false assumptions about the developmental levels of those to be served and the further assumption that little intraindividual differences exist in regard to those who participate. Such assumptions lead to crafts programs with standardized expectations about interest, skill level and needed time to complete projects; sports and fitness programs which are planned before the physical capabilities of participants are actually determined and which have no room to allow for variation in physical conditions; senior citizen centers which are designed, staffed, and programmed for a nonexistent "typical" elderly individual; and parks which provide nothing for the elderly but benches.

The elderly have to be thought of in terms of market segmentation based upon differences in developmental trajectories. Recognizing such diversity is, of course, more easily said than done. It would seem to imply that recreation leaders working with elderly must attempt to stratify services based upon level of functioning of those they serve. It also implies the heavy use of volunteers for smaller scale programs and the recruiting and training of volunteers with specialized capabilities in dealing with the strata of elderly served. Many volunteers, of course, will be the elderly themselves. Because of the wide range of functioning of older adults, the able elderly can and have been serving to help older and less-able elderly.

As has been said time and again in the literature, the recreation, park and leisure service professional must play a facilitating role and, for the elderly, doing so will likely mean serving as an intermediary rather than a provider of face-to-face programs or services. That is, such services must serve as a catalyst to bring about services from a diverse range of organizations and volunteers.

**The Critical Role of Logistics.** The logistics of providing leisure services with the elderly, from what has been previously stated, is likely to be complex and different from situation to situation. Perhaps the most important issue regarding logistics is that they are planned from an understanding of the everyday lives of those served. Many services will have to be conceptualized in the same terms in which outdoor recreation managers have been urged to conceptualize outdoor recreation visitation: anticipation, travel, participation, travel, and recall (Clawson and Knetsch, 1962). This means the service provider begins planning for and with participants by considering how and when potential participants may know about the program or service and make the decision to participate; how they will travel to the service and what logistical problems will be encountered; how and why they will participate; how they will return home or elsewhere after participation; and their recall of the event. It cannot be the assumption of those who work with the elderly that responsibility for participants begins when they set foot on the premises and ends when they leave. To provide effective leisure services, issues such as transportation must be systematically addressed even when participants provide their own transportation. For example, where can they park safely?

Not only must leisure service providers think about the travel phase of participation, but also they must also consider the possibility of bringing their services to the homes of the elderly rather than vice versa. In some cases, volunteers may go to homes of elderly who can take care of themselves but cannot travel to central locations.

Logistics are also important in the on-site experience. In terms of urban park use, for example, older park users are more likely than others to ascribe critical importance to safety, quality of maintenance, availability of restrooms and drinking fountains, and contact with the natural environment (Godbey and Blazey, 1983).

**Overcoming Constraints to Participation.** It can't be assumed that given rates or formats of participation are inherently appropriate for a given elderly individual. Overcoming constraints to participation must recognize the hierarchical nature of such constraints. That is, the first constraints to participation which must be overcome are intrapersonal ones (e.g., stress, depression, perceived self-skill, subjective evaluations of the appropriateness of and availability of various leisure activities) before interpersonal constraints (e.g., other people with whom to participate) or structural barriers (e.g., lack of transportation, cost, climate) may be handled. Certainly, leisure service providers are limited in the extent to which they can assist older people in overcoming intrapersonal constraints, but some progress is possible. First, they can think in terms of participation–nonparticipation from this perspective. Also, much can be done in providing role models and in publicizing and structuring opportunities in ways which give maximum assurance that the skill levels possessed by potential elderly participants are not only appropriate, but also welcomed. In some cases, this may mean even more specific age segregation or division of participants by gender. Some water exercise programs for elderly may need to cater exclusively to females to overcome the fear elderly woman may have about wearing a bathing suit in public or their ability to begin exercising again. There may also need to be diverse program formats even when the elderly are a primary target market. In terms of water exercise, for instance, a YMCA in Norman, Oklahoma, offers the following: an program for people with arthritis which stresses exercise of joints and is slow paced with slow repetitions designed by the Arthritis Foundation; a water exercise program which is slow paced and stresses arm and leg exercises; a basic aqua aerobics program which includes some aerobics exercise but is not too fast and includes heart rate checks; an aqua aerobics class which is fast-paced, has warmups and cool downs and heart rate checks; deep water exercise which includes warmups, alternative arm and leg exercises, water running, aerobic moves and other deep water exercises; a tummies and thighs program conducted in shallow water featuring isolation exercise for the entire stomach region, hips, and thighs; beginning water walking which is slow paced and teaches various water walking steps; and intermediate and advanced water walking which is medium to fast paced and features heart rate checks (Spannuth, 1989). Such diversity of formats may help overcome the intrapersonal barriers by letting the would-be participant know that there is an appropriate activity format which will involve people similar to them in skill level or life situation.

Another important issue in overcoming constraints to participation is a simple idea which is often ignored—the critical importance of friends. Research by Larson, Mannell and Zuzanek (1986) and others confirms that, while family members are the major source of physical and emotional support for older adults, friendships have a stronger impact on subjective well-being. This may be partly attributable to the greater frequency of active leisure activities with friends, but also to unique qualities of interaction which allow transcendence of mundane daily realities; "...friends provide an immediate situation of openness, reciprocity, and positive feedback" (Larson, Mannell and Zuzanek, 1986). Leisure service providers to the elderly must seek to not only provide opportunities for friends to participate together but also to encourage those who participate in programs to encourage their friends to participate. Opportunities to socialize and form friendships are also of critical importance to the urban elderly. Programs and services need to plan time when individuals can mix and get to know each other. Such socialization often has the added benefit of not costing much and, since urban elderly often are limited economically, lack of cost may be particularly appealing.

**Changing Roles of Leisure Service Providers.** The previous section implies much for those who work with the elderly in the recreation, park, and leisure service area. Perhaps the foremost implication is that such services must increasingly become synergistic, with recreation practitioners fulfilling a facilitating role rather than one of direct service. While this is often observed by those who study leisure service, direct leadership and service remain the norm.

The aging of the population which had higher levels of education will bring about not only decreasing participation in sport, particularly team and ice and snow sports, but also revive less strenuous forms of outdoor recreation, such as birdwatching. Tables 8, 9 and 10 (page 102) show the relationship of participation in several outdoor recreation activities by age as well as the fastest-growing and fastest-declining forms of participation.

An aging society with higher levels of education also will likely result in higher levels of participation in the arts, culture, historic visitation and activities involving plants. There will be a greater interest in gardening, and the ecological, aesthetic, nutritional and health-related aspects of plant life. For those who plan and manage botanical gardens, this would seem to indicate increases in interest, attendance and support from the general public. The renting of space for gardens by local government may become more popular, following the British tradition.

The management of botanical gardens and arboretums will, increasingly, need to be managed based upon the recognition that they serve as important forms of leisure behavior for many visitors. The "experiential" and "interactive" aspects of such facilities will need to be increased. Additionally, there will be greater need for increasingly diverse visitors to interact with such facilities at multiple levels of sophistication. Doing this may involve the use of concepts such as "flow" which assumes that optimal experiences involve a close match between the skill level of the participant and the challenge (Csikszentmihalyi, 1991b).

The increasing interest in the nutritional and medicinal values of plants will necessitate rethinking what forms of plant life should be displayed and what settings are appropriate. Interest in the environment will

Table 8    **Percent of U.S. Population Participating in Physical Outdoor Activities by Age and Activity (1994–1995)**

| Activity | 16–24 | 25–29 | 30–39 | 40–49 | 50–59 | 60+ |
|---|---|---|---|---|---|---|
| Bicycling | 37.9 | 36.1 | 37.4 | 30.7 | 21.8 | 10.6 |
| Rock Climbing | 8.3 | 5.4 | 3.9 | 2.9 | 1.8 | 0.7 |
| Mountain Climbing | 8.2 | 6.2 | 5.2 | 3.6 | 2.3 | 1.7 |
| Caving | 8.0 | 7.0 | 5.3 | 4.3 | 2.9 | 1.6 |
| Running/Jogging | 50.4 | 33.2 | 28.3 | 23.3 | 17.4 | 8.1 |
| Walking | 68.1 | 72.4 | 74.6 | 71.9 | 65.4 | 51.5 |
| Downhill Skiing | 15.5 | 14.2 | 9.9 | 8.1 | 3.8 | 1.0 |
| X-Country Skiing | 3.5 | 3.5 | 3.7 | 4.4 | 4.0 | 1.2 |
| Hiking | 31.5 | 30.1 | 29.4 | 27.0 | 18.0 | 9.6 |
| Backpacking | 14.3 | 11.8 | 8.2 | 7.0 | 4.4 | 1.4 |
| Canoeing | 10.6 | 8.8 | 7.8 | 7.0 | 4.7 | 1.8 |
| Kayaking | 1.3 | 1.0 | 0.7 | 0.7 | 0.4 | 0.05 |

Source: Dwyer (1994)

Table 9    **Ten Fastest-Growing Outdoor Activities Among Persons 16 Years or Older in the United States (1982–1995)**

| Activity | Number 16+ years 1982–1983 (millions) | Number 16+ years 1994–1995 (millions) | Percentage Growth |
|---|---|---|---|
| Birdwatching | 21.2 | 54.1 | 155.2 |
| Hiking | 24.7 | 47.7 | 93.0 |
| Backpacking | 8.8 | 15.2 | 72.7 |
| Downhill Skiing | 10.6 | 16.8 | 58.5 |
| Primitive Camping | 17.7 | 28.0 | 58.2 |
| Walking | 93.6 | 133.6 | 42.7 |
| Motorboating | 33.6 | 46.9 | 39.9 |
| Sightseeing | 81.3 | 113.4 | 39.5 |
| Developed Camping | 30.0 | 41.5 | 38.3 |
| Swimming in Natural Waters | 56.5 | 78.1 | 38.2 |

Source: Dwyer (1994)

Table 10    **Activities For Which Numbers of Participants Decreased in the United States (1982–1995)**

| Activity | Number 16+ years 1982–1983 (millions) | Number 16+ years 1994–1995 (millions) | Percentage Decrease |
|---|---|---|---|
| Tennis | 30.0 | 21.2 | 29.3 |
| Hunting | 21.2 | 18.8 | 11.4 |
| Horseback Riding | 15.9 | 14.2 | 10.7 |
| Sailing | 10.6 | 9.6 | 9.4 |
| Attending Outdoor Concerts or Plays | 44.2 | 41.5 | 6.1 |
| Fishing | 60.1 | 58.3 | 3.0 |
| Ice Skating | 10.6 | 10.6 | 1.9 |

Source: Dwyer (1994)

mean that plant displays must increasingly show interrelationships between plant life and human and other animal life.

Arboretums and botanical gardens are likely to rely increasingly on private sources of economic support during the next decade and will, therefore, be increasingly consumer-oriented and operated from the concepts of marketing.

All forms of leisure activity will be affected in some way by the aging of the population and by a more ethnically diverse society. As the demographic makeup of a city, county, state or members of a fitness club change, participation rates in various activities will change, sometimes dramatically. In spite of a general tendency for older people to participate less in activities which are physically strenuous or involve temperature extremes, many outdoor recreation researchers believe it is currently very difficult to predict how aging and a more diverse ethnic makeup will affect participation. In terms of ethnic status, Dwyer (1994) mentioned that "discrimination plays a key role in outdoor recreation participation; and future trends in participation rates will also depend upon trends in relations between various racial and ethnic groups" (p. 3). As racial and ethnic differences decline, differences in participation rates will likely be minimized. If minority groups seek to preserve racial and ethnic identity, and if discrimination continues or worsens, differences in rates of participation will become more apparent.

Dwyer (1994) drew the following management implications for outdoor recreation providers:

### Prepare for Change

1. Outdoor recreation customers are likely to increase in numbers at a slower rate than in the past, and will be increasingly older, urban and from racial and ethnic minority groups.

2. It will be increasingly difficult to predict outdoor recreation behavior.

### Possible Responses to Change

3. The changes in customers that are currently underway will have wide-ranging implications for recreation resource management programs.

4. Particular attention must be given to the management and use of resources in or near urban areas.

**Some Reflections Beyond Participation**

5. It may be necessary to review fee structures in the years ahead.

6. The selection of staff and the development of training programs should address the needs of increasingly diverse customers.

7. Managers and planners must expand their regular dialogue with their diverse customers, both on site and off site, to be certain that management plans and programs are in tune with customer needs.

# 24

# *The Emergence of a Leisure Gerontocracy*

Not only is modern society aging rapidly, but older people are wealthier, in better health, and more politically powerful than a few decades ago. The average U.S. worker now retires in his or her late fifties or early sixties. For Americans who reach the age of 65, men now have a life expectancy of 79.8 years while women's life expectancy is 83.7 years. On average, about 12 years after age 65 people will be relatively healthy. This means these people will have, on average, 15 or more years generally free from paid labor in good health.

Much of the gains in free time have been stored during the last few decades of life. Consider the following, historically unprecedented situation. Over 20 percent of our population, 52 million, are age 55 and over. Of those, only about 27 percent are in the labor force. Mass leisure has already arrived for this generation—under our very noses. While the media persist in telling us that we are working longer hours, consider that the vast majority of Americans do not work for pay during a 15-year period of adulthood in which the majority are in good health, highly mobile and own their homes.

A study by the Commonwealth Fund of New York (1993) found that of the 52.4 million Americans age 55 and over, 14.3 million are working,

26.4 million are retired and don't want to work, 6.3 million would like to work but are unable to, and 5.4 million are able to work but do not have jobs.

Of the ten percent who are willing to work but not employed, only 21 percent said they are bored with retirement, 14 percent said they want to do something useful and 37 percent cited financial need. This study recommended keeping older people working through flex-time, job sharing and phased-in retirement. Keep in mind, however, that, at present, the majority of those 55 and over are retired and don't want to work.

## Issue Questions

1. Should retirement be changed? If so, how?

2. Should tax laws give advantages to old people? Infants? Young people?

## Possible Implications for Leisure

As of the writing of this book, older people constitute a target market for all kinds of leisure services. They have the most free time, the most financial assets, the most welfare support from the government (as mentioned elsewhere, over $132,000 average subsidy for social security in excess of their payments and interest). They also have the most political clout, thanks to organizations such as the American Association of Retired Persons, which represents the interests of older people but is not concerned with younger ones. Older people are also more likely to vote. All these factors and more have produced a gerontocracy that exerts its will in numerous ways in our society.

This situation, in the emerging society where the life chances of young people may be less than those of older ones, has the potential to produce intergenerational conflict. In terms of leisure services, there may be questions of equity. "Senior Citizen" discounts, for example, go to people who are not disproportionate poor and who reside in households which are generally financially better off than those of people age 18 and under.

There is also the issue of how free time is distributed across the life span, as mentioned elsewhere. The talents of older people are needed in the labor force and the free time of the elderly are needed by parents in two-worker households who have young children. Retirement needs to be rethought in ways which allow continued participation in the labor force. Parenting needs to be rethought in ways which allow for parents to spend time with children in the most critical period of their lives—the first year of life.

# 25

# *A More Diverse Culture*

North American culture, and that of a variety of modern and developing nations, are becoming more ethnically diverse, due primarily to immigration. The perceived extent of such change, however, is currently exaggerated within the United States  The impact of ethnic change will have the greatest impact in only a handful of states, but such states have enough electoral votes to select a President. Immigration policy will become a fiercely-debated political issue. Figure 10 and Figure 11 project the extent to which the population of the United States is or will be made up of ethnic minorities and the age distribution of such groups.

The ethnic makeup of the U.S. population is being transformed, even if the rate of transformation is often exaggerated. While the 1990 percentage of the population which was Hispanic was nine percent and African-American was 12 percent, a Gallup poll found that Americans estimated these percentages as 21 percent and 32 percent respectively. While both legal and illegal immigration of Mexicans, Cubans, Haitians and those from Central America as well as those from numerous Asian countries are reconfiguring the population makeup of the emergent "third world" cities in the United States, such as Los Angeles, New York, and Miami, such immigration is partially dependent upon immigration policy and enforcement of policy which is subject to rapid change.

This situation is mirrored in Canada, where Toronto and Vancouver have experienced massive immigration. An estimated 40 percent of those who reside in metro Toronto were born in another country. While Canada is officially bicultural and bilingual from the time of the British North America Act, immigrants may now play a pivotal role in political issues as important as whether Quebec succeeds from the country. Canada now has almost twice the percentage of foreign-born residents as does the United States

In both Canada and the United States, immigrants are concentrated in a few areas. Almost two-thirds of all foreign-born residents in the United States reside in four states: California, New York, Florida and

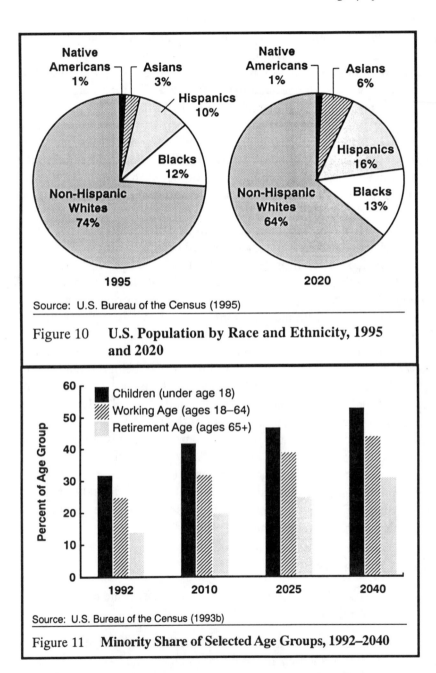

Source: U.S. Bureau of the Census (1995)

Figure 10    **U.S. Population by Race and Ethnicity, 1995
and 2020**

Source: U.S. Bureau of the Census (1993b)

Figure 11    **Minority Share of Selected Age Groups, 1992–2040**

Texas.  The African-American population in the United States is predicted to increase only modestly during the next 50 years.  Whites are
likely to remain a slim majority in the United States for the foreseeable

future but will become an even more distinct minority in the world. Future immigration policies will therefore become increasingly politicized. In Britain, immigration laws have recently changed so that children born in the country are no longer automatically citizens if their parents are not. Such changes may be considered in the United States.

Nevertheless, there will continue to be great pressure to immigrate from Mexico and numerous other countries. In terms of Mexico, for instance, it must be remembered that the largest income differential in the world between any two countries which border each other is between Mexico and the United States. About one-half of the Mexican labor force earns in one day less than what the poorest American workers earn in one hour. The official Mexican minimum wage is around $5 per day. Their version of social security may pay a retired person as little as $1 per day. Half of Mexico's 90 million residents are under the age of 15, about half of all children live in households which are female led, and about half do not complete even six grades of formal education. Forty percent of Mexican homes have no indoor running water nor indoor plumbing (Oster, 1990).

Mexico is the largest supplier of drugs to the willing United States market. It is also our third biggest trading partner, behind Canada and Japan. It has a huge oil supply and, at times, is the largest exporter of oil to the United States, which imports over one-half of its oil. Mexico's problems and its future will shape the future of the United States. Should Mexico undergo a revolution, it would shape U.S. immigration policy for decades to come.

The same may be said about numerous other countries. While this may not mean massive increases in immigration, it will mean that the United States will concern itself with the problems of poverty, ignorance and exploitation which other nations face.

## Issue Questions

1. How will a more diverse population affect the celebration of holidays?

2. Should immigrants to the United States adopt the leisure activities which are common to those who live there?

3. Should public leisure services try to help immigrants assimilate?

# Possible Implications for Leisure

As the United States becomes more ethnically diverse, a number of issues will be raised concerning leisure. Many of our large cities, for instance, have symphony orchestras but the majority, or sizable portions, of the residents of that city are not of European origin, where such music forms and organization originated. The holidays which are celebrated, the sports which are played, the literature which is "classic," the forms of dance, even the ways in which one uses a park are all essentially European. This will change, but change does not mean the world will lack a dominant culture. Such a notion flies in the face of history. There are few examples of countries with numerous ethnic factions, none of whom rules. The ability of "multiculturalism" to produce a viable culture will be tested. Leisure will be an important arena in which humans determine if they can deal with differences in ways which don't make superior-inferior assumptions. If no such multiculturalism develops, the ethnic groups which learn the most may dominate. It remains to be seen if this will be residents of European origin.

# 26

# *Increasingly Diverse Roles for Women— And Men*

Women's roles will continue to diversify dramatically. Globally, it may be argued that the women's movement in third world nations is the most important social movement in the world, since population increase may be the biggest threat to our environment and such growth occurs, to a great extent, because of the second-class status of women. The diversification of women's roles, and, to a lesser extent, corresponding changes in the roles of men, is an ongoing process not only in North America and in other modern nations but also in developing ones. Women have not only entered the labor force in record numbers, but also many are pursuing careers in ways which were once largely reserved for males. In terms of time use, we are headed toward androgyny, although there continues to be cultural lag in men's response to participation in homemaking activity (Robinson and Godbey, 1997). Women spend almost as much time traveling as men. Their continuing participation in the labor force is a given. Today's young women:

> ...probably represent the largest one-generation advance in de facto sexual equality in American history. The 13th (born between 1961 and 1981) is the first generation of women who exceed men in average educational attainment. They're first to pursue competitive athletics in significant numbers. They're the first to attend military academies, the first to enter the legal, medical, and business professions in double-digit percentages, and the first to approach male salaries in a wide variety of occupations. Knowingly or not, they're the front-line shock troops in America's feminist campaign to achieve on-the-job economic equality. For all full-time U.S. workers, the median earnings of women may linger at only 70 percent of the median for men, but that ratio varies from a low of roughly 60 percent among the 50ish Silent [generation] to a high of over 80 percent among twentyish 13ers. (Howe and Strauss, 1993)

The U.S. government and other institutions are only beginning to operate from the recognition of these changes. Considerable "cultural lag" remains. In an information economy, however, the fact that women constitute the majority of undergraduate students in universities in North America may be telling.

A number of unanswered questions remain in terms of the status of women. These include the following:

1. Will better educated, higher income women live in a culture in which men's and women's work and leisure patterns continue to become more similar with the child bearing and homemaking roles of women becoming less prevalent?

2. Will women with low education and income levels retain traditional responsibilities for child rearing and also take on responsibilities for full-time work?

3. Are various women's movements breaking up into diverse factions which have little in common?

4. Will the increasing earning power of women reshape the way in which our society is organized, such as reshaping work for both males and females to allow parents to be home when their children are?

5. Will this earning power translate into political power?

In the answers to such questions lies the ways in which our society will be transformed.

Part of the answers to such questions will be the extent to which there is continuing change in men's roles. Certainly there is evidence of numerous changes in the behavior of males, including more participation in household work, greater involvement with their children, and an increasing likelihood that they will take responsibility for their children if divorce occurs. (It should be noted, however, that only about 20 percent of divorced males pay all the alimony and child support mandated by the courts.) Many males are also coming to rely on their wife or significant other to be a financial partner in marriage or other live-together arrangements. Whether due to financial need or desire for their mate to pursue a career, such change means that women's paid work is thought of in terms more similar to that of males. It may even mean that women's right to free-time activity is more respected, although this is clearly not always the case.

## Issue Questions

1. Should women do more childcare than men? Why or why not?

2. How might more diverse roles for women reshape the leisure activities of females?

3. In college, should women adopt the male model of highly competitive team sport? Why or why not?

## Possible Implications for Leisure

As males and females cross more boundaries which were once the province of one sex or the other, lots of traditional assumptions will no longer hold true. Many leisure providers who have been able to make assumptions in advance about what gender they served will be challenged to deal with the needs of both males and females. Managing leisure services for a less gender-segregated society will be a challenge and will necessitate learning a lot more about the leisure preferences of various subgroups of females, and of males. Gender won't cease to be an important variable because males and females are different in important ways. Rather, the significance of gender will lessen—making other variables, such as education level, more important.

# 27

# *The Challenge of Crime*

High levels of crime are an issue in countries as diverse as Russia, Sierra Leone, and the United States. Issues of safety, security, crime and rehabilitation of criminals must be dealt with in new ways if the American way of life is to continue. Crime and fear of crime have become a major factor shaping everyday life in America, the most violent modern nation. Consider the following from eminent historian Paul Kennedy (1992):

> Thanks to the political power of the National Rifle Association, Americans have access to deadly weapons—and use them—to a degree that astounds observers abroad. Americans possess an estimated 60 million handguns and 120 million long guns, and kill one another at a rate of around 19,000 each year, chiefly with handguns. Homicide rates per capita are four to five times higher than in Western Europe (while rape rates are seven times higher, and forcible robbery rates are four to ten times higher). Experts suggest that this violence has cultural roots, and cannot simply be linked to poverty. New York's homicide rate is far larger than that in the slums of Calcutta, for example, and in prosperous Seattle—recently rated number one city in the United States for "livability"—the murder rate is seven times that of Birmingham, England. Nor is the violence due to lack of police efforts and deterrents; at the last count, American prisons were holding over a million convicted prisoners, a proportion of the population larger than even in South Africa or the former Soviet Union.

Our current approaches to crime primarily involve the proliferation of private security guards, high-tech monitoring and surveillance devices and building new prisons. Prison guard was the fastest growing federal government occupation two years ago.

The majority of violent crimes are committed by males, disproportionately by young African Americans, and usually by those with low levels of formal education. The cost-benefit ratio of prisons is so low that increasing reliance will be placed on seeking to identify, educate, monitor and control at-risk youth. There will also be increased monitoring of those who have previous records of crime. Security will be an increasingly important variable in everyday life. Gun control will continue to be an uphill battle since those who favor the ownership of pistols and assault weapons are highly organized and zealous about the issue. Bullet control may be tried. Terrorism will be a factor in everyday life in the United States, as it already is in Britain and numerous other countries.

On the positive side, our population is aging and older people commit fewer crimes (and are less likely to be the victim of crime than any other age group). Crime rates have dropped in North America during the last few years and may continue to.

# Issue Questions

1. How may crime rates shape leisure behavior in the future?

2. Is crime a critical issue in establishing tourism? Are any tourist areas high crime areas?

# Possible Implications for Leisure

Crime and fear of crime have obvious implications for use of leisure. People who fear crime stay inside at night (and sometimes during the day). Older people and women have higher than average fear of crime and their behavior is more shaped by such fear (even though the most likely victims of most crimes are young and are overwhelmingly male). Leisure service providers will have to be able to document to their customers or clients that using their service presents no more than a small risk in terms of crime. This will be particularly critical in terms of tourism, since potential tourists will have access to an increasingly sophisticated system of information concerning the crime rates at various tourist sites. Tourist areas may limit the access of "natives" to the area or rely on sophisticated security forces, sometimes disguised as tourists, to secure tourist areas.

In urban parks, high-tech monitoring devices may be used to scan park areas for potential crimes. Crime prevention and surveillance will become an increasingly important issue of state and federal land managing agencies.

# 28

# A Society With More Education
# (and an Obsolete Education System)

Most modern societies are characterized by a population which has increasingly higher levels of education even as the education systems which provide it are becoming more and more obsolete. In the United States, from 1950 to 1991, the increase in the number of years that adolescents stay in school and defer full-time employment is pronounced. While in 1950, 83 percent of 14 to 17 year olds were in school, that figure jumped to 96 percent in 1991. It was among postsecondary students, however, where the biggest gain was realized. Among 18 and 19 year olds, the jump from 1950 to 1991 doubled—from 30 to 60 percent. For 20 and 21 year olds, the jump was from 19 to 42 percent.

The percentage of 25 to 29 year olds who have completed high school leaped from 53 percent in 1950 to 85 percent in 1991, while those who completed an undergraduate college degree zoomed from eight percent to 23 percent. Thus, Americans, like those in many other modern nations, are entering the labor force considerably later and have considerably more years of formal education than in previous decades. The quality of higher education, however, appears to be rapidly deteriorating even as a higher percentage of the population attends a college or university. Peter Sacks (1996), author of *Generation X Goes to College: An Eye Opening Account of Teaching in Postmodern America,* expresses the concerns of many educators that college students today, on average, have developed a psychology of entitlement in which, as consumers, they should be catered to without too much effort. The hours spent in study, for many undergraduates, has declined from the old rule of thumb of three hours of study outside the classroom for every hour of class to about one hour or less.

Grade inflation is evident even as standardized measures of academic attainment are not rising. Nearly 30 percent of high school students graduate with a 4.0 grade point average (that is, an A), and that on the college level, the average grade is somewhere between a "B and a B+" and on some campuses up to 70 percent of students graduate cum laude or above (historically the percentage has been only about 10 to 15 percent). All this while Scholastic Aptitude Test (SAT)—which measure achieved ability—scores have been declining.

Thus more years of formal education may not automatically mean higher levels of knowledge. Since the bases of employing people is likely to increasingly be their skills and knowledge rather than their degrees, many college graduates may find their degree was not the ticket to the middle class that they assumed.

While a higher percentage of the population is staying in school, there are obvious signs that the systems which provide education are obsolete. First and foremost, the notion that spending high percentages of one's time in formal education during the first third of one's life will prepare one for the next two-thirds makes less and less sense, as the rate at which knowledge is created expands exponentially. While most who study education believe lifelong learning models must be adapted, modern nations are usually not organized under such assumptions. (Although some Scandinavian countries have a proud tradition of continuing education.)

The fact that government has not responded to this need has caused many corporations to become continuing educators as are many professional organizations. Such education is usually not degree granting but is based upon the changing needs of their workforce or profession.

Colleges and universities, as presently organized, are increasingly obsolete, according to many analysts. Peter Drucker predicts:

> Thirty years from now the big university campuses will be relics. Universities won't survive. It's as large a change as when we first got the printed book. (1997, p. 127)

College and university costs have risen as fast as health expenditures and, like healthcare, massive change will result. Part of this change will be due to various forms of distance learning, which can deliver coursework by satellite or two-way video at a fraction of the cost. These technologies will supplement and, in many cases, replace traditional residential educational experiences. Figure 12 shows learning technologies classified by time and place.

As may be seen, there are numerous forms of education which do not involve the teacher and learner being in the same place at the same time. More of these techniques will be used in the future, simply because they are dramatically cheaper and more flexible than in residence higher education. "The college won't survive as a residential institution. Today's buildings are hopelessly unsuited and totally unneeded" (Drucker, 1997, p. 127). This revolution will touch off many others, in which young

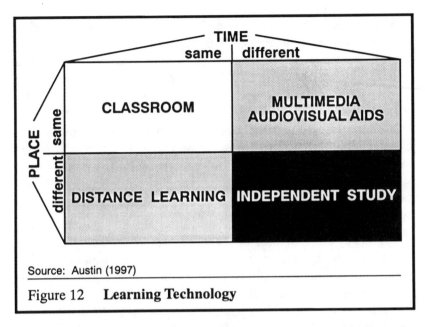

Source: Austin (1997)

Figure 12    **Learning Technology**

adults pursue numerous combinations of work, education, family and community life. University campuses may be reorganized into educational corporations serving whatever clientele can pay for services. Corporations and associations of employees may be among such clientele, along with the governments of other countries. Some universities, however, may simply sell off their buildings and disappear.

Those universities and colleges who do survive will change radically. As Galen Godbey, Executive Director of the Center for Agile Pennsylvania Education, observed:

> Drucker's predictions regarding large universities are probably true; however, for smaller institutions, there is an alternative scenario built around cooperation, radical reshaping of faculty roles, the capacity to teach teaming (which large universities find difficult to do), the attractiveness of smaller organizations to first-rate people, and using technologies to prepare people to function in geographically distributed, technologically mediated, team-based production processes. (personal communication, March 5, 1997)

Whether such changes can take place fast enough to make small colleges viable (or even large universities) remains to be seen. For the large university, one tactic may be to stress the leisure amenities of the residential campus, including sports, culture, and entertainment. Such campuses may become tourist attractions and centers for socialization and recreation as well as learning for young people with wealthy parents.

Because of this, education itself will become an export of immense importance, requiring reconfiguring the way education is organized and delivered. As education becomes a major export of many modern nations, the way in which education is delivered will need substantial reorganization.

> The day of the stand-alone, geographically-driven institution, with its concomitant zero-sum game approach to interinstitutional relationships, is over. However, this counterproductive traditional mode of organizational life still drives many of our policies and practices. (Galen Godbey, personal communication, December 13, 1995)

Universities, as well as secondary schools, will need to learn to cooperate, share, find new ways to affect economies of scale, develop win-win strategies and, in general, become more "agile." (More about agility later.)

Many countries, such as Britain, already understand that higher education is a critical component of their economy but studies to measure this effect have concentrated on the numbers of international college and university students who come to study. The challenge ahead will be to use the existing technology to enhance distance education in ways which allow education to become an export to students who do not leave their home country to participate. The use of satellite-assisted, interactive video learning and other virtual means of delivering education will increase exponentially.

As this happens, countries which export education, such as the United States, will need to develop more policies which promote education as a resource. Just as many modern nations have developed industrial policy, they will now have to develop educational policy which is based on an understanding of education's central role in the national economy and the economy of other nations.

The increase in distance learning will likely involve numerous leisure services, who will provide numerous on-line opportunities for people to learn about leisure interests, skills and opportunities. The decline of the residential university may mean that young people will not be exposed to many forms of leisure expression, such as the fine and performing arts, in as systematic a way as before.

Past this is the issue of how to restructure all learning throughout a person's lifetime. Our current systems often assume that one can learn everything he or she needs to know for the rest of his or her life during the first third of his or her life—even though such an assumption is ridiculous. The assumptions made about education seem out of touch with how we live. Education of a child isn't taken seriously until the age of four or five even though the most important learning he or she will do in his or her live is during the first two years of life. In secondary school, children are let out in summer, based upon the custom of our ancestors who needed their children to help them farm. Schools often let out at three in the afternoon on the assumption that "Mom" is home, although increasingly she is not. Colleges prepare students for highly specific occupations even though the requirements for such occupations and even the existence of the occupation itself changes with increasing speed.

As the value of products and services is increasingly a matter of the intelligence which is used to develop them, all aspects of formal and informal education will have to be rethought—and quickly.

## Issue Questions

1. How might changes in the education system affect the amount of free time which people have at different periods in their lives?

2. Can formal education become leisure?

3. How might school systems be changed by the increased importance of a highly and continuously educated citizenry? What changes might take place in the operation of colleges and universities during the next 20 years?

## Possible Implications for Leisure

People with more education make more demands of those who provide leisure services. They ask more questions, wanting more information about the activity or facility in question. They are more willing to experiment or try something new. They integrate learning into a variety of leisure experiences, such as tourism.

Better educated people draw less distinctions between males and females in terms of leisure activity. They are more likely to exercise, more likely to read and more likely to travel. The increase in education level of the public means that more demands will be made of leisure service providers and that second rate service is less likely to be tolerated.

In terms of the restructuring or decline of colleges and universities, an important question is the extent to which present campuses will become learning-leisure infrastructures geared to the tourists which has an educational component, conferences, high culture and entertainment, and other forms of leisure expression.

*29*

# Information-Based Products and Services

Information-based products and services will become a major, if not dominant part of the economy of the United States and many other modern nations. We already exist in a "postcapitalist" society in which the basis for economic success is increasingly knowledge rather than capital to invest. Those countries or organizations which do the best job of educating their citizens or employees are likely to dominate. It may be argued that intelligence and cooperation are the dominant issues in terms of economic growth. Thus, many countries can rapidly change their standard of living by improving the educational system. A leading geneticist, Steve Jones, observed:

> Over the past 20 years the average IQ score of Japanese children has risen to more than ten points higher than that of Americans. Not even the most radical hereditarian claims that this is due to a sudden burst of genetic change in Japan. Instead, the schools are getting better. (Jones, 1993, p. 243)

Thus, the stage is set for a shifting of wealth and power in the world based upon which educational systems succeed and which ones fail. It is by no means assured that such systems will be in the United States. Indeed, international comparisons of U.S. secondary school students have generally rated educational accomplishment among U.S. students in the lower half of modern nations, although some more recent studies show the United States gaining ground. Countries where there is a belief that those of a given race, ethnic group, caste or gender are not capable of learning will be at an extreme disadvantage in this competition for intelligence.

Part of this competition reflects changes in how products and services are being delivered. A key issue in whether a given product or service succeeds is how much intelligence or information is built into it. "Smart" cars, houses and tourist sites are likely to be developed by "smart" people.

The key to economic success is increasingly intertwined with education. A literate, skilled, problem-solving labor force is critical. The ability to add value to products and services through an information-rich working environment determines which products and services are purchased and exported; price is increasingly a less important variable. While it mattered that the Yugo cost less than half the price of a Honda, for instance, the critical variable in Honda's success and the Yugo's failure was the amount of information added to the production process, since it differentiated the quality of the two cars.

## Issue Questions

1. As information becomes a more central part of products and services, how might a leisure activity such as going to a play, visiting a national park or taking a vacation in Hawaii be transformed?

2. How might some of your personal leisure activities be changed by "smart" equipment and facilities?

## Possible Implications for Leisure

It is difficult to predict how this trend will reshape recreation and leisure. Certainly, use of leisure will be increasingly intertwined with learning, among both the have and have-not segments of society. Demands for leisure services which contribute to learning will likely increase, especially for youth who are "at risk," as it is increasingly realized that they represent a resource which, if wasted, will further contribute to the economic problems of the rest of society.

An additional change may be the extent to which many leisure services provide information to their clients. Such information may be delivered in ways which allow the receiver to understand more about the quality of a given leisure opportunity. Additionally, there is likely to be ongoing communication between the provider and receiver of services. (More about this later.) A golf course, for instance, may be wired to a mainframe computer in such a way that a golfer can find out statistics, layout and other information about each hole prior to teeing off. Conversely, some golf formats may demand that the player be limited in the amount of information he or she can use while playing the course.

Whether or not to undergo a given leisure activity without information may become a big issue. Should the tourist know what to expect, or be surprised, or discover it for himself or herself? Should the musician interpret a score by himself or herself or should his or her oboe provide information to him or her about the way in which a piece should be played—or sound?

# 30

## Increased Debt Within Government, Corporations and Households—A Test of Will

The debt structure within government, corporations and households is increasing in many modern nations and may necessitate lowering economic standards of living. In a period of "prosperity" and in peacetime, the United States, Canada and many other modern nations are running up massive debts. Debt in the corporate sector is such that two-thirds of all spending goes to amortize debt—an all-time high. The acknowledged federal government debt amounts to about $18,000 per person and an increasing amount of this debt is being financed by governments of other countries. Almost four out of every five dollars spent by the federal government are "entitlements," money that must be spent by law on numerous programs such as Medicare or unemployment compensation. Thus, the debate about how much money to spend for education, environmental protection, and other government interests is really a debate about one-fifth of the budget. About one dollar out of every seven spent by the U.S. government is spent to pay the interest on debt. Reducing deficits will involve cuts to entitlement programs and, likely, increasing taxes. While the federal government has begun to make some progress in lowering this debt, helped by the wildly successful stock market of 1997, the coming retirement of the baby boom generation will raise costs for healthcare and social security payments significantly. Also, "balancing" the budget will make no progress toward eliminating the huge, built-up deficit of 5.4 trillion dollars ($5,400,000,000,000)!

Household debt has increased to maximum affordable levels and household saving rates are the lowest among modern nations. Additionally, the amount of credit card debt in early 1996 had increased to an average of $4,000 per card holder. Credit card debt among young people is a growing problem. The cumulative effect of such debt will necessitate a generation of sacrifice or of printing more money, thus risking fierce inflation.

Perhaps as a consequence of such debt, many Americans who are approaching retirement have not saved much money for the period of life after work. A study by Public Agenda (1997) found that 30 percent of those between the ages of 51 and 61, and 40 percent of those age 33 to 50 have saved less than $10,000 for retirement. Only 29 percent and 16 percent of these groups, respectively, had saved over $100,000.

In spite of huge debt, there is enough economic "fat" in the system to deal with such debt if Americans, Canadians, Australians, and other endebted nations have the political courage to do so. Residents of modern nations are living at a material level unprecedented in the history of the world which continues to increase. The United States also continues to subsidize consumption and the lifestyles of wealthy people more than other modern nations.

The standard of living for most modern nations has grown tremendously since the end of World War II. Americans currently have about 100 million dwelling units, nearly two-thirds of them owner occupied. *They have almost tripled in average size until they now average a remarkable 600 square feet of living space per occupant.* Most are single-family detached homes with a patio or balcony and garage or carport. About five million Americans own second homes. Children typically have their own bedrooms and bathrooms. Water consumes less than one percent of households budgets and is used prodigiously. Ninety-three percent of households have telephones, usually more than one operating on private lines. More than nine out of ten contain an audio system, more than eight out of ten have a microwave oven, more than seven out of ten have a videocassette recorder. More than 25 percent have a personal computer. In terms of air conditioning, 76 percent of American homes are so equipped while 95 percent have adequate heating, 98 percent have complete plumbing, 54 percent have automatic dishwashers, and 78 percent have clothes washing machines (U.S. Census Bureau, 1997). Radios are ubiquitous and clothing is so plentiful that it is rarely worn out.

About 140 million vehicles are registered in the United States; most for household use. Daily adult food intake in the United States has risen to 3,500 calories, more than twice the minimum energy intake needed for survival. Seventy percent of the enormous grain supply of the United States is consumed by cattle to fatten them and 100,000 head of cattle are slaughtered every day to fatten Americans (Rifkin, 1992). On almost every measure of consumption, the United States is the world's "leader," using a quarter of the world's petroleum with only a little more than four percent of the world's population, and more wood than any other country (see Ornstein and Erlich, 1989; Kennedy, 1992). In terms of medical care, Americans have also gained. There were, for instance, only 14,000 heart bypass operations in 1970 but 407,000 in 1990. In terms of education, 60 percent of high school students now go to college, up from 50 percent in 1960.

While there is the impression that incomes have not grown since the 1970s, economist Paul Samuelson (1995) shows that they have continued to grow. Hourly wages, in inflation corrected dollars, are shown in Table 11.

| Table 11 | Hourly Wages | |
|---|---|---|
| Year | Hourly Wages | Hourly Compensation |
| 1950 | $5.61 | $5.92 |
| 1970 | $9.49 | $10.64 |
| 1990 | $10.72 | $12.87 |

Source: Samuelson (1997, 29 April)

While our incomes may not have increased as fast as the baby boomers expected, they have gone up. There has also been a huge gain in our spending for healthcare and benefits of workers to pay for them.

There are also huge amounts of fat in the system because of U.S. government policies. The prices paid for gasoline are less than almost every country in the world because it is taxed so little. The United States taxes most forms of consumption less than other modern nations and taxes the wealthy far less than other modern nations; allowing people to write the interest paid on mortgages for houses costing one million dollars off their owed income tax; and subsidizing huge timber, mining, ranching, and agribusinesses. Americans rebuild the large beach houses of wealthy people who foolishly built them too close to the ocean. They subsidize wealthy elderly people by paying them back far more money than they put into social security—even those who don't need it. They subsidize the price of water for large farming interests who grow rice in the desert or dump water onto arid land to graze cattle. They have zoning laws which prohibit people of modest means from living over gas stations or in "substandard" housing which used to be "standard." Huge sport stadiums are built in cities at the taxpayers expense merely to allow millionaire owners and athletes to conduct their business. There are huge amounts of financial "fat" in the economic system, but greed, stupidity and arrogance have allowed the richest nation in the history of the universe to run up a huge bill. The biggest problem Americans face in terms of changing such policy is our inability to appreciate the absolutely enormous wealth with which we live.

In spite of these examples, a large portion of U.S. citizens are experiencing a decline in their economic standard of living. As discussed elsewhere, the gap between rich and poor is growing daily and this gap may ultimately be a bigger problem than the absolute amount of income the average American has.

## Issue Questions

1. What are some ways in which being in debt may reshape the leisure behavior of Americans?

2. What are the consequences of this debt for the management of public recreation and park services?

3. To what extent do you think satisfying and meaningful leisure activity can be decoupled from high rates of material consumption?

## Possible Implications for Leisure

Both the use and style of many leisure activities may be changed by how Americans and their government react to debt. If gasoline is taxed at higher rates some tourist destinations may suffer, while other closer to home destinations benefit. If mortgage subsidies for second homes disappear, there may be less building of such residences. If luxury items such as yachts are more heavily taxed, leisure may be used less to display wealth (and a few yacht builders will go out of business). Consumers of leisure equipment may be more price conscious and interested in durability, rather than fads or style.

The "simplicity" movement may become more mainstream. How much stuff does one need for leisure experience? What is enough? Why do we label people as "consumers?" Many leisure opportunities for those with higher levels of education may consciously shy away from huge amounts of consumption.

Past that, many recreation and park services of government are likely to be pushed more into a role of either generating their own revenue through fees, charges, lease agreements and other means, or demonstrating their benefits in the areas of health, juvenile delinquency or tourism.

# 31

# Infrastructure Problems

The United States, and many other developed nations who started open-ended growth after World War II, have an infrastructure problem which will increase. Currently, there are more roads, bridges, national parks, university buildings, tunnels, sewer systems, and other infrastructure components in need of repair than can be maintained. Table 12 lists the infrastructure problems North Americans face.

---

Table 12    **Serious Infrastructure Problems**

- Large segments of our streets and highways are deteriorating.
- Gridlock traffic conditions exist in a growing number of areas.
- Nearly half of our bridges need repairing.
- The water storage and distribution systems in some older urban areas have seriously deteriorated.
- Sewage treatment capacity in many areas is in short supply.
- A shortage of affordable housing exists in many areas of the country.

---

Source: Population Reference Bureau (1990)

---

Much of this infrastructure in the United States, was built in the years following World War II when economic assets were enhanced by the temporary destruction of much of its economic competition in the world. Some of this will have to be simply written off or abandoned. Additionally, there is a surplus of office space in many regions. Some actions which would have been unthinkable in the 1970s, such as selling off some federal lands devoted to parks, are already being contemplated.

In the previous era of unlimited growth, emphasis was upon building rather than maintaining. In the coming years, maintaining roads, water supplies, government monuments, airports, and the other parts of the county's infrastructure will be difficult.

# Issue Questions

1. Do public recreation and park departments have an infrastructure problem? If so, describe what it is. How might it be improved?

2. How important are these infrastructure problems to tourism? Why?

3. What can be done to prevent infrastructure problems in the future?

# Possible Implications for Leisure

All sorts of leisure service organizations have infrastructure problems. There are more residential centers for the emotionally disturbed, public tennis courts, state parks, national recreation areas, retrofitted buildings which comply with the Americans with Disabilities Act, wildlife refuges, urban recreation centers, public golf courses, and state fish hatcheries than the government can pay for, unless the public will increase taxes for such purposes.

Another implication is that those who work in public recreation and park agencies will have to change their orientation. As one of the better known recreation and park directors in the country told me when he resigned from his job: "I'm a builder; not a maintainer." We are going to need more and better maintainers, since maintaining what exists will become relatively more important than building new facilities.

# 32

# Investing in Those Who Will Make Society Competitive

While America has made a huge investment in those with a variety of disabilities and disadvantages, retirees, welfare recipients and those with special needs, it has made very little in those who will determine international competitiveness in a world economy—newborn children, gifted students, young people in general (particularly those who don't go on to college), working mothers, and displaced workers in need of retraining.

In the emergent knowledge economy, the tendency to invest huge sums in subsidizing the elderly and those with disabilities through social security, the Americans with Disabilities Act, and other forms of help must be weighed against the need to support the needs of the young, the gifted and those whose work lives are largely ahead of them. The percentage of federal spending for education which is devoted to "gifted" students, for example, is about one-tenth of one percent. While the United States spends the least on education per capita of any modern nation, it spends the most on the education of the mentally retarded. Unlike European countries, the United States has comparatively little job training opportunities available to those who do not continue on to college. Similarly, it is a follower, rather than a leader, in taking care of newborn children and investing in their health and early learning experiences.

With good intentions, in summary, the United States has failed to help those who will determine its economic viability in the emerging international economy.

## Issue Question

1. What role, if any, do various public and private, nonprofit organizations concerned with recreation and leisure have to play in improving the quality of life for newborn children, gifted students, young people (particularly those who don't go to college), working mothers and displaced workers?

### Possible Implications for Leisure

Part of the investment made in these groups will be by leisure services organizations, not only in targeting recreation programs for them but also seeking to make existing programs and services more accessible and relevant to them. Recreation services are likely to be combined or work in teams with other social services in concerted efforts to improve the life chances of these groups.

# 33

# Tourism as the World's Largest Composite Industry

It is difficult to say what is the world's largest industry because it depends on how you define an industry and how accurately its revenue can be measured. The United Nations Research Institute identifies the three largest "industries" as (1) the military — $800 billion, (2) illicit drugs—$500 billion, and (3) oil—$450 billion (Ayres, 1996). By other measures, however, it may be argued that tourism has emerged as the world's largest composite industry so rapidly that its consequences cannot yet be understood. It is decreasing cultural diversity in the world much the same way as agribusiness is decreasing biodiversity.

Domestic and international tourism accounted for $3.5 trillion in 1992, tourism growth is expected to double by 2005, with over 600 million international arrivals. According to the World Tourism Organization (1994), the American region (North, Central and South America) will receive 147 million international travelers by the year 2000, and 207 million by the year 2010, nearly double as many arrivals as in 1993. In the United States, total tourism services to both domestic and international travelers in 1993 reached over $416 billion in revenues and supported 6.2 million jobs. Much of the growth in tourism in North America has come from recently more prosperous Southeast Asian visitors and Europeans seeking greater value for their money.

The extent to which people travel, and the extent to which such travel is done voluntarily and for pleasurable purposes increases throughout the world with massive consequences. The largest industry in San Antonio, Texas, is tourism, as is the largest industry in Spain. The changes in attitudes of human beings toward travel is revolutionary. As Cohen (1972) observed:

> Whereas primitive and traditional man will leave his native habitat only when forced to by extreme circumstances, modern man is more loosely attached to his environment, much more willing to change it, especially temporarily, and is remarkably able to adapt to new environments. He is interested in things, sights, customs, and cultures different from his own, precisely because they are different. Gradually, a new value has evolved: the appreciation of the experience of strangeness or novelty. This experience now excites, titillates, and gratifies whereas before it only frightened.

While tourism has massive impacts on the economy, environment and culture in which it takes place, these impacts are just beginning to be understood. Even theories of tourism reflect this uncertainty, viewing tourism variously, as a form of play, of imperialism, of relations among strangers, as a search for the authentic, as a form of economic development, as a means of promoting understanding and world peace, and as a postmodern phenomenon which diminishes both ideology and sense of place.

Most tourism in the world continues to be "mass tourism," that which is done using travel agents, tourist hotels, standardized "packages" of travel, lodging and sometimes transportation. In such experiences, travelers never get too far outside their "cultural bubble." Ecotourism, however, which, while hard to define, includes rural tourism, heritage/cultural tourism, nature-based tourism, and adventure/experience-based tourism, has been experiencing growth in excess of mass tourism. Ecotourism is experiencing 30 percent annual increases between 1990 and 1995, far in excess of mass tourism, which is estimated at eight percent during the same period (Stanford Research Institute, quoted by Ivanko, 1995).

> According to the Travel Industry Association of America, over 50 percent of the United States, adult traveling public—147 million people—have taken "adventure" trips in their lifetime; included in this "adventure" activity roster are camping, hiking and biking. While a small segment of

the overall tourism industry, ecotourism products' average costs—and profit margins—tend to exceed that of mass tourism products. In 1994, the average ecotourism two-week package cost between $2,000–$3,500, depending on location and activities. (Ivanko, 1995, p. 3)

Whatever ecotourism is, it has grown with startling rapidity.

Other pronounced tourism trends include more frequent, shorter vacations, experienced closer to home. Such travel is usually less than 100 miles and involves a stay over from two to four days. Since travel has become more stressful, and many tourists themselves have higher stress levels, many tourists seek stress relief on their vacation and in the travel phase.

The vast majority of American tourists continue to travel by car, with about 80 percent of domestic vacation travel done in automobiles. More people are traveling with children today and travel with grandparents is also becoming more popular. Resorts and other lodging sites sometimes specialize in family vacations.

The biggest group of tourists, however, is older people. In the United States, for instance, while people over 50 make up only about 25 percent of the population, they account for 80 percent of all leisure travel, 35 percent of all packaged tours, 44 percent of all U.S. passports, 60 percent of all cruise passengers, and 57 percent of all golf vacations (Maas cited by Ivanko, 1995). These older tourists are more likely than others to use travel agents and to take longer trips. Seventy percent take vacations which are one week or longer.

It appears that today, people are increasingly able to make their own travel arrangements with personal computers. Many airlines have already established such programs for their frequent fliers. Travel agents will have to find ways to sell information about where the tourists are going, what they might do, what decisions would make their trip more pleasant, informative or relaxing. This information, rather than commonly shared information about the price and time schedule of trains, planes and buses, may be what keeps some travel agents in business.

## Issue Questions

1. Under what conditions is tourism a "good thing" from a moral standpoint?

2. When people from "developed" countries visit "developing" countries for tourism purposes, should attempts be made to protect the way of life of the natives of the "developing" country? If so, why? How? If not, why?

3. Should the United States promote itself as an international tourist destination more than it currently does?

## Possible Implications for Leisure

As ecotourism emerges as a major component of the economy of most countries, government will increasingly develop policies to promote tourism, establish and protect or develop tourism areas, target desirable visitor groups, and otherwise plan for it. In terms of urban planning, rural development, urban redevelopment, environmental protection, transportation policy, and even diplomatic relations between countries, tourism will be planned for.

Tourism will also be central in land management policy. The most important function of the publicly owned land in modern nations will increasingly be recognized as leisure and tourism. Outdoor recreation, often by tourists, is emerging as the most important use of the one-third of the landmass of the United States which is administered by the federal government. This is not to argue that timber production, flood control, grazing of cattle and other animals, mining, or other functions are no longer important, only that outdoor recreation has increased in importance faster than any of the other functions of land management. One of the problems of such rapid change is that the skills and orientations needed for jobs change faster than do the employees. While none of the federal land-managing agencies were originally created with recreation as a specific part of their mandate, all of these agencies are today involved, to some extent, in both recreation and tourism. These missions are sometimes not comfortable ones for those who manage forests, waters, and the deserts of the United States. In many cases, for instance, foresters have received little training dealing with human behavior or with leisure experience and would prefer that these lands be managed in ways which minimize the public's use of them. Nevertheless, federal land-managing agencies such as the Bureau of Land Management (BLM), which currently manages about one-eighth of the landmass of the United States, have become heavily involved in recreation management. The BLM long-range plan for recreation, *Recreation 2000: A Strategic Plan*, identifies several major objectives which must be met to successfully manage these lands. These include:

- Improving visitor information and interpretation;

- Strengthening resource protection and monitoring;

- Studying land ownership and improving public land access;

- Creating partnerships with private and other government agencies;

- Recruiting volunteers;

- Tapping into state and local tourism programs;

- Studying permits, fees, and concessions; and

- Developing budgeting/marketing strategies.

Other land managing agencies are similarly in the process of developing plans for outdoor recreation and tourism for the next decade. In doing so, many decisions have to be made concerning the extent to which public use of lands and waters can be accommodated within environmental and financial constraints.

Outdoor recreation sites will increasingly serve as tourist destinations, and, like other North American tourist destinations, will serve international tourists who are more and more likely to be from the Pacific rim and less likely to be from Europe. In managing for such tourism visitation, care must be taken:

> ...to strike a balance between promoting American culture
> and history and ensuring that attractions are made friendly
> to visitors with a variety of cultures and languages. Other
> challenges in preparing for international visitors include
> the endangered status of the United States Travel and
> Tourism Administration, which has provided marketing
> information about international visitors to communities
> across the country, and the safety concerns of international
> visitors to the United States. (Trussell, 1996)

Many public and private, nonprofit institutions such as museums, art galleries, nature conservancies and arboretums, municipal and country recreation and park departments, theaters, symphony orchestras, and other various institutions, will increasingly recognize their role in tourism and seek to "reposition" themselves as sustainers and promoters of tourism.

# 34

## The Decline of the Medical Model of Health

New concepts of health emphasize that our state of health is largely determined by factors other than medical treatment. Over 80 percent of the factors which determine our state of health have to do with our environment, our relations with friends and enemies, the quality of our education, our status in the community, and how we think about ourselves. It has only been during the last 30 years that medical practice could be said, on balance, to do more good than harm (Ornstein and Erlich, 1989).

Our state of health, then, is largely determined by how we live our everyday lives, our behaviors, emotions and, sometimes, our luck. Other than having the right parents, what is most important in determining health is our own personal habits and daily behaviors and our collective actions. If all forms of cancer were cured immediately, life expectancies would go up an average of only two years, but if "good nutrition, exercise and good health habits (especially not smoking) were followed, average life expectancy would increase by seven years" (Ornstein and Erlich, 1989).

Illness, like life itself, may be thought of as a complex web of interrelationships throughout the universe or as something negative which happens to the body of an individual. This variation in thought extends to issues surrounding specific illnesses, such as cancer. Cancer expert Carl Simonton has argued that cancer must be understood as a disorder of the entire system "...a disease that has a localized appearance but has the ability to spread, and that really involves the entire organism—the mind as well as the body. The original tumor is merely the tip of the iceberg" (in Capra, 1988). Cancer, according to Simonton's psychosomatic model, is not so much an attack from the outside but rather a breakdown from within in which a person's immune system doesn't recognize and breakdown abnormal, cancerous cells as it would usually do. The factors which inhibit a person's immune system from doing this at a particular time are both physical and psychological. Stress may both suppress the body's immune system and also lead to hormonal imbalances which increases production of abnormal cells.

It may also be argued that stress produces "social illness," pathological responses such as violent and reckless behavior, crime, or drug abuse. Antisocial behavior is a common reaction to stressful life situations that has to be taken into account when we talk about health. If there is a reduction in illness but at the same time it is offset by an increasing violent crime rate, we haven't done anything to improve the health of the society.

Sense of community is critical in our well-being in our everyday lives. As psychologist Robert Ornstein and physician David Sobel (1987) concluded, need for community is a key part of our evolutionary heritage. The brain's primary function is not to think but rather to guard the body from illness, and "It now appears that the brain cannot do its job of protecting the body without contact with other people. It draws vital nourishment from our friends, lovers, relatives, lodge brothers and sisters, even perhaps our coworkers and the members of the weekly bowling team" (Ornstein and Sobel, 1987). Perhaps it is no wonder that a University of Michigan study found that doing regular volunteer work, more than any other activity, dramatically increased life expectancy (Rockefeller-Growald and Luks, 1988). The feeling of warmth from doing good may well come from endorphins, the brain's natural opiates which produce not only runner's "high" but also, apparently, volunteer's high.

Community is related to the belief that the world makes sense. Antonovsky and Sagy (1986) argued that the capacity to mobilize resistance resources, and the key to holistic wellness, is based on a sense of social coherence which Antonovsky defines as:

> ...a global orientation that expresses the extent to which one has a pervasive, enduring though dynamic, feeling of confidence that (1) the stimuli deriving from one's internal and external environments in the course of living are structured, predictable and explicable; (2) the resources are available to one to meet the demands posed by these stimuli; and (3) these demands are challenges, worthy of investment and engagement.

Wellness models are replacing medical models of health. Use of leisure is being recognized as an important variable in health-related policy. Americans spend a higher portion of their GNP (between 11 and 14 percent) on healthcare than any other nation but, in some cases, get less for it. There is increasing evidence that much of what is done is not effective or done to avoid litigation. Billing costs, in some federal programs, represent 20 percent of total costs. Large chunks of total healthcare spending go to people during the last six months of their life, often keeping them alive only in a technical sense.

As the medical model becomes more apparently dysfunctional, health is being more broadly defined. The opposite of illness is perhaps not health, but wellness:

> The concept of well-being or optimal health involves a
> delicate balance among physical, emotional, spiritual in-
> tellectual and social health. Physical health may be
> thought of in terms of fitness, nutrition, control of sub-
> stance abuse, medical self-help, and so on. Emotional
> health may refer to such areas as stress management and
> care for emotional crises. Examples of spiritual health are
> those themes dealing with love, charity, purpose and medi-
> tation. Intellectual health encompasses topics in the
> realms of education, achievement, career development,
> and others, while subjects concerned with social health
> may include relationships among friends, families and
> communities. (Alberta Centre for Well Being, 1989)

Wellness leads to radically different assumptions from the medical model. Wellness theory, and an increasing number of studies, infer that, on average:

- happy people are healthier than sad ones;
- people who laugh frequently are healthier than people who don't;
- people who have numerous friends are healthier than people who don't;
- people who are optimists are happier than people who are pessimists;
- people who can celebrate their lives are happier than people who can't;
- people who help others are healthier than people who don't;
- people who have things they love to do are healthier than people who don't;
- people who joyfully exercise their body are healthier than people who don't;

- people who joyfully exercise their mind are healthier than people who don't;

- people who acquire higher levels of skill in leisure activities are healthier than people who don't; and

- people who feel they can control their destiny are healthier than people who don't.

These assumptions lead to a vastly different notion of what providing healthcare may mean. Inherent in preventive notions of wellness is that use of leisure is a critical variable in determining state of health. That is, what people do when they have maximum choice, what, if anything, gives them pleasure such that they are likely to incorporate it into their style of life is of vital importance to their health. Our physical and spiritual selves are one. When people are joyfully absorbed in a crossword puzzle, for instance, the dendrites in the brain expand. Depression has a spiritual and a chemical dimension. The leisure choices people make have real health consequences and such consequences are beginning to be understood and valued.

In spite of what has been learned about health, there is very little evidence that much money is being spent on preventing poor health as opposed to treating it or doing research to understand how to treat it once a health problem has occurred. In regard to cancer, for instance, only about one cent of every dollar on cancer research gets spent on understanding how to prevent it (Montague, 1996).

## Issue Questions

1. How is "leisure" related to "wellness?"

2. How should healthcare policy be changed based on new findings about the basis of good health?

3. Are municipal recreation and park departments really "wellness" departments?

# Possible Implications for Leisure

Many of the changes regarding the decline in the medical model of health mean that recreation and leisure will increasingly be recognized as an important component in maintaining and enhancing good health.

This conceptualization is also in keeping with a definition of leisure which does not view work and leisure as opposites. Both are seen "...as responses to a biological need for optimization of arousal (Berlyne, 1960, 1966, 1971), complexity (Walker, 1980), challenge (Csikszentmihalyi, 1975, 1991, 1993) or stress (Antonovsky, 1987). That is, satisfying recreation or leisure, like satisfying work, involves the creation and acceptance of challenges which "make sense," and which one has acquired skills and otherwise has the resources with which to deal. We need certain levels of arousal, challenge, complexity, stress, or stimulation to make us respond in ways which promote healthy growth and also need the resources to have a reasonable chance of dealing with such challenges. In short, healthy leisure involves acting rather than being acted upon. For children, healthy play means the ability to have some "effect" on the environment. Vicarious leisure, being acted upon by television or narcotics or displays in a shopping mall, does not present such challenges and, as principal uses of leisure, would not be healthy.

Such vicarious leisure is also positively related to addictions. As addictions expert Stanton Peele (1989) argued, many parents are no longer trustful of their children, having lost the idea that children can learn and grow from exploration, independence, risk and adventure. "Yet the abilities to manage oneself, to accept the responsibility of independence, and to generate adventure and excitement without behaving antisocially are skills that enable people to avoid drug or alcohol abuse and other addictions" (Peele, 1989). Leisure activity which is vicarious, in which the individual is passively entertained, does not produce the ability to manage oneself, accept responsibility or become independent. Indeed, the individual in question is likely to become more dependent upon outside sources for stimulation rather than develop the ability to entertain himself or herself.

Perhaps such abilities are related to the concept of self-efficacy. Self-efficacy is the feeling that one can control the outcomes in life which are important to them (Bandura cited in Peele, 1989). Those individuals with low levels of self-efficacy would seem to be less likely to seek to control their own use of leisure and more likely to rely on vicarious experience. While leisure behavior, in the ancient Athenian sense, is self-regulating, in addictive behaviors there is no self-regulation. Such self-regulation is related to self-regard or self-esteem. That is, an individual with higher self-esteem is more likely to be self-regulating.

Not only is individual self-efficacy important in how leisure is used, so, too, is community efficacy. In communities which appear to be powerless, unable to control outcomes which are important to successful community life, there is a greater tendency toward passivity.

Where self or community efficacy are low, leisure behaviors are more likely to be passive, and such passivity is related to addictive behavior. Television viewing, for example, among children is positively related to obesity in children since it interferes with burning calories through active play. Like excessive eating, drinking or drug taking, it is a passive, consumer-oriented form of entertainment.

> The link between watching television and obesity and other addictions is that watching television depletes the child's resources for direct experience and interaction with the environment in favor of vicarious experiences and involvements. (Peele, 1989)

Not only is television linked to obesity, the content of programs produced for mass audiences is increasingly vulgar.

> Television is not vulgar because people are vulgar; it is vulgar because people are similar in their prurient interests and sharply differentiated in their civilized concerns. All of world history is moving increasingly toward more segmented markets. But in a broadcast medium, such a move would be a commercial disaster. In a broadcast medium, artists and writers cannot appeal to the highest aspirations and sensibilities of individuals, manipulative masters rule over huge masses of people. (Gilder, 1994, p. 49)

Television viewing, for people who are by themselves, like drugs, may keep the mind from having to face depressing thoughts. According to Csikszentmihalyi (1991a), "...what drugs in fact do is reduce our perception of both what can be accomplished and what we as individuals are able to accomplish, until the two are in balance." While drugs may produce an alteration of the content and organization of consciousness, they do not add to our ability to order them effectively.

Sexual activity, too, may simply be used as a way to impose an external order on our thoughts of killing time "...without having to confront the perils of solitude" (Csikszentmihalyi, 1991b). It is, therefore not surprising that television viewing, sexual activity and drinking are relatively interchangeable behaviors within many households. What such activities do is focus attention naturally and pleasurably but what they fail to do is to develop attentional habits which might lead to a greater complexity of consciousness. Addictive behavior, then, is undertaken to relieve the pain which may creep into the unfocused mind.

Finally, all these issues are related to a person acting rather than being acted upon. People who have high levels of wellness are more likely to "act" during their free time than merely to be acted on. Such "action" must be thought of holistically rather than merely in terms of physical behavior if we are to understand it. The many benefits of physical exercise occur because the individual has found something worth doing, because he or she has a strong sense of self-efficacy. The most critical constraints to such involvement are not those which have to do with lack of time, money or resources, but rather those which:

> ...involve individual psychological states and attributes which interact with leisure preferences rather than intervening between preferences and participation. Examples of intrapersonal barriers include stress, depression, anxiety, religiosity, kin and nonkin reference group attitudes, prior socialization into specific leisure activities, perceived self-skill, and subjective evaluations of the appropriateness and availability of various leisure activities. (Crawford and Godbey, 1987)

The most fundamental constraints to "acting" during leisure in ways which may produce positive physical activity are those which have to do with how individuals feel about themselves and what they think it is appropriate to do during free time. This recognition has caused some organizations concerned with physical fitness to broaden the way they seek to promote fitness. In Canada, Fitness Canada has adopted a campaign called "Active Living," a concept which:

> ...connects the mind, body and spirit in physical activity within various stages of life and as an integral part of our

daily routines and leisure pursuits. It contributes to increased feelings of personal worth, energy and vitality for
living, as well as to maximizing our human potential physically, emotionally and socially. The process and experience of being physically active in everyday living is self-
empowering; it increases our sense of personal control over
our lives and stimulates feelings of self-confidence in our
ability to manage our own health. (Fitness Canada, 1992)

The benefits of physical fitness, it is slowly being realized, are more
likely to occur when physical activity is conceived within a broad frame-
work which considers the individual's total being.

The relation of leisure services to public health agencies and other
health and wellness organizations will intensify. At the municipal level,
there are already some precedents for state or local health agencies providing funding targeted to specific facilities or services of recreation and
park agencies which have measurable wellness outcomes. The *Healthy
People 2000* statement of national opportunities, coordinated by the U.S.
Department of Health and Human Services and involving a coalition of
22 expert working groups, specifically targeted increases in community
availability and accessibility of physical activity and fitness facilities.
These include hiking, biking and fitness trails, public swimming pools
and acres of park and recreation open space (U.S. Department of Health
and Human Services, 1990).

There is also evidence that the American public associates wellness
benefits with local recreation and park departments. The national telephone survey of the benefits of local recreation and park services found
that the benefits the American public most frequently associated with use
of such services at the individual, household and community level were
exercise and fitness benefits (see Table 23, page 203; Godbey, Graefe and
James, 1992). At the individual and household level, relaxation and
peace (stress reduction) was the second most frequently mentioned benefit. These benefits and others, which respondents identified in their own
words, are not only in keeping with the concept of wellness, but refer to
most of the components in the definition of wellness given previously.
Another large scale study of older people's use of local parks found that
older park users commonly got significant amounts of exercise during
their park visitation and that, in interviews, about one-half of them
"...said they felt different about things after visiting the park and the

typical descriptions of such feelings were intensely positive and of an emotional, spiritual or psychological nature. Negative change was almost nonexistent" (Godbey and Blazey, 1983).

In summary, recreation and park services provide opportunities to individuals which have positive health effects. These effects can and must be measured and analyzed in terms of cost savings in public health expenditures. Doing so will often involve collaborative efforts with public health agencies. This measurement process must proceed from a paradigm which expresses the outputs or consequences of such services. That paradigm is wellness.

Such changes also mean that some vocational specialties, such as therapeutic recreation, will become more highly integrated with both those in other "therapeutic" professions, such as occupational therapists and physical therapists as well as those in both public, commercial and private, nonprofit leisure services. Therapeutic recreation's critical mission will continue to be leisure education, but will change from mainstreaming to "best fit" facilitation, from open-ended thinking to systems approaches, from seeking professional identity to seeking integration, from striving for recognition to receiving recognition by the medical and health establishment.

As our population ages dramatically, as many people with disabilities who would have died in previous generations are kept alive, as our awareness and compassion increase for those who must struggle with a multitude of conditions which create constraints to the enjoyment of life, therapeutic recreation may grow in importance. Also contributing to the increasing need for therapeutic recreation is the huge split between haves and have-nots which is taking place in the United States, in which the disparity between rich and poor is already greater than any other modern nation. One need only look at the fastest growing jobs in the United States to see that "therapeutic recreation" is an occupation with a huge growth rate. Therapeutic recreation was among the fastest growing jobs during the last decade, although all occupations in the rapidly changing healthcare system are, themselves, subject to rapid change.

Therapeutic recreation will also be reshaped by changes in the way healthcare is provided.

The traditional therapeutic recreation department, with a certified therapeutic recreation specialist (C.T.R.S.) as director, is often replaced by a 'product line' or 'program'

model. Such models organize rehabilitative services according to the disability, diagnosis, or medical goals of the
client or patient, rather than the discipline of the service
provider. Thus, there is a movement away from hierarchi-
cally organized, discipline specific services toward services that require multidisciplinary cooperation among allied health professionals. (Smith, 1995, p. 67)

As with many other areas of leisure services, then, therapeutic recreation
practitioners find themselves working in multidisciplinary teams. Part of
this has occurred due to managed care systems. Under such management,
which is concerned with cost effectiveness, the length of stay of a patient
in a hospital is decreasing dramatically, making traditional forms of therapeutic recreation services impossible. This requires forms of extended
care to be provided after the patient has been discharged from an institution. Community reintegration is increasing in importance, with emphasis
on functional skills that allow a client to return to the community as
quickly as possible (Smith, 1995). This is leading to the need for increased
collaboration between therapeutic recreation specialists and community
recreation practitioners. Additionally, assessment of clients or patients is
being sped up, cooperative ventures with government agencies and private businesses are increasing, and client to staff ratios are increasing.

Therapeutic recreation personnel are increasingly involved with
co-treatment programs involving one or more allied health disciplines
collaborating and delivering a service to a client more rapidly.

Therapeutic recreation has always operated primarily from a situation
of limited resources, but it will increasingly have to conceptualize from
such limits, envisioning what is possible rather than in terms of rights as
must every other occupation in our society. Those who only "advocate"
and think in open-ended terms about resources do no one a favor. Similarly, pretending that disabilities aren't real and placing real limitations
on people leads to, ultimately, making things worse. Recent restraint-free
laws passed in Florida for nursing homes, for instance, make certain the
realistic possibility that many frail elderly may be seriously harmed because they have no restraints. Terms like "barrier-free environment" may
lead to such thinking but none of us will ever be free of barriers.

Those who work in therapeutic recreation will focus more on facilitating and educating rather than open-ended advocacy. That is, rather than
in advance, arguing for their clients rights, sometimes at the expense of
others in society, they must think in terms of what trade-offs can be

made, what compromises can be struck, what incremental improvements can be made in the lives of those with disabilities. Such facilitation must consider the lives of others as well as the lives of those with disabilities. If a child is mainstreamed into a classroom but moans throughout the class, there must be a recognition of the costs to the students whose learning may be hindered as well as the needs of the child who moans.

Part of the changes which take place in therapeutic recreation may have to do with mainstreaming or inclusion. The goal of including those with a disability in the everyday lives of those without disabilities has sometimes been an unquestioned ideal of therapeutic recreation professionals, but it needs to be examined for several reasons. First, in a society which is increasingly tribalized, where the mass culture is disappearing, it is difficult to say just where the "mainstream" is. Our culture shows increased diversity by ethnic status, income, values, and membership in subcultures. Mainstreaming or inclusion are less and less evident in the lives of people without disabilities; thus making it more difficult and sometimes impractical for this to take place among people with disabilities.

There is also the issue that many people with a disability prefer to form their community from others with a similar situation or disability. Among the deaf, for example, many prefer to remain within the deaf community, forming their own organizations for recreation and other purposes. Since many leisure activities are successful only where there is appropriate competition levels, such activities, and the social groups which emerge from them, may not be inclusive, nor should they be. Play occurs, as Huizinga (1950) noted, only when the outcome is in doubt. Keeping the outcome in doubt may mean the players must segregate based upon physical or mental condition, or life stage. Finally, of course, there is the issue of cost. Inclusion may simply be prohibitively expensive or may provide less benefit to the individuals involved than a noninclusive leisure format.

All of this means that many therapeutic recreation services will be concerned with what might be called "best-fit facilitation." That is, given the financial, environmental, social and moral aspects of the situation, what model of provision will best contribute to enhancing the quality of life of both those with a disability and the rest of society.

Therapeutic recreation will also deal with the issue of what constitutes a "disability." In a changing world, the fundamental basis of disability is rapidly becoming ignorance or inability to learn. Hence, education for leisure is a concept which must be more widely applied to populations whose "disability" is becoming more serious. This includes school dropouts, youth gangs, the rural and urban poor, and others.

When the former Surgeon General of the United States, C. Everett Koop, looked back on his challenges, he commented: "When I look back on my years in office, the things I banged my head against were all poverty" (Coontz, 1992). Poverty is linked to the likelihood of possessing a number of forms of disabilities and, in the emergence of what Drucker (1993) calls the "knowledge economy," ignorance will be more directly linked to poverty, becoming the greatest disability.

The Equal Opportunity Commission of the federal government has attempted to clarify what is a disability under the law. A legal impairment is a physiological disorder affecting one or more body systems or a mental or psychological disorder. The following, however, are not legal impairments: environmental, cultural, and economic disadvantages; common personality traits; homosexuality and bisexuality; pregnancy; and normal deviations in height, weight, or strength that are not the result of a physiological disorder. For example, not being able to read due to lack of educational opportunity is not a disability. Not being able to read because of dyslexia is a disability. Having a quick temper is not a disability but behavior that can be traced to bipolar mood disorder is a disability. Major life activities can include such mental and emotional processes as "thinking, concentrating, and interacting with other people." This is in addition to "caring for oneself, performing manual tasks, walking, seeing, speaking, breathing, learning, working, sitting, standing, lifting." Surely, one can see the problems here. To say that not being able to read due to lack of educational opportunity is not a disability ignores the fact that reading is critical to middle-class life.

Conversely, many "disability" groups must be thought of as having the potential to be in good health or bad health. In many surveys, for instance (Godbey and Graefe, 1993), people who listed a physical or emotional disability also frequently listed their health as "good" or "excellent." One may be, for instance, an amputee who is in good health, a person with a spinal cord injury who is in good health, or a person who has mental retardation who is in good health. Thus, while "ill" and "handicapped" used to be considered synonymous, they no longer should be, but we sometimes continue to think they are.

Also, from the previous definition, one can see that many conditions not classified as a "disability," in reality are statistically related to "disabling conditions." It is not by chance, for instance, that gay teenagers are markedly more likely to commit suicide than those who are not. Thus, being gay as such may not be a disability but the reactions of those around the gay person may cause it to be.

It will be up to professionals in therapeutic recreation to move "hospitality" to the new level which historian Theodore Zeldin described in 1994 (and as was quoted on pages 13–14). Such hospitality expresses itself in concern for the well-being of strangers, in the acceptance of diverse ideas and conditions of other people, and in the willingness to act in ways which help those who are less fortunate. Therapeutic recreation, in the most profound sense, is a "hospitality" occupation. (If one wants further evidence of this, think about why the words "hospitality" and "hospital" have a common derivation.)

# 35

# Deteriorating Health in Modern Nations

The health of individuals who live in modern nations is declining, even as they are living longer. While in most modern nations, life expectancy continues to increase, the state of health of such individuals, on average, appears to be deteriorating. Much of this decline is unlikely to be attributable to frail people being kept alive longer. Scientific studies have found deteriorating health in Canada in the 1970s, Australia during the 1980s, and Japan from the 1950s through the 1990s.

In the United States, the National Health Interview Survey, initiated in 1957, examines two measures of health of 100,000 people annually. One of these measures is "limitation of activity" which is a measure of long-term disability that is due to chronic conditions and diseases which have usually lasted at least three months. A person is limited in activity when he or she has difficulty performing his or her usual activity that is normal for his or her age group (Montague, 1996). The other measure is "restricted activity days" which is how many days during the past two weeks the individual had to cut down on normal activity because of health. Restricted activity can be due to either acute conditions, such as colds and sore throats, or chronic conditions, like heart disease. It is an indicator of both acute and chronic illness.

In the United States population, between 1957 and 1989, "activity limitation" has increased 43 percent. The number of "restricted activity days" has increased 28 percent between 1961 and 1989. Some of the reasons for this, in addition to an older population, include: technologically keeping people alive who would have previously died, overeating and a junk food diet, lack of exercise, higher stress levels, increased chemical exposure which may be degrading the immune system, giving rise to increased infections and autoimmune disorders such as asthma, rheumatoid arthritis and diabetes (Montague, 1996).

There has also been a shift in the causes of death due to chronic illnesses which humans can exert some control over. Table 13 shows the changes in the top ten causes of death in 1900 and 1990. As may be seen, the causes of death in 1990 are more often those over which humans can exert some control by how they lead their everyday lives. Figure 13 makes this clear by showing the role of many contributors to cardiovascular disease such as smoking, exercise, diet and hypertension.

Cancer rates are generally higher and such increases are not attributable just to an older population. The age-adjusted increases in the incidence of all cancers has increased 54 percent during the last 45 years and the death rate has increased almost ten percent. Numerous studies show that environmental factors are far more important than genetic, inherited factors in terms of contracting cancer. "Migration studies" show that when

Table 13     **Top Ten Causes of Death in the United States (1900 and 1990)**

| Rank | Cause of Death | Deaths per 100,000 | Percent of All Deaths |
|------|----------------|--------------------|-----------------------|
| | **1900** | | |
| 1 | Pneumonia | 202 | 12 |
| 2 | Tuberculosis | 194 | 11 |
| 3 | Diarrhea and enteritis | 140 | 8 |
| 4 | Heart disease | 137 | 8 |
| 5 | Chronic nephritis (Bright's disease) | 81 | 5 |
| 6 | Unintentional injury (accidents) | 76 | 4 |
| 7 | Stroke | 73 | 4 |
| 8 | Diseases of early infancy | 72 | 4 |
| 9 | Cancer | 64 | 4 |
| 10 | Diphtheria | 40 | 2 |
| | **1990** | | |
| 1 | Heart disease | 290 | 34 |
| 2 | Cancer | 203 | 24 |
| 3 | Stroke | 58 | 7 |
| 4 | Unintentional injury (accidents) | 37 | 4 |
| 5 | Lung diseases | 35 | 4 |
| 6 | Pneumonia and influenza | 32 | 4 |
| 7 | Diabetes | 19 | 2 |
| 8 | Suicide | 12 | 1 |
| 9 | Liver disease | 10 | 1 |
| 10 | HIV/AIDS | 10 | 1 |

Source: Montague (1996)

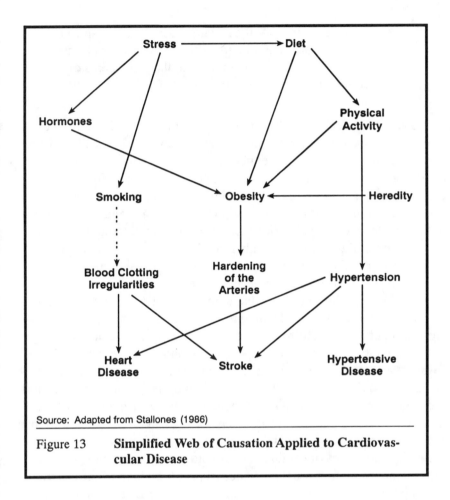

Source: Adapted from Stallones (1986)

Figure 13    **Simplified Web of Causation Applied to Cardiovascular Disease**

people migrate from one country to another, they tend to develop rates of
cancer which reflect the country they have moved to (Montague, 1996):

> So long as we continue to bathe ourselves in carcinogens
> in air, water and food, and in chemicals which degrade our
> immune systems, more of us each passing year will have
> to learn to live with cancer. Present policies are exceed-
> ingly expensive (estimated at $72.5 billion in 1985) and
> don't make much sense from a public health standpoint,
> but they make eminently good sense from the viewpoint

of the cancer industry—those who cause it and those who
sell services that ameliorate its effects. The cancer industry
is robust and healthy; by comparison, the proponents of
prevention are sickly, weak and pallid. (p. 4)

Part of the declines in health may be due to recent declines in exercise and sport and the increase in television viewing. Ironically, leisure service professionals rarely see themselves as being in competition with television. Those in the various recreation "movements" from which present-day leisure services evolved, however, would have indeed recognized television as part of the competition. J. B. Nash and others warned of the problems of "spectatoritis," passive forms of recreation in which the individual did not exercise either mind or body. The writing of Charles Brightbill (1960) and others also reflect this sentiment.

In spite of efforts to promote sport and exercise, participation in sport will likely continue to decline in modern nations. In spite of earlier increases in the 1970s, the decline in sport in North America is increasingly evident and not attributable only to deteriorating health or the aging of the population. Based on large-scale and nationally representative surveys of the American public conducted by the National Center for Health Statistics, Robinson and Godbey (1993) found that participation in sport and fitness activity declined by ten percent between 1985 and 1990. Contrary to expectations, such declines were greater among females than males, thus increasing the gender gap in sport and fitness. Young women showed greater rates of decline than did older women, and the largest declines, amounting to more than 30 occasions of sport and fitness participation per year, were among the youngest group of females in the sample. Such differences continued to be pronounced even when the influence of a variety of variables were accounted for pertaining to biological, social, economic and lifestyle statuses were accounted for.

## Issue Questions

1. Do you think public leisure services are in competition
   with television? Why or why not?

2. Based on the previous discussion, should society put
   more emphasis on "prevention?" If so, how?

3. What forms of leisure activity do you believe contribute
   the most to good health?

## Implications for Leisure

As with many other trends, the deteriorating health status of those in modern nations has vast implications for leisure services. First, many leisure services will redefine themselves more directly as health services. Second, adapting activities for people with some health problems and physical limitations will become increasingly important. Therapeutic recreation will be a service in more demand and will work with people who have health limitations of types that therapeutic recreation has traditionally not worked with (such as allergies).

While the long-term solution to many problems of health is environmental change, the short-term solutions will involve use of leisure in more central ways.

# 36

# Increased Rushing and Stress

Americans feel significantly more rushed and under more stress. Almost four out of ten Americans say they "always" feel rushed (Godbey and Graefe, 1993). In numerous surveys, it is evident that Americans believe they have less free time (this is probably not true), want more time away from work, and want the pace of life to slow down. Table 14 (pages 154–155) shows the characteristics of people who are most likely to feel time crunched. There are numerous other indicators that residents of postmodern societies feel more stressed. Insufficient attention has been paid to the effects of the deskilling of work, accelerating pace of production, increasing work loads, and new forms of coercion used to force worker compliance. An increasing number of workers act solely as observers, watching information processes unfold on a machine which has been programmed to carry out tasks with an inhuman exactness. While Japan has been the model in the efficiency revolution, consider that one study found that 124,000 of Toyota's 200,000 workers suffered from chronic fatigue. Lean production systems require stressing the system to find out where the weak points are. *Karoshi* is a Japanese term to describe the pathology of production-related illnesses and, in an internationalized economy, such approaches to work and resulting illnesses have spread to Britain, the United States and elsewhere. Between 20 and 35 percent of all clerical workers in the United States, for instance, are now monitored by sophisticated computer equipment. It is not surprising that a large U.S. study

| Table 14 | The Time Crunch and Who Feels Crunched |
| --- | --- |

| A. Item | % Agreeing |
| --- | --- |
| 1. I often feel under stress when I don't have enough time | 43% |
| 2. When I need more time, I tend to cut back on my sleep | 40% |
| 3. At the end of the day, I often feel that I haven't accomplished what I set out to do | 33% |
| 4. I worry that I don't spend enough time with my family or friends | 33% |
| 5. I feel that I'm constantly under stress—trying to accomplish more than I can handle | 31% |
| 6. I feel trapped in a daily routine | 28% |
| 7. When I'm working long hours, I often feel guilty that I'm not at home | 27% |
| 8. I consider myself a workaholic | 26% |
| 9. I just don't have time for fun anymore | 22% |
| 10. Sometimes I feel that my spouse doesn't know who I am anymore | 21% |

Source: Hilton Time Values Survey, 1991 continued on page 155...

found that clerical workers who use computers suffer inordinately high levels of stress (Rifkin, 1995). The distance we have traveled from the dark, satanic mills of England's industrial revolution may be a short distance indeed. All of this may mean that the pace of life and of work will become an increasingly political issue, particularly since our society is aging.

Economist Staffan Linder theorized that the speed up of the pace of life in America occurred as follows. An equilibrium existed between the work and leisure of Americans in terms of what was accomplished during each of these periods of life. As output per worker increased, the time of each worker became more valuable and therefore thought of as more scarce. This destroyed the balance between work and leisure, since people had increased the yield on their work but not their leisure. People then began to attempt to increase the yield on their leisure both by speeding up their participation in various activities and by combining given activities with additional material goods. This caused a shift away from leisure activities which could not be easily sped up or combined with additional material goods, such as contemplation, singing and dancing or writing short stories and increased time spent in activities which could be sped up and combined with material goods, such as driving for pleasure,

Table 14    **The Time Crunch and Who Feels Crunched** (continued)

**B. Demographic Differences in the Time Crunch**
**(average number of agreements with ten statements)**

|  | Women | Men |
|---|---|---|
| **TOTAL** | 3.5 | 2.9 |
| **AGE** | | |
| 18 to 29 | 3.6 | 2.8 |
| 30 to 49 | 3.8 | 2.9 |
| 50 to 59 | 2.4 | 2.8 |
| 60 and older | 2.7 | 2.8 |
| | | |
| **EMPLOYMENT** | | |
| Full-time | 3.7 | 2.8 |
| Part-time | 3.3 | 4.1 |
| Not employed | 3.1 | 2.7 |
| | | |
| **CHILDREN AT HOME** | | |
| Under age 6 | 4.0 | 2.8 |
| Aged 6 to 11 | 4.1 | 2.7 |
| Aged 12 to 17 | 4.1 | 3.2 |
| No children under 18 | 3.3 | 2.8 |
| | | |
| **RACE/ETHNIC ORIGIN** | | |
| White | 3.3 | 2.8 |
| Black, Hispanic | 4.4 | 2.8 |
| | | |
| **MARITAL STATUS** | | |
| Single | 3.2 | 2.9 |
| Married | 3.3 | 2.9 |
| Divorced/widowed | 4.3 | 2.5 |

Source:   Hilton Time Values Survey, 1991

shopping and tourism.  Linder (1969) argued that this situation led to a general perceived scarcity of time.

Every culture, of course, is haunted by some specter seemingly beyond its control:  weather, war, disease, religious prejudice, boredom, starvation.  Presently, our own society is starving—not the starvation of Somalis or North Koreans, who die for lack of food—but the ultimate scarcity of the postmodern world—time.

Starving for time does not result in death, it results, as ancient Athenian philosophers observed, in never having begun to live.  The examples of time scarcity surround us include:

- Condensing of birthday parties into restaurant meals at which the wait staff assemble to sing a quick chorus of "Happy Birthday," perhaps accompanied by a cupcake with a lit candle that is extinguished within 20 seconds after it is lit.

- Running red lights; risking life and limb to save a few seconds.

- Gulping food at meals too quickly to savor the flavor; such habits are a major factor in obesity.

- Using drive-through windows in "fast food" restaurants. You drive through throwing money at them and they throw grease, salt and sugar back at you.

- Advising parents to spend "quality time" with children, which simply means doing more with them in less time.

- Spending rarely more than a few seconds in front of a painting in a museum.

- Complaints of retired couples claiming that they always feel rushed, even though there is almost nothing they have to do.

- Wrecking a car while simultaneously driving, talking on the telephone, listening to a taped lecture and eating lunch out of a McDonald's bag (as actually happened to a colleague of mine).

- Playing endless and perverse games of communication tag, made worse by call waiting, fax machines, and voice mail.

- Following the new social taboos—being late, taking too long to get to "the point" in a conversation, or waiting—for anything.

- Increasing reliance on guns and violence as a quick way to resolve conflicts.

- Experiencing the massive decline of patience in everyday life—except for those who are "patients" in hospitals, but even patients are getting impatient.

To "rush" is a bit more sinister than we might suspect. In a culture that is particularly rushed, this may be hard to discern since it takes lots of unrushed reflection to recognize what rushing means.

The word "rush" has many related meanings. It may be either a swift advance, or an attack or charge. To rush means "to move, act, or progress with speed, impetuosity, or violence" (*Random House College Dictionary*, 1988). Thus, to rush may mean not only speed of action or progression but also rash or unthinking action or an injurious, rough, or destructively forceful action. The range of synonyms for rushing has expanded to include:

> speed, race, hasten, hie, hurry, run, dash, tear, scramble, dart, hustle, scurry, scamper, speed up, accelerate, dispatch, expedite, perform hastily, finish with speed, work against time, hurry, spur, whip, urge, goad, drive, pressure, push, press, keep at, go carelessly, go headlong, act thoughtlessly, leap, plunge, precipitate oneself, attack suddenly, storm, charge, descend upon, have at, run, dash, sprint, haste, speed, dispatch, and urgency. (*Random House Thesaurus—College Edition*, 1989)

In most of these meanings, there is the quality of aggression. Surely aggression is a widely admired trait in our culture—from business to sport to politics to matters of the heart—aggression is encouraged.

There is also the quality of violence in rushing—it is no accident that the high speed train system in Japan is called the "bullet train." There is rushing in football, in dating, and in fraternities. In many cases, rushing indicates going after some objective independent of the feelings of others. If you move slowly, the other individuals involved have time to consider what you are doing and make judgments about it. If you rush—they may not.

Among the antonyms one finds are walk, crawl, slow, dawdle—and leisure. Leisure requires an absence of rushing, tranquillity, an end to hurrying; a letting go. Thus, questions of amounts of "free time" in a society may not tell us much about the extent to which that society experiences leisure.

Rushing, then, is a complex term. It is easy to see situations in which rushing would be worthwhile and functional. If your house is on fire, you *should* rush out of the building; if a mugger is chasing you, run away; if the wind blows your hat across the field, rush after it. As a way of life, however, rushing doesn't sound very inviting or even functional.

Effortless speed, of course, is something very different from rushing. The leopard does not "rush" after its prey. Mozart did not rush to create music; it simply poured out. One who is a "quick study" does not have to necessarily "rush" for answers and a savant seems to receive his or her magical skills as a gift from God. Indeed, much of what we can do quickly without rushing appears to be God's gift. Barry Sanders of the Detroit Lions is remarkably gifted at rushing, yet, like most highly talented running backs, he never seems in a hurry. Rushing, then, is something different from speed; it is an attempt at greater control—often after control seems to have been lost. If you stomp an anthill with your boot, the ants will rush around. Sometimes our culture resembles one big stomped anthill.

The term "time deepening" describes the leisure behavior of many Americans. Time deepening assumes that, under pressure of expanded interest and compulsion, people are capable of higher rates of doing. Rather than thinking of leisure behavior in "either-or" terms, that is, a person does either one activity or another, some people develop the capacity to do both activity A and activity B. Time deepening occurs in four ways. First, people may attempt to speed up a given activity. Drive-through zoos, for instance, in which individuals go through an animal park in their cars, are visited more quickly than zoos where you must visit on foot. Second, individuals may substitute a leisure activity which can be done more quickly for one which takes longer. For instance, a person may substitute aerobic dance for tennis, since tennis usually takes longer. Third, a person may do more than one activity at once, watching sports events on a big screen television while dining and drinking in a restaurant. Fourth, one may undertake a leisure activity with more precise regard to time, perhaps planning an evening of cocktails, dinner and attending the theater with only a five or ten minute tolerance in the schedule.

Time deepening, while it may have some advantages in terms of accomplishments, may produce great stress, if such behaviors result in feeling rushed. In one nationwide study, those who felt rushed were significantly more likely to describe themselves as having high levels of stress than those who were less rushed (Godbey, Graefe and James, 1992). Time deepening also means that, during leisure, Americans rarely experience anything fully—never live in the moment. Additionally, they may avoid activities which require a long time to learn the necessary skills.

While Americans may use time deepening techniques due to the speed up of the pace of life, there is considerable evidence that such rushing produces stress and dissatisfaction. Godbey, Graefe and James (1992), for example, found a positive relation between feeling rushed and high-stress levels as well as between feeling rushed and low self-esteem.

In the United Kingdom, it is estimated that job stress costs up to ten percent of the annual gross national product (Rifkin, 1995). Such high stress often leads to health-related problems, including ulcers, high blood pressure, heart attacks and strokes, alcohol and drug abuse. In the United States a Metropolitan Life Insurance Company study estimates that one million workers miss work on any given day because of stress-related illness. Then, too, there is an increase in accidents. A major study concluded that "a person under stress is an accident waiting to happen" (Rifkin, 1995).

Our bodily functions, which are attuned to the forces of nature, have upward limits in terms of their adaptability to the rhythms of the computer. The nanosecond culture of the computer must inevitably cause stress. Imagine that two computers are having a conversation. They are then asked by a human being what they are talking about. In the time the human takes to pose the question, the computers have exchanged more words than the sum of all words exchanged by human beings since *Homo sapiens* appeared on the earth two or three million years ago (Simons, 1985).

There is a revolution going on at work as severe as that which occurred during the Industrial Revolution. The fallout from this new revolution is stress—which has become perhaps the greatest killer in our society. As futurist Hazel Henderson noted:

> I have this vision of stress as a ball being pushed around the system. Everybody is trying to unload the stress in somebody else's system. For example, take the economy. One way to minister to the sick economy would be to create another percentage point of unemployment. That pushes the stress back onto the individual. We know that one percentage point of unemployment creates about seven billion dollars' worth of measurable human stress in terms of morbidity, mortality, suicide and so on....Another way of doing this is that the society can shove the stress onto the ecosystem, and then it comes back 50 years later, as in the case of Love Canal. (in Capra, 1988)

Physiologically, when the mind is stressed the body responds by rising metabolism, heart rate, blood pressure, breathing and muscle tension. Such reactions are a lasting vestige of our prehistoric ancestors who, when faced with danger, prepared to fight or run away. The hormones which are released under high stress, such as epinephrine, speed up the heart. If your heart is weak, of course, or the small arteries feeding blood to it are clogged with fat, epinephrine might overload your heart. The ability to relax and relieve such stress is positively associated with a variety of health issues, from high blood pressure to headaches and backaches to diabetes to depression to heart attack.

**Is a Slowdown Beginning?** In 1995, the Americans' Use of Time Project replicated much of the previous research on people's perceptions of time and found that Americans are feeling slightly less stressed than they were a few years ago. They are also somewhat less likely to say that their free time has declined.

The proportion of people aged 18 to 64 who say that they always feel rushed fell from 38 percent to 34 percent in 1995. For those aged 65 and over, the drop is more dramatic. The proportion of people who say they had experienced at least some stress in the past two weeks was 54 percent in 1995, hardly changed from 56 percent in 1993. The share who would rather have an extra day off than an extra day's pay is also declining, from 49 percent in 1991 to 47 percent in 1995. Perhaps the most interesting reversal of all is that 45 percent say they had less free time than in the past, down from the 54 percent obtained by the Roper poll in 1991. Thus, while it is too early to tell, people may be starting to slow down.

# Issue Questions

1. Are there advantages to rushing through life?

2. Do you feel more rushed than five years ago? Why?

3. How can recreation and park professionals help the public reduce stress?

# Possible Implications for Leisure

It may be that the most important function of leisure in the coming decades will be to reduce stress. This means opportunities to slow down, for solitude, to be as close to nature as possible, to have quiet. Making these opportunities come about will mean, in some ways, limiting personal freedom in order to increase group freedom. Right now, if one wishes to buy a motorcycle which will interrupt the lives of a thousand people who live near the road it is driven on, one has the "freedom" to do so. Any "developer" can make life busier; the needs of the airline industry ignore the needs of those whose houses are below the roaring planes. This may begin to change, limiting individual freedom in return for communal well-being.

Limiting stress will also mean limiting the recreational use of natural areas. This may mean limiting use of natural areas to walking, limiting boating to sailboats, rowboats, canoes or kayaks, and otherwise controlling the extent to which outdoor recreation activities can use vehicles which make noise and pollution.

3 7

## The Increasingly Central Role of Free Time in Modern Nations

Leisure has become an increasingly expected and important part of people's lives in modern societies. Privileged people, however, do not get more free time than less privileged people in such societies; rather, they get the good jobs. While the work ethic is supported almost everywhere and, in particular, held up as a way to get ahead economically, leisure and its use is increasingly replacing work as the center of social arrangements. Monetary spending for leisure increases, use of federal land for leisure purposes increases, resorts fill up, major professional sports events routinely sell out, participation in avocational organizations shows overall increases, gardening surges, sports bars are crowded, and the leisure use of libraries, museums, and botanical gardens increases.

In regard to relative importance of work and leisure, one national survey found that 41 percent of the public thought leisure was more important than work, while only 36 percent thought work was more important than leisure, and 23 percent thought they were equally important (Roper Organization, 1990). This question had been asked by the Roper Organization since 1975 and, from 1975 to 1985, more people thought work was important, but leisure slowly rose in importance. Another study, using a national sample of 1,300 households, found 38 percent said work and leisure were equally important, 36 percent said work was more important and 26 percent said leisure was more important (Godbey, Graefe and James, 1992).

Leisure, then, is of critical importance to the public even if it is not widely recognized.

## Issue Questions

1. What is more important to you—work or leisure, or are both equally important? Why?

2. If leisure is as important as people say it is to them in survey questions, why do you think studying recreation and leisure as an academic specialty is sometimes not taken seriously?

3. Have people's expectations about what they can do during leisure increased or decreased during the last decade?
Why?

## Possible Implications for Leisure

The increased importance of leisure in the lives of individuals argues that
more systematic attempts to prepare children and adolescents for leisure is
a more important task for families and schools as well as other social institutions such as religious organizations. There also needs to be a more
general recognition of the importance of leisure as a powerful force for
good or evil among physicians, counselors, city planners, and others.
People's use of leisure is an issue which transcends corporations, government organizations or specialists in leisure studies. It must be thought
about in designing highway systems, building hospitals and in redevelop-
ing rural areas.

# 38

# *Increasing Free Time Across the Life Span*

Peter Drucker (1993) and others argue that where business has succeeded
in the noncommunist world, it has succeeded so well that people can consider satisfying noneconomic needs. "[H]alf of the expansion in wealth-
producing capacity was used to create leisure time by cutting the hours
worked while steadily increasing pay" (p. 177). Drucker further notes that:

An additional third of the increased wealth-producing capacity has gone into healthcare, where expenditures have
gone from less than one percent of gross national product
to 8–11 percent (depending on the country) in fifty years.
There has been almost equal growth—from two percent of
GNP to 10–11 percent—in the expenditure on formal
schooling; and with more and more schooling taking place
outside the formal school system, especially in and by employing institutions, the portion of GNP that now goes to
education is much higher than the ten percent officially reported. Leisure, healthcare and schooling require goods;

they are not spiritual. Very little of the new leisure is used for intellectual pursuits. The free hours are more likely to be spent in front of the television set watching 'Dallas' or sports. Still, neither leisure nor healthcare nor education were ever considered economic satisfactions. They represent values quite different from those of the 'business society.' They bespeak a society in which economic satisfactions are a means rather than a good in themselves, and in which business therefore is a tool rather than a way of life. (pp. 177–8)

This same phenomenon is shown to be taking place in most other modern nations (Ausubel and Grubler, 1994). Table 15 shows that, not only has there been a decline in hours of work per year in the countries shown, but that the American worker is not overworked compared to his or her counterparts in Germany or Japan.

Table 15    International Comparision of Hours Worked
(Effectively) per Person per Year

| Year | France | FRG | UK | USA | Japan | Ratio of Japan/USA |
|------|--------|------|------|------|-------|--------------------|
| 1870 | 2945 | 2941 | 2984 | 2964 | 2945 | 0.99 |
| 1890 | 2770 | 2765 | 2807 | 2789 | 2770 | 0.99 |
| 1913 | 2588 | 2584 | 2624 | 2605 | 2588 | 0.99 |
| 1929 | 2297 | 2284 | 2286 | 2342 | 2364 | 1.01 |
| 1938 | 1848 | 2316 | 2267 | 2062 | 2361 | 1.15 |
| 1950 | 1926 | 2316 | 1958 | 1867 | 2166 | 1.16 |
| 1960 | 1919 | 2081 | 1913 | 1795 | 2318 | 1.29 |
| 1973 | 1771 | 1804 | 1688 | 1717 | 2093 | 1.22 |
| 1987 | 1543 | 1620 | 1557 | 1608 | 2020 | 1.26 |

Data refer to annual hours worked effectively (i.e., contractual working time plus overtime minus holidays and sick leave). Other definitions are also used frequently in international working time comparisions (e.g., contractual working time, excluding overtime and sick leave), or actual working hours (derived from detailed time budget surveys including also "informal" overtime). Definitions and data sources are discussed in detail in Maddison [31, pp 255–258]. Methodological issues (and resulting uncertainties) in international comparisons are discussed in Marchlang [32, pp 33–38].

Source: Maddison (1991)

Additionally, work is taking a smaller and smaller fraction of the hours of one's life. An analysis of British citizens, for instance, found that:

> Although the average career length has remained around
> 40 years, the total life hours worked shrank from 124,000
> hours in 1856 to 69,000 in 1983. The fraction of dispos-
> able lifetime hours spent working declined from 50 per-
> cent to 20 percent. (Ausubel and Grubler, 1994, p. 195)

Even if we have not achieved a society of leisure, we have gained free time—not only on a daily basis but as a percentage of our total lives. Free time is increasing in a wide range of countries and the increases of free time are positively related to increased gross domestic product, in line with Drucker's thinking.

A central feature of the declining portion of life spent working is later entry into the labor force and earlier retirement with longer life expectancy. United States workers now retire, on average, in their late fifties or early sixties, and American men who reach the age of 65 now have a life expectancy of 80 years, while women's life expectancy is 84 years. On average, about 12 of these years after age 65 will be relatively healthy. The elderly are not only no longer disproportionately poor but, if wealth is measured as financial assets, among the wealthiest groups in society (ages 55 to 64 is the wealthiest). Their potential for free time use has increased dramatically.

Our current society hoards huge amounts of free time to be spent only in the last fifteen to twenty years of life. The Prussian bureaucrat who is reputed to have established 65 as the age of retirement payment, is said to have done so completely arbitrarily. He probably never imagined that the institution of retirement that he helped establish would today consume almost one-fifth of a person's life. Less than one out of five of the 52 million Americans age 55 and over is in the labor force—a stunning indicator of where free time has grown most quickly. Does this retirement policy recognize the vastly differential rate at which people age, or transfer adequate free time or provide more tranquillity for those in earlier life stages who must scramble to fulfill the multiple roles of parent of young children, full-time employee and spouse? (Even though an increasingly small portion of young people have all these roles).

Not only retirees but children as well may be considered to have more free time. School-age children attend public school only about 180 days per year in the United States (compared to 240 in Japan) and the amount of time they spend doing schoolwork at home is thought to have declined. They may also spend less time helping parents with housework or other chores.

The portion of our lives devoted to both paid work and housework is decreasing and it appears that such declines are predicted by rising economic standards of living within a country. Gershuny (1992), after a meta-analysis of time use in 15 countries drew this conclusion and added: "...there is no basis, theoretical or empirical, for thinking that we are 'running out of time'" (p. 18).

## Issue Questions

1. If you were reorganizing your country with regard to the way free time is distributed across the life cycle, would you make any changes? Why or why not?

2. Is the school year organized in ways that make sense for parents and children? Why or why not?

3. Should the largest block of free time be experienced during the final fifteen or twenty years of a person's life?

## Possible Implications for Leisure

The pronounced decline in the percentage of life spent at work will increasingly bring leisure to the center of social arrangements and economic well-being. This means first and foremost that more must be understood about the consequences of leisure for individual happiness, family cohesion, sense of community, health, the environment, the economy, and so forth. In short, leisure needs to be understood more completely. Such an understanding can only happen if interdisciplinary research focuses on leisure constraints, choices, attitudes, behaviors, monetary spending, the leisure problems faced by those with disabilities and by specific subgroups of the population such as ethnic minorities, and a host of other subjects.

The increased portion of life spent away from work also means that a reexamination of how everyday life is organized, when and by whom work is done, and what kinds of policies should be enacted or changed which affect our patterns of work, free time, travel, child rearing, shopping and every other aspect of life.

# 39

# The Decreasing Workweek and the Maldistribution of Free Time

The total number of hours per week devoted to paid work, the commute to work and total family care declined 6.2 hours a week for women and 6.0 hours a week for men from 1965 to 1985, as shown by nationally representative time diary studies. Preliminary analysis of 1995 time diaries and other data sources generally show amount of free time has held steady since 1985 (Robinson and Godbey, 1997).

Free time has increased since 1965 by about six hours per week. Both men and women average about 40 hours of free time per week. Basically, all sectors of the population have gained free time, although the main gain in free time occurred between 1965 and 1975. While the gain since 1975 has been only one to two hours per week, this six-hour average gain per week is of considerable significance. It translates to a gain of more than six 40-hour workweeks of additional free time per year, or an additional month and a half of vacation.

While free time has increased across the workweek, most free time occurs during weekdays, not the weekend. Free time increases from five hours a day on weekdays, to six hours on Saturdays, to 7.5 hours on Sundays. Across the week, then, 25 of the 40 weekly hours of free time occur on weekdays. Free time during the week may have more limited value in terms of its possibility for leisure. That is, with a whole day of free time, a broader range of activities is possible, such as taking a trip, sailing a boat or perusing books in the local library. These activities would be very difficult to squeeze into 45 minutes per day gains during workdays.

This distribution may be a problem, since free time in larger segments has expanded potential for leisure purposes. For instance, the nature of free time differs dramatically on vacation. Even though the 7.4 hours of free time on vacation days are barely more than a typical Sunday, there is a dramatic decline in television viewing to less than 20 minutes a day (Hill, 1985). In its place, reading time more than doubles and communication time almost doubles (although visiting time is cut in half). The biggest increase is in sports, walking and other outdoor activity—nearly two hours. The increases in sleep and meal time, and the decrease in grooming time, also suggest a more leisurely pace.

Survey respondents generally report they would rather have their increases in free time in the form of three-day weekends or larger blocks of time. In spite of this, the chores of weekdays appear to be expanding into the weekend, even as free time expands during weekdays. The expansion of free time on the weekday may help explain the greater amount of time devoted to television viewing during the last few decades (Robinson and Godbey, 1997).

## Issue Questions

1. Can the amount of time devoted to work continue to decline in modern nations? Why or why not?

2. How many hours would a person choose to work a week, if given a choice? Why?

3. What would make the increased free time, which most Americans have, more useful or pleasurable?

4. Should most free time be stored during the last decade or two or life? Why or why not?

## Possible Implications for Leisure

As work has seeped into the weekend and free time has seeped into weekdays, changes appear to be taking place in people's use of free time which are not very satisfying. One reason for this may be that the many short segments of free time do not provide a psychological escape from necessity. People do not feel the transition from a rushed work pace to relaxed and tranquil leisure. Indeed, as we have seen previously, large segments of the public feel rushed at both work and during their free time.

Thought must be given to the reorganization of free time in ways which produce longer time segments away from work and, if possible, beyond the reach of work. Advanced technologies have made it more difficult for some to ever feel that they have escaped work, but ways must be found for them to do so.

# 40

# The Rise of Television as the Primary Use of Free Time

As may be seen in Figure 14, of the almost 40 hours of free time per week which Americans average, only 2.2 are devoted to participation in outdoor recreation, active sports, hobbies, crafts, art, music, drama, games and other forms of recreation. Social activities such as attending sports events, going to the movies, parties, bars and lounges, and social visiting account for 6.7 hours per week. Religion and cultural events each take less than an hour per week. By far the largest time consumer is television, with 15 hours per week (and another five hours per week as a secondary activity).

Almost all the gains in free time since 1965 have been used for more television viewing! Such TV viewing overwhelms all other uses of free time, accounting for about 40 percent of all free time. As scholar of architecture James Kunstler (1993) observed:

> The American house has been TV-centered for three generations. It is the focus of family life, and the life of the house correspondingly turns inward, away from whatever occurs beyond its four walls. (TV rooms are called 'family rooms' in builders' lingo. A friend who is an architect explained to me: 'People don't want to admit that what the family *does* together is watch TV.') At the same time, the television is the family's chief connection with the outside world. The physical envelope of the house itself no longer connects their lives to the outside in any active way; rather, it seals them off from it. The outside world has become an abstraction filtered through television, just as the weather is an abstraction filtered through air conditioning. (p. 167)

Thus, television has become the pivotal use of free time, and most of its content is based around both escapism and consumption. The cultural historian Christopher Lasch (1979) describes how:

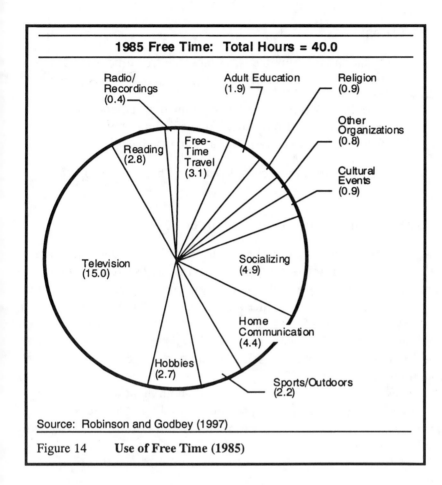

**1985 Free Time: Total Hours = 40.0**

Radio/Recordings (0.4)
Reading (2.8)
Free-Time Travel (3.1)
Adult Education (1.9)
Religion (0.9)
Other Organizations (0.8)
Cultural Events (0.9)
Television (15.0)
Socializing (4.9)
Home Communication (4.4)
Hobbies (2.7)
Sports/Outdoors (2.2)

Source: Robinson and Godbey (1997)

Figure 14     **Use of Free Time (1985)**

The appearance in history of an escapist conception of 'leisure' coincides with the organization of leisure as an extension of commodity production. The same forces that have organized the factory and the office have organized leisure as well, reducing it to an appendage of industry. (p. 217)

Leisure, then, is organized by large corporations rather than the people in local communities. Any thoughts of reordering leisure in society will have to start by considering TV.

# Issue Questions

1. What do you think the ways in which free time is used tell us about our society?

2. Should efforts be made by government or others to discourage people from watching television in favor of other forms of leisure activity? If so, on what basis?

3. Can TV viewing be considered a health issue? If so, why?

# Possible Implications for Leisure

To a great extent, modern leisure has been organized around television. The growing recognition of this and the controversy surrounding how appropriate television is as a principle use of leisure may cause systematic efforts to minimize TV's influence and its use. Unlike in many other countries, in the United States, television exists almost exclusively to sell goods and services, since most TV viewed by Americans is sponsored by large corporations who wish to sell something in turn for sponsoring the programming.

Social movements to reform leisure are nothing new. Previous social movements targeted brothels, saloons, gambling and other forms of leisure considered to be evil or disruptive of family life. Perhaps TV will be the new target.

# 41

# *Increasing Economic Significance of Free Time*

Free time increases as countries become more affluent and leisure and its use become a more important engine driving the economy. While "leisure studies" is not often taken very seriously within universities, the well-being of the economy is increasingly tied to use of leisure. Gershuny (1992) and others have recently argued that leisure, in modern societies, creates the jobs which most people have, allowing for consumption of an ever-expanding variety of goods and services.

> When consumption is the main activity of a day or a life, most work in restaurants, hotels, schools, media, fitness centers, banks and healthcare organizations. Service dominates employment and over the long run may especially favor medicine and recreation as well as information handling. In a society in which we live longer and work less, people can worry more about youth, beauty, and health. (p. 211)

To the extent that leisure is the generator of jobs, it will have to be more systematically understood.

While a comprehensive count of leisure industry jobs is hard to find, there are some leisure-related jobs in every industry, including defense. Crandall (Academy of Leisure Sciences, 1992) claimed that travel and tourism employs nine million people in the United States. There are about 250,000 public sector jobs in federal, state, county and local recreation, park and other leisure agencies. There are nearly two million writers, artists, entertainers and professional athletes. No one has completely sorted out all of the jobs that are linked to leisure and converted these to full-time equivalents. The simplest way to get a total leisure-job estimate is to convert leisure spending to jobs.

> If about $40,000 in consumer spending generates a job (full-time equivalent), a trillion dollars in leisure spending

translates into 25 million jobs—about a quarter of all jobs in 1990. If this isn't enough, figure that every leisure job generates another job in a supporting industry. This ties nearly half of all jobs to leisure. (Stynes, Academy of Leisure Sciences, 1993)

Thus, free time has increased and leisure has become of central importance in our lives and the economy.

## Issue Questions

1. Can an economy which grows based upon leisure activity provide high-quality jobs? Why or why not?

2. What kind of leisure services will grow in the next ten years? Why?

3. Will leisure grow as a creator of jobs in developing countries such as Mexico? Why or why not?

## Possible Implications for Leisure

As leisure becomes a more central part of the economy of modern nations, there may be increasing competition to export forms of leisure from one country to another along with the goods and services which go with them. The United States has been a leader here, exporting mass media, theme parks, and other forms of leisure activity in a world in which many other countries will seek to export their leisure industries.

# 42

# *Jobs Will Become the Critical Issue of the Next Decade*

Many analyses of work find that the same process of technological change which led to agriculture workers declining to two percent of the population has moved through manufacturing and is now producing a huge decline in the need for service workers and, shortly, for information workers. The majority of jobs are technologically replaceable right now by computers, robots or other technological means. The process of "reengineering" currently going on in corporate America is at only its beginning stages. Reengineering begets reengineering, just as marketing begets marketing. In the banking industry, this may lead to 30 to 40 percent of all employees being laid off in the next ten years. As a vice president of Taco Bell said recently, the company's goal was to shrink the kitchen in its restaurants as small as possible and get rid of all employees except for point of sale. While Americans often think that jobs which are exported to third-world countries are not subject to reengineering—they are. The phenomenon is worldwide. Additionally, some jobs are not deported; they just disappear.

Job sharing, with a corresponding reduction of hours worked, is an idea whose time has come and is beginning to be recognized in countries like Germany and France. (The French acknowledged unemployment rate was 12 percent in 1997.) The choices may be either massive unemployment or shorter workweeks for many employees, more free time, less financial resources and more dependence upon the public and private, nonprofit (third) sector for leisure.

The ways in which work may be spread out are still being thought about and experimented with but include:

1. Job sharing—This usually involves two persons filling a single job, both dealing with the same customers, clients or files.

2. Flex-time and compressed workweeks—Under flex-time a person may choose the time he or she starts and finishes work. Compressed workweeks give employees the right to take time off on one day—often to stretch the weekend

to include a Friday or Monday—if they make up the time by working slightly longer hours the other days of the week.

3. Leading-edge employers—Such employers have sought to attract and retain desirable employees by becoming much more flexible in the work patterns of their employees, in effect customizing the work schedule to fit the life of the worker.

4. Four-day workweek—This alternative, which has been initiated by Volkswagen in Germany and elsewhere, involves employees working only four days a week. There are many alternatives under this model, some in which workers work 36 hours over four days and others in which they work as few as 30. In some cases, employees may choose what additional day of the week they want off from work but, since most want either a Friday or a Monday to produce a three-day weekend, many companies may assign or limit the right to choose the additional day.

5. Reduced work time and job creation—Some recent union or other worker agreements have reduced the hours of current employees in order to create new jobs or to avoid layoffs. In some cases, these agreements have meant a proportionate reduction in salary or other forms of pay; in some cases they have not.

6. Limiting overtime—Under such arrangements, the extent to which employees could work overtime were minimized, with overtime after a certain number of hours being compensated by additional time off rather than more pay.

7. Early retirement—Under this arrangement, employees are given financial incentives to retire from work at an earlier age than previously.

8. Flexible and phased-in retirement—This allows for workers to retire gradually; cutting back their hours, usually with attendant cutbacks of pay and benefits.

None of these techniques, of course, guarantees that more jobs will be created or work shared. In any of these alternatives, the employers in question may simply use the technique to cut back on the number of employees.

Not only is the distribution of work changing, so are the types of employment available. In the emerging economies, work may be redefined and redistributed as follows (Handy, 1990):

**The Professional Core**—Well-qualified people, professionals or technicians or managers. They get most of their identity and purpose from their work. They *are* the organization and are likely to be both committed to it and dependent upon it. They will work long and hard, but in return they want not only proper rewards in the present but some guarantee of their future. They think in terms of careers, of advancement, and of investing in the future. The number of people in this group may decline by 50 percent.

**The Contract Fringe**—Made up of both organizations and individuals who will do much of the work formerly done by core professionals. They will be paid for results, not for time, in fees, not wages. Work will be subcontracted to them.

**The Flexible Labor Force**—Hired help which employers hire as needed for as little money as they can pay. Part-time and temporary workers, the flexible labor force will do low- or no-skill jobs both to supplement income in a two-worker family or because they have no choice.

**Consumers**—Those who purchase products will increasingly be asked to do some labor as part of the purchase—pumping the gas they buy, assembling the furniture, clearing the table at a fast-food restaurant and recycling the products they use.

**Volunteers**—Those who choose to do work for reasons other than pay. They will increasingly be recruited, trained, "hired," evaluated, promoted, fired, and in other ways serve the same functions as paid workers. As Peter Drucker (1997) stated: There are no more volunteers; there are only unpaid employees.

This new redistribution of work will have fundamental implications for how people experience different stages of life as well as their life chances.

## Issue Questions

1. Will the changes in the way work is done and the need for workers affect recreation and leisure? If so, how?

2. If society had no need for some people to work, how could their lives be made meaningful?

## Possible Implications for Leisure

This configuration of the labor force will possibly mean that people are less alike in their economic resources, amount of free time and when it occurs, and in the extent to which they stay in continuous learning. Leisure services will sometimes have to be specifically targeted to one such worker group to succeed. Past that, the central life orientation for some people will be leisure while for others work will dominate. Individual self-definition will come from leisure behavior in one case and work in another.

There is also the real possibility that not everyone will be needed to do paid work. This situation will force a reordering of society as fundamental as the changes caused by the industrial revolution. While it is already true, as reported earlier, that the majority of U.S. citizens and those in many other countries think their leisure is as important or more important than their work, the political and economic systems in place do not assume that there can be another organizing principle of society than paid work. Will "leisure" become the penalty of an underemployed or unemployed subgroup of society? If so, we will see turmoil and strife. A society of leisure will not necessarily make things easier. Indeed, without a fundamental rethinking of every aspect of our society, it may be a huge problem.

There is some precedent for a society of leisure, however. It may be seen in the almost one out of five people in our society who are "retired" from work but generally, not from life. Older people provide an ongoing experiment for the leisure society.

# 43

# "Management" Is Changing in Meaning and Function

Management is changing its meaning and function. While "management" may have meant "someone who is responsible for the work of subordinates" immediately after World War II, that meaning changed in the early 1950s to "someone who is responsible for the performance of people." Today, however, according to Peter Drucker (1993), it means one who "is responsible for the application and performance of knowledge" (p. 44).

> Land, labor and capital are important chiefly as restraints. Without them, even knowledge cannot produce; even management cannot perform. But where there is effective management, that is, application of knowledge to knowledge, we can always obtain the other resources. (p. 45)

Managers must also manage for change, which means the organization in question destabilizes. "The task of management in the knowledge-based organization is not to make everybody a boss. It is to make everybody a contributor" (Drucker, 1995, p. 109). Thus, employees must increasingly be convinced that what they are doing makes sense and is worthwhile. While those who do unskilled labor may still be treated as "subordinates," increasingly such jobs are being done by machines. For most organizations which do "work," the issue will be determining and obtaining the knowledge needed to do the job and then continuing to change as the requirements of the organization change. Ben Franklin said that time is money, but today knowledge and cooperation are money. Managers will have to deal with this shift.

## Issue Questions

1. What implication do these changes have for the management of hotels and restaurants?

2. Will therapeutic recreation ever become essentially a provider of knowledge to people with disabilities?

3. Should the manager of a golf club be essentially a manager of knowledge? If, yes, why? If no, why? With what kinds of knowledge would should a manager deal?

## Possible Implications for Leisure

Managing knowledge means that leisure service organizations, like others, "must be organized for systematic abandonment of the established, the customary, the familiar, the comfortable. ...It is the very nature of knowledge that it changes fast and that today's certainties will be tomorrow's absurdities" (Drucker, 1993). Managers of all forms of leisure services will need to experiment, reconceptualize, and to let go of what they have been doing based on changing conditions. There is a tendency to seek greater efficiencies rather than to change—keep doing what we are doing but do it better. While efficiency will continue to be important, rethinking what an organization does and then quickly changing when necessary may become more important.

44

## The Rise of Corporate Power

As the economy of all countries becomes increasingly internationalized, large corporations have become the most powerful organizational entities, with little allegiance to the country within which they operate. While corporations vary in their environmental sensitivity, they are ultimately driven by the profit motive and must operate in ways which are profitable. In numerous cases, the inability of corporations to restrain themselves has contributed to a world of haves and have-nots; in which some people make athletic shoes in one country for four dollars a day which are sold in another country for two hundred dollars a pair. A world in which a mining company in the United States can mine gold using techniques which produce one ton of slag for the mining of enough gold for only one wedding band.

Of the largest ten organizational budgets in the world, four are not national governments but corporations. Countries and states compete for corporate relocations, often trashing environmental laws in the process. In numerous modern nations, corporations have come to be the dominant political power. In South Korea, Japan, Taiwan and other Asian perimeter countries, corporations directly shape both the domestic and foreign policies of government.

In many developing nations, corporations determine who will govern and take steps to kill off those they oppose. They also pollute the environment to a remarkable degree. Shell Oil, for instance, has caused 784 separate oil spills in Nigeria, admits to 3,000 polluted sites, has flared off 1.1 billion cubic feet of natural gas, causing acid rain about ten percent of the days of the year and generally devastating the environment. They have also set up a system described by the World Council of Churches as one in which Shell executives become Nigerian political officials and Nigerian political officials become Shell executives. In countless ways, corporations exploit economically weak nations for short-term profit (*New York Times* cited by Montague, May 15, 1997, pp. 1–8).

In the United States:

> Urged on by a coalition of big industries, one state after
> another is adopting legislation to protect companies from

disclosure or punishment when they discover environmental offenses at their own plants. (*New York Times*, April 7, 1996 cited by Montague, 1997)

Corporations are being given exemption from environmental laws if they self-report such offenses. Documents reporting such self-reporting are secret by law and can't be divulged to the public or used in any legal proceedings.

In both developed and developing nations, corporations are part of a "permanent government" that rules regardless of who is elected to political office. As the editor of *Harper's Magazine*, Lewis Lapham, recently stated:

The permanent government, a secular oligarchy... comprises the Fortune 500 companies and their attendant lobbyists, the big media and entertainment syndicates, the civil and military services, the larger research universities and law firms....Obedient to the rule of men, not laws, the permanent government oversees the production of wealth, builds cities, manufactures goods, raises capital, fixes prices, shapes the landscape, and reserves the right to assume debt, poison rivers, cheat the customers, receive the gifts of federal subsidy, and speak to the American people in the language of low motive and base emotion. (1996, p. 34)

Thus, many of the assumptions made about democracy—that people vote in or vote out those who will carry out the policies they favor—aren't true.

Certainly, however, corporations do much good. Many of the advances in science have been due to corporate research and development, many of the comforts of life, improved medicines, advances in communication and other positive changes have come from corporate involvement. More people visit Disneyland than England each year and they seem free to choose where they go on vacation. If power corrupts, however, then increased corporate power is an increasing problem in the modern world, particularly to the extent that such corporations have no goal or vision other than short-term financial profit by any means.

In terms of leisure, corporations shape the majority of hours of free time for those in modern nations. In the United States, for instance, television exists only because it is sponsored by corporations seeking to sell their goods and services. (There is a public television network but it receives less than ten percent of the viewing audience.) Thus the content of TV is shaped to reach a maximum audience and generally presents programming which appeals to the lowest common denominator.

The vast majority of tourism in the world is managed and controlled by large corporations—tourists flying to a destination on an airline owned by a large corporation, staying in a hotel owned by a large corporation, taking photographs with a camera and having them developed by large corporations, eating in "chain" restaurants owned by large corporations, drinking beer brewed by large corporations, and perhaps playing golf on a course owned by a large corporation. It may be argued that "marketing" techniques represent the ultimate in democracy, simply finding out what people value, believe and want, and then supplying it to them. Such claims, however, ignore the fact that most Americans have spent thousand of hours watching and reading commercials for the products and services supplied by corporations. Marketing might actually work well as a device for insuring democracy if advertising did not exist and if people had sufficient education and exposure to various alternative ways of life to make intelligent choices.

Commercial forms of recreation may be satisfying for some people, but they are ultimately supplied to make money for stock holders of a company rather than improve human beings or contribute to their well-being. (It might be said, of course, that government sponsored recreation is often used as a means of social control, or to keep elected officials in office, or to divert attention from many societal problems with which government has failed to deal.)

Minimizing corporate control of much of the modern world would involve limiting corporations by law in ways in which they often formerly were. Such limitations would include: requiring corporations to have a specific purpose, with penalties or removal of corporate privileges if that purpose were not fulfilled or exceeded, requiring a percentage of stockholders to live in the state in which the corporation is licensed, prohibiting corporations from owning stock in other corporations, issuing corporation charters for a fixed period of time, prohibiting all political donations and imposing strict liability on corporate officers and stockholders (*New York Times* cited by Montague, May 15, 1997). Until such steps are taken, corporations will continue to be a central component of the permanent government.

Fortunately, some corporations are beginning to believe that their own well-being is dependent upon the well-being of the environment.

Large corporations which sell insurance have become concerned about global warming—perhaps because such warming is probably responsible for the increases in violent weather which is raising insurance claims at an alarming rate. There is profit in environmentally sensitive corporate behavior, such as recycling, light weighting of products and other environmentally friendly behavior.

In spite of this, the enormous power of corporations to control mass media, constantly advertise and engage in massive public relations efforts to promote their services and products, to influence legislation in their favor, and to get rid of small competitors remains a problem of growing proportions.

## Issue Questions

1. What personal leisure activities do you participate in and what products do you buy for leisure purposes which come from large corporations?

2. Could private, nonprofit organizations provide some of the leisure activities Americans want rather than corporations? Why or why not?

3. Do government-sponsored recreation, park and leisure services provide a real alternative to corporate-sponsored leisure? Why or why not?

## Possible Implications for Leisure

The huge power of corporations to shape the use of leisure among those in every modern nation is increasingly apparent. People dine for pleasure in chain restaurants; try every new device produced by corporations for use during leisure; riding jet skis and snowmobiles which go 75 miles per hour; rent endless video tapes; visit theme parks developed by corporations which make beer or candy; and otherwise make use of what corporations provide during free time. Is this a waste of one's life? Corporate-sponsored leisure is the dominant mode of free time use and questions surrounding such use are critical in determining whether or not free time in modern nations is used wisely.

There is massive evidence that people want much of their free time experience organized by someone else and corporations have a number of advantages in doing so. This should not, however, open the door to unlimited corporate privilege. If private, nonprofit or government organizations providing leisure services had the power to advertise which corporations do, it would be interesting to see what changes took place in people's use of free time.

# 45

# *The Loss of Social Capital Critical to Governance in a Democracy*

Recent research by Robert Putnam documents the decline of "social capital." By social capital "I mean features of social life—networks, norms and trust—that enable participants to act together more effectively to pursue shared objectives" (Putnam, 1995). Documentation of the decline in social capital includes greatly decreased membership in voluntary organizations such as the Boy Scouts, League of Women Voters, Parent Teacher Associations, the Red Cross, volunteers in many organizations, and even league bowling. Since the governance of a democracy is dependent upon voluntary participation, these declines are ominous. While the reasons for this decline are not completely understood, Putnam believes that increased time spent in television viewing is a critical reason, citing a roughly 25 percent decline in time spent in informal socializing and visiting since 1965 and the nearly 50 percent decline in the time we spend in clubs and organizations. The progression by which television is causing this problem may be conceived as seen in Table 16 (page 186).

Social capital is necessary not only for a democracy, it has been argued that the inability of the Soviet Union to move from a communist state to a capitalist state has to do with the lack of social capital.

Finding ways to reinvent and encourage social capital, in some cases making use of modern communication technology, is a critical issue which will ultimately determine whether democracy, as we know it, will continue at the local level.

Not all social critics agree with Putnam that social capital has declined. It has been argued that Putnam has ignored grass-roots political groups, religious organizations and soccer leagues. It is also contended that such "social capital" organizations may be more interested in excluding other people than including them (Perlstein, 1997). Such groups may

| Table 16 | The Consequences of Television |
|---|---|
| **Possible Television** | **Consequences** |
| 1st Order | People have a new source of entertainment or information in their home. |
| 2nd Order | People stay home, less socializing. |
| 3rd Order | Residents of communities do not meet as often, therefore do not know each other. |
| 4th Order | Community residents are strangers, find it difficult to deal with common problems, isolation and alienation. |
| 5th Order | Isolation from neighbors, members of a family depend on each other for satisfaction of psychological needs. |
| 6th Order | When spouses are unable to meet heavy psychological demands that each makes on each other, frustration, possible breakdown. |

Source: World Future Society (1991)

also now be using home computers to do their work. It may be that Americans are redefining the forms and nature of their engagement with the community (Stengel, 1996). In spite of such criticisms, time spent watching TV has increased, displacing other uses of free time. Time devoted to social life has declined—as has time spent in voluntary organizations and in religion. While in survey research Americans report that religion is of central importance in their lives, they spend an average of 42 minutes per week in religious activity.

# Issue Questions

1. Is "social capital" declining on your campus or in your community? Why or why not?

2. What role could public recreation and park departments play, if any, in promoting social capital?

3. Does participation with others on the World Wide Web or by e-mail constitute a form of social capital?

# Possible Implications for Leisure

This decline in social capital has numerous negative consequences for society including lack of participation necessary for democratic government to function, increased alienation and loneliness, and decreasing ability to solve problems in groups. It may also mean that sense of caring about one's neighborhood, community or other group in which one resides may decline.

Building social capital will be an increasingly important task of all leisure services. Leisure services play multiple roles which can help restore social capital. Many local government recreation and park departments help organize their community to plan communitywide celebration, festivals that celebrate the heritage of a community or ethnic group within a community and other all community events which enhance social capital. Such planning will, increasingly, need to be inclusive and involve the active participation of community members. To do this, such organizations will need to become more "agile" (see pages 216–225). Those who work in resort hotels and convention centers also play a role in increasing social capital. Part of hospitality training must be the development of skill in building social capital among tourists who are, perhaps, on a cruise for a week, conference attendees playing in a two-day golf tournament or visitors touring the sights of a city.

Leisure service organizations will also likely play a larger role in facilitating the adjustment of new residents to a community. Such new residents will include not only those who have moved from another state or part of one state, but also immigrants from other countries and refugees— those who have fled their country due to persecution, or environmental or economic disasters. Seeking to integrate such new residents will require that leisure service professionals actively learn about such new residents; their backgrounds, the circumstances under which they moved, and about their leisure interests and their culture.

Leisure service organizations which deal with individuals with a disability will also increase their efforts to develop social capital. This will mean, in some cases, rethinking how services are offered and assuming that the process by which the leisure services are developed is as important as the services themselves. Social capital is more difficult to develop if the leisure service staff take the role of "expert" and "prescribe" what services are needed. (You rarely see much social capital developed in a medical doctor's office.) Thus, the professional in leisure services will increasingly need skills in community development, group dynamics, and community organization. While these ideas are a century old, they will be rediscovered.

Most recreation, park and leisure services are in competition with home entertainment/information centers for free time more than other providers in the commercial and private, nonprofit leisure service sector. The decline in social capital makes this competition even greater.

# Government Will Need Substantial Restructuring, Reinventing and Downsizing

As presently designed, the U.S. federal government, as well as those of other nations, is too small to deal with one set of problems, such as pollution or international trade, but too big to deal with others, such as local school systems. It is inefficient, slow and often incapable of making tough decisions.

There are many efforts beginning to reinvent government. Whether such efforts succeed remains to be seen—historically, government changes only when it is threatened by outside forces. The assumptions made by those who wish to reinvent government are as follows:

1. There is a need for more governance, but less government.

2. If an analogy to a boat is made, government must do more steering, but less rowing.

3. Government agencies must be judged on what their outputs are rather than what their mandates or intentions are.

4. Government agencies must be concerned with prevention rather than treatment, e.g., U.S. fire departments are second-rate in international terms because they concentrate on putting out fires rather than preventing them through code enforcement, educating the public about fire prevention, and performing onsite inspections.

5. Competition is preferable to monopoly in both the public and private sectors.

6. Citizens are valued customers who must be listened to and given options and choices.

7. Government functions are in a constant state of change and should be. In such a state, flexibility and capacity to change are critical. Thus government employees must also be flexible, continuously educated and trained. (Osborne and Gaebler, 1992)

Much of what the federal government does will be passed down to states and to "third sector" private, nonprofit organizations and those in the market sector. This is not to argue for the irrelevancy of federal government, only that it is poorly equipped to do much of what it does, seems incapable of rapid change, and shows little ability to create policy which reflects the increasing economic, ethnic and political diversity of the country. Outsourcing will become more common as a way of achieving efficiency.

At the same time, other tasks will require greater participation from our federal government in multinational organizations. Problems of pollution, terrorism, technological transfer, the economy and immigration all require multinational involvement for effective solutions to emerge. These problems affect many countries and need systematic international cooperation to be solved.

Government workers will need to be substantially reorganized, retrained, and retired. Government is the biggest employer of service workers, yet they have the lowest productivity.

In every single developed country, governments have reached the limits of their ability to tax and their ability to borrow. They have reached these limits during boom times when, according to modern economic theory, they should have built up sizable surpluses. The fiscal state has spent itself into impotence. (Drucker, 1993, p. 133)

Government has, by and large, not shown itself to be very good at "doing" things. (The Department of Defense, in 1994, spent as much on travel billing and procedures as on the actual travel.) Government can set the rules or standards; it can provide, but it doesn't provide direct services as well as other forms of organization. Part of the reason for this is that the traditional "productivity by command" approach doesn't work very well. "In knowledge and service work, partnership with the responsible worker is the *only* way to improve productivity. Nothing else works" (Drucker, 1993, p. 92). Government organizations must become learning and teaching organizations which allow and insist that employees increase the productivity of knowledge about what they are doing. It will also involve considerably more outsourcing, getting rid of almost all management layers, reengineering in ways which will result in layoffs of employees, and more reliance on "third sector" organizations. Such private, nonprofit organizations, from the Catholic Church to Trout Unlimited, have become America's biggest employer. Ninety million Americans work three or more hours per week for such groups as unpaid staff.

## Issue Questions

1. How will the downsizing of government, particularly at the federal level, reshape public recreation and park services, libraries, museums, therapeutic recreation and other similar services?

2. Is it possible for public leisure services to grow even as government is being downsized? If so, how?

3. Should recreation and leisure services be left strictly to the commercial sector? What would be lost if this were done?

## Possible Implications for Leisure

Recreation, park and leisure services, like other services of government, are being reshaped by attempts to reinvent government. Leisure services sponsored by government will be reinvented, reorganized and outsourced. They will become more important.

Part of the changes in government leisure services will be due to the need and desire to reinvent government. Part, also, will be due to the litany of changes described previously. These changes have considerable impact for all forms of recreation, park and leisure services. A Delphi study by Whyte (1992) asked a panel of experts from the American Academy of Park and Recreation Administrators and the Academy of Leisure Sciences to identify key trends and issues impacting local government recreation and park services in the 1990s. There was a high level of agreement concerning such issues and the trends listed in Table 17 were identified as having "extreme impact" on such services. Issues which were rated as having extreme impact are shown in Table 18.

As shown, the most pressing trends and issues identified involve finance. Perhaps we should put these ideas in some perspective. First,

---

**Table 17   Trends Having Extreme Impact on Local Government Recreation and Parks Services**

• Deteriorating park and recreation infrastructure.
• Increasing crime (e.g., violence, drug use, vandalism, gangs) in communities and parks.
• Declining park and recreation budget relative to costs.
• Increased competition for shrinking federal, state, and local tax resources.
• Massive public sector debt.

**Table 18   Issues Having Extreme Impact on Local Government Recreation and Parks Services**

• How to insure adequate finance for capital development (e.g., land/open space, facilities).
• What spending priorities should be set in the face of budget cuts or when services are stretched too thin.
• How to make parks safe places (from crime, vandalism, gangs, substance abuse) while maintaining visitor enjoyment.
• How can public parks and recreation strengthen its political position and shape the future through affecting state and national policy.
• How to compete successfully for funding against other community services (e.g., education, health, police).

---

these trends and issues do not necessarily mean that recreation and parks is a less valued service of local government. Indeed, recreation and parks as a percentage of local government has generally not declined and net expenditures have increased during the last decade.

Growth of spending for local government recreation and park services has been substantial from the late 1980s and early 1990s. Municipal expenditures for recreation and park services increased in inflation adjusted dollars from an average of $19.76 in 1964–65 to $32.72 in 1990–91 (see Table 19, page 192). Variation among states is dramatic, reflecting different political traditions as well as economic circumstances.

A major study by Crompton and McGregor (1994) found that employment of staff had also increased during this period but had remained, essentially unchanged from 1978 to 1990 (see Table 20). Their study concluded that the immediate effects of the tax revolt movement had ended in 1984 but that "its lasting effects extending beyond that period have been an increase in the proportion of revenue that is self-generated, and an increased tendency to use part-time employees and to contract out services" (Crompton and McGregor, 1994, p. 35). These authors also point out that there is great variation in what has happened to funding and staffing of these services from town to town, reflecting, perhaps, the Balkanization of society discussed elsewhere. Nevertheless, if local government expenditures are declining, as they are in many cities, all government services must do more with less. For municipal and county recreation and park services, part of the problem is the deterioration of the recreation and park infrastructure built

| Table 19 | The Actual and Adjusted per Capita Expenditures on Recreation and Parks in the United States | |
| --- | --- | --- |
| **Year** | **Actual Dollars** | **Adjusted Dollars** |
| 1964–65 | 5.69 | 19.76 |
| 1965–66 | 6.05 | 20.03 |
| 1966–67 | 6.53 | 20.41 |
| 1967–68 | 7.06 | 20.83 |
| 1968–69 | 8.14 | 22.42 |
| 1969–70 | 9.29 | 23.70 |
| 1970–71 | 10.22 | 24.39 |
| 1971–72 | 11.16 | 25.14 |
| 1972–73 | 12.20 | 25.52 |
| 1973–74 | 13.96 | 26.44 |
| 1974–75 | 16.24 | 27.95 |
| 1975–76 | 18.00 | 29.03 |
| 1976–77 | 17.89 | 27.07 |
| 1977–78 | 17.81 | 25.05 |
| 1978–79 | 19.26 | 24.79 |
| 1979–80 | 21.21 | 24.61 |
| 1980–81 | 23.28 | 24.93 |
| 1981–82 | 25.11 | 25.11 |
| 1982–83 | 26.61 | 25.44 |
| 1983–84 | 28.28 | 25.73 |
| 1984–85 | 29.57 | 25.74 |
| 1985–86 | 31.97 | 27.05 |
| 1986–87 | 34.99 | 28.45 |
| 1987–88 | 37.57 | 29.19 |
| 1988–89 | 40.94 | 30.30 |
| 1989–90 | 42.62 | 30.16 |
| 1990–91 | 47.71 | 32.72 |

Note: Base year is 1981–82

Source: Crompton and McGregor (1994). Adapted from *Economic Report of the President,* transmitted to Congress January 1990; *Census of Government Finances* for the given years, U.S. Department of Commerce.

during the 1930s and 1940s due to work creation programs sponsored by the federal government to help deal with massive unemployment. There is also deterioration of the recreation facilities built with Land and Water Conservation Fund moneys from the federal government during the 1970s and 1980s, all of which were developed with no accompanying funds to maintain, renovate and operate them. These building programs,

Table 20    **Park and Recreation Employment in Local Government (in thousands)**

| Year | Full-time | Annual Difference In Full-time Employees | Part-time | Annual Difference In Part-time Employees | Total Full-time and Part-time |
|------|-----------|------------------------------------------|-----------|------------------------------------------|-------------------------------|
| 1966 | 104 | — | 34 | — | 138 |
| 1967 | 107 | 3 | 41 | 7 | 148 |
| 1968 | 111 | 4 | 42 | 1 | 153 |
| 1969 | 114 | 3 | 42 | 0 | 156 |
| 1970 | 117 | 3 | 43 | 1 | 160 |
| 1971 | 122 | 5 | 42 | −1 | 164 |
| 1972 | 126 | 1 | 48 | 6 | 174 |
| 1973 | 132 | 6 | 59 | 11 | 191 |
| 1974 | 120 | −12 | 79 | 20 | 199 |
| 1975 | 128 | 8 | 90 | 11 | 218 |
| 1976 | 131 | 3 | 77 | −13 | 208 |
| 1977 | 141 | 10 | 80 | 3 | 221 |
| 1978 | 145 | 4 | 76 | −4 | 221 |
| 1979 | 141 | −4 | 85 | 9 | 226 |
| 1980 | 135 | −6 | 84 | −5 | 219 |
| 1981 | 131 | −4 | 89 | 5 | 220 |
| 1982 | 128 | −3 | 86 | −3 | 214 |
| 1983 | 127 | −1 | 93 | 7 | 220 |
| 1984 | 127 | 0 | 92 | −1 | 219 |
| 1985 | 132 | 5 | 98 | 6 | 230 |
| 1986 | 135 | 3 | 98 | 0 | 233 |
| 1987 | 135 | 0 | 102 | 6 | 237 |
| 1988 | 144 | 9 | 108 | 6 | 252 |
| 1989 | 142 | −2 | 112 | 4 | 254 |
| 1990 | 144 | 2 | 122 | 10 | 266 |

Note:    Statistics are estimates as of October 1 of each year.

Source: Crompton and McGregor (1994). Adapted from *Public employment* for the given years, U.S. Department of Commerce.

while highly worthwhile, increased the infrastructure which had to be maintained without increasing the local government's ability to do so.

Notice that the last issue sees funding for municipal government as "them against us." This way of thinking is likely to change as government organizations become more agile.

While public leisure services will be reinvented, the private, non-profit sector (third sector) is likely to become increasingly important in the provision of leisure services. A number of trends in combination seem to point toward private, nonprofit organizations becoming more influential in the provision of leisure services. Such organizations are already extremely important. As Peter Drucker observed, church-run schools have had startling successes in tough neighborhoods, improvements in major healthcare areas such as the prevention and treatment of cardiac disease and mental illness have largely been the work of private, nonprofit organizations such as the American Heart Association and the American Mental Health Association. Fostering such autonomous organizations in the social sector is critical. Consider that some private, nonprofit organizations in leisure services include those found in Table 21.

In the future, a combination of government debt, the increasing importance of leisure to the public, the tribalization of society, and other trends may make private, nonprofit organizations even more important. As this occurs, questions of whether such organizations operate more like government agencies, seeking and obtaining tax-exempt status as well as, in some cases, government grants or continuous financial support, or whether they operate more like corporations, aggressively marketing their services and seeking to maximize "profit," will become critical issues.

---

Table 21    **Selected Recreation and Conservation Nonprofit Associations**

**Recreation Programs**

Boy Scouts of America
Camp Fire Inc.
Girl Scouts of America
YMCA
YWCA
Intercollegiate Outing Club
   Association

**Natural Resources**

Izaak Walton League
The Nature Conservancy
American Forestry Association
Appalachian Mountain Club
Environmental Defense Fund
Friends of the Earth
National Parks & Conser-
   vation Association
National Wildlife Federation
Sierra Club
Wilderness Society
World Wildlife Fund

**Activity Interest Groups**

American Hiking Association
American Motorcycle Association
Appalchian Trail Conference
Balloon Federation of America
Bikecentennial
Boat Owners Association of U.S.
Federation of Fly Fisherman
Federation of Western Outdoor
   Clubs
League of American Wheelman
National Gardening Association
Road Runners Club
Sports Car Club of America
Trout Unlimited
U.S. Ski Association
U.S. Yacht Racing Union
Ducks Unlimited
National Audubon Society
National Campers & Hikers
   Association
National Rifle Association

Source: Adapted from Szwak (1989)

# 47

# The Increasing Importance of Managing Federal Lands for Recreation

In many countries, much of the land is managed by the national government. Such land has traditionally been managed for a variety of purposes: timber, mining, flood control, grazing land for cattle and sheep, irrigation, preservation and other purposes. While, traditionally, the recreational use of such lands was not even recognized in legislation, a revolution is underway in which the recreational use of such land is becoming the most important management objective.

In the United States, where the federal government manages one-third of the land mass, many traditional land managing agencies which have traditionally ignored recreation have now decided it is critical to their mission. For the Bureau of Land Management, for example, recreation has become the primary management objective. For the U.S. Forest Service, a tradition-bound organization staffed by those trained primarily in forestry, a revolution is taking place.

The head of the U.S. Department of Agriculture in 1997, James Lyon, envisioned a future for national forests where the lakes are full of fish, damage is healed from clear-cut logging, and riparian habitat along streams is restored and protected.

> 'Unfortunately, too many know us as a roading and timber business,' Lyon said. 'But we're changing. We are the Number One provider in America of the outdoor recreation experience.' (Stienstra, 1997, p. C-16)

In a critical transition in the U.S. Forest Service, new chief Mike Dombeck pledged he would ask Congress for more money for recreation needs, even if it meant less money for logging. "There is a tremendous demand for recreation," Dombeck said. "You will see me asking for more money for recreation in the appropriation process." While about three-fourths of the contribution of the U.S. Forest Service to the gross national product comes from outdoor recreation, especially from camping, fishing and hiking, Congress allocates only 2.5 percent of the Forest Service budget to recreation. This is likely to change.

New programs which collect fees from recreation users of federal lands are generally showing that people will gladly pay a few dollars to enjoy and protect the natural environment. While the Forest Service used to subsidize large corporations who clear-cut large chucks of the publicly owned forest, things have changed. National forests provide a vast landscape for camping, fishing, hiking, boating and hunting, especially in California and the rest of the West. In California alone, there are 20 million acres of land with roughly 125 lakes one can drive to, 450 lakes (with fishing) that one can hike to across 35 significant wilderness areas, 175 major streams and 800 drive-to campgrounds, many of the latter remote and low cost.

Since the comparatively few national and state parks are filling to capacity, the importance of national forests providing public access has become one of the most important elements in the outdoor experience in California and the rest of the West.

The Forest Service now has 35,000 employees, a budget of three billion dollars, and a new era in which there will be: far less logging, new fee charges to the public, new services (starting with restrooms) for campers, hikers and boaters, better resource management (especially for streams), and more predictable standards from area to area.

The emphasis on recreation comes at the same time when the impact of logging on national forests will be diminished, reduced from 12 billion board feet nationally in the Reagan years (supposedly "to reduce the federal deficit") to four billion board feet at the present.

## Issue Questions

1. What kind of training would a manager of a federal land-managing agency need to deal primarily with outdoor recreation?

2. Can federal lands be successfully managed for both recreation and conservation?

## Possible Implications for Leisure

As recreation becomes a more critical function of federal land management, numerous changes may occur. First, the training of those who manage such lands may change or broaden to include a better understanding of people's use of leisure in the outdoors. This is not to argue that an

understanding of the environment, forest ecology, or wildlife management of related subjects will be unimportant. Only that they must be integrated with a knowledge of how people may pleasurably use such areas
while making a minimum impact.

   Additionally, the increased importance of recreation will be yet one
more reason to stop subsidies for the mining, logging and grazing of livestock on federal lands. If recreation must pay its own way, so should
competing uses of such land.

# 48

# Local Government Will Become More Important

Local government is going to become increasingly important. We are no
longer a mass culture. We are a mosaic culture in which values, economic conditions, social problems and a willingness to address them vary
tremendously. Economically, we are a postindustrial society; not an industrial one. As Peter Drucker (1993) observed:

> ...postindustrial society has to be *decentralized*. Its orga-
> nizations must be able to make fast decisions based on
> closeness to performance, closeness to the market, close-
> ness to technology, closeness to the changes in society, en-
> vironment and demographics, all of which must be seen
> and utilized as opportunities for innovation. (p. 60)

There are a number of reasons why fundamental changes taking place in
our world will elevate local government to the most important level of
government. Not only is the nation-state less and less able to deal effectively with problems which are increasingly either supranational, regional
or local, but also the changing characteristics of our population. Such
changes include the increasing number of people in service sector jobs
whose productivity cannot be raised quickly enough to keep them in the
middle class; the increasing percentage of the population that is elderly,
live alone and want to live in their own homes; and rises in violence. As
Peter Drucker (1993) argues, local government will be concerned with

two growth areas in social needs: "charity, or helping the poor, the dis-
abled, the helpless, the victims" and second, "services aimed at changing
the community and at changing people." Prevention will become the
watchword in shaping social policy in areas such as health, crime, pollution control, welfare, unemployment, safety, and other areas. Such pre-
ventative approaches will be applied at the local level, rather than the national level, based upon radically differing local conditions. In all these
endeavors, however, government will be forced to change the way it operates. Government workers are the least productive of service workers
and, given huge deficits, that situation has to change.

## Issue Questions

1. Is local government the most important government level
   for the provision of recreation, park and leisure services?
   Why or why not?

2. What role should local government recreation and park
   services play in the provision of "charity" and changing
   the community and its people?

3. What role can local government leisure services play in
   prevention?

## Possible Implications for Leisure

This trend may mean that more will be asked of local government recreation and park departments. The tasks that Drucker identifies are not ones
which are thought of as "proprietary" functions—tasks where government
acts more like a small business, undertaking activities which aren't really
crucial to public well-being. Such tasks are central to public well-being
and the traditional method of paying for such crucial tasks is through taxa-
tion. Thus, there is a contradiction between the idea that local government
should "contract out" such services, which are presumed to be dealing
with "amenities," and Drucker's forecast which sees local government
taking on critical issues, such as health, crime, unemployment and safety.
Local recreation and park departments will have to be equipped for these
critical functions, and the students who become employees will need an
understanding of the have-nots if they are to be effective.

What seems certain is that local government recreation and park services will move more quickly toward becoming: (1) a market-driven, revenue-generating organization which is largely self-funding; (2) an essential function of local government with demonstrated impact on reducing costs and improving people's lives in regard to health or crime; or (3) a tourism agency involved with generating tourism and managing tourist sites.

In the United States, as in other developed nations, the vast majority of the public will continue to use local government recreation and park services, identify benefits from them, and be willing to pay for them. There is increasing evidence that local government leisure services are important to the public, such as in studies conducted in the United States (Godbey, Graefe and James, 1993) and in Canada (Harper, Neider and Godbey, 1996) which examined the use and benefits of local government leisure services.

These studies consisted of telephone interviews administered to a broadly representative national samples of individuals age 15 and over. Additionally, a follow-up questionnaire dealing with leisure behavior and selected health and wellness variables was conducted in the United States.

**Use of Local Recreation and Park Services.** In both the United States and Canada, there is a surprisingly high rate of use of local government park and recreation services throughout the country. In terms of use of local parks and playgrounds, slightly over seven out of ten respondents reported having a park or playground within walking distance while in the more urban Canada, 85 percent of respondents had them.

The United States study found that 75 percent of all respondents had used parks and playgrounds during the previous 12 months, 51 percent using them occasionally, and 24 percent using them frequently while in Canada 77 percent used parks and playgrounds, 50 percent occasionally, and 27 percent frequently.

Respondents were also asked if they had participated:

...in any recreation activities organized by your local government's recreation and parks department. This would include such things as sports leagues, educational and instructional classes, and special artistic or cultural events in your community. During the last twelve months, have you participated in any recreation or leisure activity

that was sponsored by or took place on areas or facilities
managed by your local government's recreation and parks
department?

Not only did 30 percent of the U.S. respondents say they had participated in such activities during the previous 12 months, but another 35
percent said they had done so prior to the previous 12 months. Table 22
shows that the vast majority of respondents made use of recreation and
park services during the previous 12 months. In Canada, 42 percent of
the public had participated in recreation services other than park use.

Use of both parks and other recreation services increased with both
educational and income level but there was no relation between them and
one's gender—women were as likely to report using both parks and other
recreation services as were men. While older people used such services
somewhat less than younger ones, decline of use with age was gradual
and those between the ages of 66 and 74 were more likely to use local
parks frequently than another age group (see Table 22). U.S. local parks
were used more by Hispanics than whites and more by whites than African Americans but those of different ethnic statuses were equally likely to
use other recreation services.

**Nonuse of Services.** While the vast majority of respondents used
local recreation and park services, those who did not were asked to agree
with several statements concerning the reasons for their nonuse. Only 14
percent of nonusers said they were not interested in recreation and park
services. Lack of time was the most frequently agreed to reason for lack
of participation, with 52 percent of nonrespondents citing it. Fees and
charges were not a significant deterrent to participation, since only six
percent of nonusers cited local recreation and park services being too expensive as a reason for nonparticipation. Lack of information, however,
appears to be a bigger problem, since fully one-third of all nonrespondents
said they didn't have enough information about such services. Additionally, 23 percent of nonusers agreed that "local park and recreation services
aren't planned for people like me" and 15 percent concurred that "there
aren't other people for me to participate with."

In Canada, lack of time was also cited most frequently, by 44 percent of the respondents.

**Benefits From Such Services.** Respondents to the telephone survey were asked about benefits received from local parks at an individual,
household and community level ("By benefit we mean anything good that

Table 22    Use of Local Government Recreation and Park
Services in the United States

| | Extent of Personal Park Use | | | Individual Participation in Locally Sponsored Recreation Programs | |
|---|---|---|---|---|---|
| | Not at All | Occa- sionally | Frequently | No | Yes |
| **Age** | | | | | |
| 15–20 | 20 | 57 | 23 | 61 | 39 |
| 21–35 | 18 | 56 | 25 | 67 | 33 |
| 36–55 | 22 | 53 | 25 | 66 | 34 |
| 56–65 | 38 | 42 | 21 | 80 | 20 |
| 66–75 | 39 | 35 | 26 | 82 | 18 |
| 76–95 | 56 | 29 | 15 | 89 | 11 |
| **Level of Education** | | | | | |
| High school or less | 31 | 49 | 20 | 76 | 24 |
| Some college to college grad | 22 | 52 | 26 | 67 | 33 |
| More than 4 years of college | 19 | 49 | 31 | 63 | 37 |
| **Income** | | | | | |
| Less than $20,000 | 32 | 49 | 19 | 79 | 21 |
| $20,000–$60,000 | 22 | 52 | 26 | 67 | 33 |
| More than $60,000 | 23 | 50 | 27 | 64 | 36 |
| **Race** | | | | | |
| White | 26 | 49 | 25 | n/a | n/a |
| Black | 29 | 52 | 19 | n/a | n/a |
| Hispanic | 10 | 69 | 21 | n/a | n/a |
| Other | 18 | 60 | 22 | n/a | n/a |
| **Size of Household (people)** | | | | | |
| One | 38 | 41 | 21 | 80 | 20 |
| Two | 31 | 47 | 22 | 73 | 27 |
| Three or four | 19 | 54 | 26 | 64 | 36 |
| Five or more | 16 | 59 | 25 | 69 | 31 |
| **Age of Children in Household** | | | | | |
| 12 and under | 14 | 54 | 32 | 66 | 34 |
| 13–19 | 21 | 58 | 21 | 70 | 30 |
| Both 12 and under and 13–19 | 17 | 57 | 26 | 58 | 42 |
| No children under age 20 | 33 | 46 | 21 | 74 | 26 |

Source: Godbey, Graefe and James (1992)

happens because parks are there. To what degree do you feel you personally benefit from your local parks?"). Next they were asked about benefits
to other members of the household and finally the community as a whole.

Perhaps what is most startling about these results is that the vast majority of respondents perceived benefits at all levels and the strongest

level of perceived benefit was the community level, where over six out of ten respondents said their community received "a great deal" of benefit from local parks. Only six percent of the respondents said there was no community benefit derived from local parks.

In terms of participation in activities sponsored by recreation and park departments, respondents were asked what specific activities they had participated in during the last twelve months and then asked what was the most important benefit they received from such participation and then if there were other benefits. These answers, in the respondents own words, were then coded into categories. Personal benefits was composed of the following major benefits: exercise, fitness and conditioning (134); fun and entertainment (86); learning and education (28); relaxation (25); and health (24). Personal benefits clearly have a strong health and wellness orientation. They accounted for 42 percent of all benefits cited. Social benefits had the following components: getting to know people (34); group participation (23); interaction of adults and kids (23); community awareness (22) and team spirit (20). These benefits also reflect wellness ideals and combined with personal benefits, accounting for four out of five of all benefits cited. Recreation and park benefits, then, are primarily "people" benefits and they are strongly related to health and wellness.

Facility/activity benefits included: having instructional classes (10); the joy of playing (8); place to go (8); place for recreation (7); exposure to arts (7); and crafts (8); and watching organized sports (7). Environmental benefits included: fresh air (12); nature (9); and a place to be outdoors (7). Finally, under economic benefits the major benefit listed was affordability.

What people did not mention is also important. While respondents clearly saw local recreation and park services as benefiting the entire community, not one of 1,305 respondents mentioned service to the poor, the disadvantaged or ethnic minorities. While a Canadian study of benefits found that recreation and parks professionals identified "basic services to poorer residents" as the number one ranked benefit, respondents saw community benefits in inclusive terms and did not associate such agencies with service to the poor (Balmer and Harper, 1989). Similarly, while the Canadian park and recreation professionals rated "protection of the natural environment" second highest, the study found environmental benefits secondary to personal and social benefits.

It should be noted that those who do not use local government recreation and park services also perceived substantial benefits from recreation and park services. While those who used such services perceived a higher level of benefits, 53 percent of those who never used local parks said their community received a great deal of benefit from such resources.

In terms of specific benefits, Table 23 shows the most frequently mentioned benefits of local park and playground use at the individual, household and community level. These benefits show that individuals go to local parks both *for* recreation and *as* recreation. That is, one may realize a benefit because one goes there to exercise or one may view the simple act of going there as a benefit in and of itself.

Table 23    **Most Frequently Mentioned Benefits of Local Parks**

| Specific Individual Benefits | Count | Percent |
|---|---|---|
| Exercise, Fitness, Conditioning | 236 | 11.5 |
| Relaxation and Peace | 125 | 6.1 |
| Open Space | 88 | 4.3 |
| Place for Kids to Go | 67 | 3.3 |
| Nature | 63 | 3.1 |
| Family Time Together | 57 | 2.8 |
| Fun and Entertainment | 56 | 2.7 |
| Enjoy Being Outdoors/Natural Resources | 52 | 2.5 |
| Place to Go | 51 | 2.5 |
| Place for Recreation | 51 | 2.5 |
| **Specific Household Benefits** | **Count** | **Percent** |
| Exercise, Fitness, Conditioning | 144 | 13.5 |
| Relaxation and Peace | 58 | 5.4 |
| Fun and Entertainment | 53 | 5.0 |
| Place for Kids to Go | 46 | 4.3 |
| Place to Play | 41 | 3.8 |
| Facilities, Play Area for Kids | 33 | 3.1 |
| Family Time Together | 32 | 3.0 |
| Keep Kids Busy/Occupied | 27 | 2.5 |
| Open Space | 26 | 2.4 |
| Enjoy Being Outdoors/Natural Resources | 25 | 2.3 |
| **Specific Community Benefits** | **Count** | **Percent** |
| Exercise, Fitness, Conditioning | 136 | 6.4 |
| Place for Kids to Go | 132 | 6.2 |
| Gathering Place | 87 | 4.1 |
| Activities | 79 | 3.7 |
| Community Awareness | 79 | 3.7 |
| Place for Recreation | 75 | 3.5 |
| Fun and Entertainment | 68 | 3.2 |
| Family Time Together | 66 | 3.1 |
| Good for Kids | 65 | 3.0 |
| Place to Go | 63 | 2.9 |
| Play Organized Sports | 63 | 2.9 |
| Keep Kids Off Streets | 61 | 2.9 |

Source: Godbey, Graefe and James (1992)

While the most frequently mentioned benefits are exercise-related, the second most frequent at the individual level is relaxation and peace. Thus, individuals change their level of stimulation in parks both by becoming more active and narrowing their field of attention, such as by playing a sport, or becoming less active and broadening their field of attention, such as by relaxing.

In terms of both household and community benefits, children are mentioned in three out of ten responses. While this study documented that large segments of the 65 and older population use local parks, the majority of respondents do not associate local park benefits with older people. Parks are, however, identified as gathering places which help foster community awareness.

Those sampled rarely mentioned increasing "cultural awareness" as a benefit of parks and exercising pets was mentioned only once, even though many people use parks to do so.

In terms of the benefits of participating in specific activities sponsored by local government recreation and park services, the vast majority of benefits identified were personal and social. Also, the majority of benefits are clearly from sport and exercise. They account for more then one-third of all benefits identified by respondents. Perhaps of equal importance, however, is the extent to which cultural and educational activities are prominent. Cultural activities were the second most frequently mentioned source of benefits and classes were mentioned fifth most frequently.

In terms of services to specific populations, however, such as "senior citizens" and special populations, the sample attributed a relatively smaller number of benefits. With regard to the elderly, as we have previously seen, this does not mean such services don't reach the elderly, since those 65–74 are slightly more likely to use local parks "frequently" than any other age group represented in the sample (age 15 and over). Rather it means that age-segregated programs, such as senior citizen centers, are not a significant source of benefits. This should not be surprising since, according to Kelly (1992), such centers serve only about one out of ten of those 65 and over.

In Canada, there were similar responses but community awareness and sense of community were also mentioned by about one out of nine participants.

**Economic Value of Local Recreation and Park Services.** Over three-fourths of the entire sample thought that park and recreation services were worth $45 per person per year or more. More than 20 percent thought they were worth from $60 to $150 per person per year and only 16 percent thought they were worth $25 or less.

In summary, the increasing urbanization of the world, in North America and elsewhere will likely mean that leisure services will become more critical as people become more dependent on organizations for satisfying leisure.

A related but extremely important issue is going to be what role recreation plays in keeping people in rural villages to slow down or stop the migration to cities. Lack of recreation opportunity is one of many variables contributing to urban migration. Additionally, many forms of recreation, including tourism, hold the promise of providing much needed jobs in rural areas where the need for agriculture workers or other forms of work have declined. Rural recreation projects are springing up in many countries in an attempt to improve the quality of life and economic stability of villages and rural areas. The success of these attempts is a critical component in stopping the world's huge migration to urban areas.

# Government Policies May Begin to Shift Based Upon What Makes People Happy

Currently, U.S. government policies encourage consumption in open-ended fashion. America taxes consumption at the lowest rate of any modern nation. What is the consequence of such policies?

There is considerable survey evidence that the public is beginning to recognize the folly of open-ended consumption. Humans have a tendency to shift their comparison levels when they earn more money, have more experiences or do more things to put on their résumé. As the basis for comparison changes, they aren't much happier than they were before. In one study of lottery winners, for example, while such individuals were much happier immediately after winning the lottery, one year later their average happiness, as measured on a nine-point scale, had increased only from 6.5 to 6.8. Conversely, those who had become paraplegics, after one year, had dropped only from 6.5 to 6.0 (Sobel and Ornstein, 1987).

While it does appear to be true that people in dire poverty are significantly happier if they gain somewhat economically, after the initial gain, additional income doesn't seem to make much difference in their happiness. As psychologist Robert Ornstein and physician David Sobel (1987) concluded:

> ...in our own culture, once a person has attained a minimal standard of wealth—owning a car (even if it is not the best) and an adequate, if not palatial, place to live, when you get education (even in state schools) and adequate, if not gourmet, food—increases in wealth don't seem to matter as much as we think and certainly don't merit planning our whole lives around them. The bottom line: if you want money to make you happy, you'll have to be poor. (p. 67)

In an increasingly stressful world, we need to remember what makes us happy. We don't remember, however, continuing to buy more stuff, producing an endless cycle of dismal changes.

As an economist might say, the marginal utility on more wealth, experience, or success declines dramatically after a minimum acceptable level has been reached. One reason for this is that expectations are easily inflated. When we owned a black-and-white television, we were pleased with it but now that we own a large color set, our expectations increase so we assume color sets are normal and are no longer impressed with them. If we give a speech and receive a fee for doing it, we are initially thrilled but soon expect to receive that much and are no longer particularly happy about such a fee.

Our minds, then, try to make an inconsistent world seem consistent. How we view an event or situation, Ornstein and Sobel (1987) tell us, depends upon what we are comparing it to at the moment.

> ...many people search for happiness and status. And they are mislead to do so. It is not those unforgettable and sought after great events or memorable sucesses or excesses of power that bring happiness. Instead many small and often overlooked daily events, even trite and obvious experiences, add up in the long run. (p. 131)

Open-ended living ignores both our need for balance and our need for routine. While we cannot, perhaps, take continual pleasure in constant routine, as a dog can, joyfully sniffing the same trail it has sniffed one-hundred times before, we can find happiness in a balance between routine and new experience. There is comfort in the familiar which open-ended living denies. There is, for instance, great joy and comfort in the endless cycle of nature, the perpetual circle of seasons which revolves around us, the ebb and flow of tides or the waxing and waning of the moon. Nature, to be sure, is not a series of uniform routines. There is, however, a kind of modified repetition which is the basis for our lives. Open-ended living denies this basis. We are, in short, somewhere between the animals and the gods in regard to pleasure. Thus, for example, our lives are not determined by the events of autumn as are other animals but are shaped by them.

If we totally reject the repeated and cyclic pleasure of animals we are left with no choice but to become lonely little gods. But we cannot be godlike given the limited amount of time we live. We cannot be happy with a life of constant routine, like dogs or cats, because our brains have evolved with such startling rapidity that we often need to seek more complexity than they for happiness to take place. If everything is perpetually new and complex, however—the basis for open-ended living—there will never be enough time. If everything is routine—simple and familiar— time may weigh heavy on our hands.

Balance or moderation is needed—an old lesson. To balance the scales we need to be more like dogs or cats and less like gods. There is no time to notice the luminescent drops of rain or hear their sound on dark leaves. We drive faster and faster and the shooting white stripes on the highway seem tied to something up ahead in the darkness. Both fish and fisherman, we are reeled—and reel. Time has become the ultimate scarcity. And as we rush after life we rush past it.

Government may begin to act on the recognition that the pursuit of happiness will more likely be successful if we expect less and appreciate more. Such a course of action will take political leadership and reform.

None of this, of course, means that government can, or should, promote a culture in which material things are largely denied to people. Historian Theodore Zeldin (1994) observed that a particular ideology which individuals profess says less about them than how they practice it. Materialism will likely continue to be our ideology; it must be practiced better. Additionally, as Zeldin concluded, while consumption is not the end that modern societies seek, voluntary poverty is unlikely to be adopted in the foreseeable future:

> It is consummation rather than consumption that people increasingly seek, taking pleasure to its ultimate degree of intensity, and not just having free time. Filling time with

the most profound experiences, in most cases, involves other people. The advise from the first generation of the Green Movement was to consume as little as possible, but that was a leftover from the ancient tradition of asceticism, which the world has repeatedly rejected, and will doubtlessly continue to reject as long as there is inequality, as long as there are people struggling to come out of poverty who have not tasted satiety. (pp. 295–296)

In a society in which the divisions between haves and have-nots are increasing, it seems unlikely that voluntary poverty will find a large niche. What will need to happen is for government to implement policies that help us practice a more limited and enlightened materialism in which what we own serves as the means to the end of human happiness rather than an end in itself.

## Issue Questions

1. Based on the previous information about what makes people happy, what kinds of leisure activity would seem likely to make people happiest?

2. What do you think "enlightened materialism" mean? How would you practice it?

3. How can people be made to appreciate what they have more than they do now?

## Possible Implications for Leisure

It will increasingly be realized that satisfying work and satisfying leisure will have many elements in common—the concept of "flow" identifies many of these common elements.

To maintain the gains from the past and to keep increasing psychic complexity, it is necessary for people to take part in activities that are themselves differentiated and integrated. Challenges are the stimulus for differentiation, while skills lead to integration. Working adults experience flow on the job three times as often as during free time. During leisure, highest levels of flow occur when people are involved in active leisure—

singing, bowling, biking, building a chair on the basement lathe, writing a story. Children enjoy flow but the mismatch between opportunities and abilities leads to a progressive atrophy of the desire for complexity. Having learned that boredom and worry are the norm in the family, in the school and in the community at large, children lose their curiosity, their interest, their desire to explore new possibilities. They no longer perceive the many opportunities for action around them. Even though passive leisure provides no joy, they see it as the only way to spend free time that is within their means.

Finally, the external energy invested in a leisure activity is slightly negatively related to happiness people report while being involved. People are happier when their activity takes less energy from the environment. Csikszentmihalyi reported a slightly negative relation (and significantly negative for women) between the happiness people reported while being involved in various leisure activities and how much external energy was consumed:

> In other words, people are happier when their leisure takes less energy from the environment. (1991b, p. 29)

# Rethinking Leisure Services

## Personal and Organizational Strategies

*You know the way spirit*
*W. S. Merwin*

How does one react to the huge changes taking place in the world, which this book has attempted to identify? Denial is not very helpful, nor is simply giving in to what is forecast as if nothing could change it. In this final section, some strategies are examined which may be useful to organizations and individuals involved in leisure services in adjusting to and then thriving in a world of change.

## *Organizational Strategies*

The organizations which provide recreation, park and leisure services are in a process of constant change. While there is no prescription for the future, those who work for leisure service organizations may consider the following.

### Responding to Change in All Organizational Sectors

Many of the same forces that are driving changes in the way business organizations function are also reshaping the way leisure services must function in all sectors: private-nonprofit, government and businesses. These drivers, as identified by Preiss, Goldman and Nagel (1996) include:

- The worldwide spread of education and technology, which increases global competition and accelerates the rate of marketplace change

Almost all customers or clients of leisure services have more options as to what service they will or will not use and the rate at which these options increase is accelerating. A tourist who wants to plan a vacation may do so through a travel agent, a credit card company, a tourism promotion bureau, an airline, a guided tour company, a local university, or other providers. The flight arrangements and booking of hotels can be done by the customer via personal computer, e-mail, the Web, telephone, or by a travel agent, or by the hotel locally or through a national 800 number. The opportunities when selecting an aerobic dance class are huge and diversified.

Changes also take place more rapidly in people's leisure interests and the constraints they encounter in trying to fulfill them. While many forms of leisure activity have been highly associated with a stage of life, life stages themselves are more various and subject to change than a decade ago.

- The continuing fragmentation of mass markets into niche markets

Mass recreation activities, products and services are disappearing along with mass culture, and even when it looks as though a "mass" activity is occurring, such as an arts festival, closer examination reveals most festivals are multiple niche markets being served by the same festival. Likewise, the options for a customer who wants to learn about refinishing furniture, playing golf, or enrolling his or her children in a summer camp have grown exponentially. Part of this represents a kind of mass customization, in which mass leisure markets which grew out of the mass culture produced by the baby boomers, are coming apart into niche markets. Thus, in terms of children's summer camps, there are now camps to learn French, lose weight, or enhance self-esteem. There are camps for suburban girls to learn to play soccer, camps for children in wheelchairs, and camps for gay teenagers.

- More demanding customers with higher expectations

Today, clients or customers of almost all leisure services have increasingly high expectations about how clean a park should be the morning after a special event, how quickly they can register for an evening class on vegetarian cooking, how many birds they will spot on a guided birdwalk, or how few delays there will be in being assigned a campsite for their motor home in a state park. Such increasing demands, combined with more alternatives for participation, mean that successful leisure services must become more agile.

• The spread of collaborative production with suppliers and customers who comprise the value-adding chain

The old way of thinking about clients or customers in many leisure services, as with most businesses, was to keep them satisfied but out of your hair in terms of organizational operation. Thus, there were surveys done about satisfaction with programs or facilities but little ongoing dialogue with customers or clients. There might be an advisory council but it operated on the assumption that the organization already knew what its mission was and that such a mission wasn't subject to question; only the logistics of how it was provided.

Today, to be successful:

> ...companies are responding to a new competitive environment by proactively linking dynamically and intimately with customers, not only to give those customers the solutions they ask for, but to work beyond that to find opportunities the customer had never imagined existed. In turn, what interprises do for their customers, they expect their suppliers to do for them. (Preiss, Goldman and Nagel, 1996, p. 8)

Doing this, of course, means that such a company or organization must establish relationships with clients which may take the organization in unknown directions—it becomes wrapped up in process, not product or service. For those in therapeutic recreation, this must surely mean that the lines between physical, occupational and therapeutic recreation blur, as do the lines between client and family and friends or between clinical and community practice. The "TR" employee is wrapped up in the process of assisting the client in adjusting to and minimizing the impact of a disability, and does so in terms which have value to that client and/or his or her family and friends.

For undergraduate university students majoring in recreation and park management or leisure studies, this means the "options" within the curriculum must be understood as arbitrary divisions which will frequently make little sense in isolation after they graduate. Thus, outdoor recreation will possibly lead them into tourism issues which lead to environmental issues which lead to health issues which lead to poverty issues which lead to education issues. Those who want to work with people with "disabilities" in leisure settings will see the basis of "disability" evolve throughout their lifetime. The complaint of some students—"I'm never going to use this because it's not in my area"—will make less and less sense, since the student's "area" is more likely to be a moving target which evolves throughout their working life.

Many urban recreation and park agencies are in the process, or will be, of forming coalitions with law enforcement and with healthcare agencies in order to respond to the issues their clients identify as critical, such as stress reduction, lowering healthcare costs, fear of crime and concern about the lives of at-risk youth. These coalitions are already beginning. The California Physical Activity and Health Initiative of the California Department of Health Services, for example, involves a team representing work site wellness, local government intervention and youth and education outreach. The team's efforts involve developing school sites for safe and convenient community recreation activities, nutrition/physical activity programs which involves working with both the USDA and the state Medicaid program as well as intervention programs for the elderly which specifically target ethnic minorities and other initiatives.

In the United States, the National Recreation and Park Association has also begun to encourage such alliances with health organizations through its Active Living, Healthy Lifestyles Project. This project, funded through a grant from the Centers for Disease Control, and with the help of Ben-Gay, is an example of both partnering and agility. It recognizes that local government recreation and park services are directly in the health business, based upon the benefits sought and received by their clients. The project, which has a goal of reaching 1,000 communities nationwide through recreation and park agencies, seeks:

1. To promote the personal health benefits of physical activity in the context of recreation activities and park resources, and

2. To position the recreation and park profession as a national leader in promoting active lifestyles and as a catalyst for communities to adopt strategies in support of a healthy environment where people live, work and play. (National Recreation and Park Association, 1997, p. 1.)

These coalitions may be threatening to some leisure service employees, who are seeking distinct professional status through stand-alone organizations and exclusive certification. Thus, therapeutic recreation professionals have established a national certification plan, partly to gain equivalent status to those in occupational and physical therapy, who also operate as "stand alone" vocations seeking to be professional. As those in various therapies begin to work in teams, however, the relevant question may become not who is certified but who provides solutions to problems which the client values (and their health services will pay for).

Likewise, the program of the National Recreation and Park Association to accredit leisure professionals or municipal recreation and park departments may need to be rethought. While some good can come out of such efforts, including a greater awareness of what can be improved, it is essentially the ability to solve problems for the client which will determine the fate of such agencies and professionals, not whether or not there is a plaque on the wall saying the agency or professional is certified.

Some recreation, park and leisure services currently suffer from the delusion that their success is determined by how they are judged by others in their profession. It is not. Success will increasingly be determined by the ongoing relationship with clients or customers discussed above. Likewise, whether or not a university or college curriculum in recreation and parks or leisure services is accredited by a group of educators may mean less than whether or not the graduates value the program and recommend it to prospective students.

- The increasing impact of changing societal values, such as environmental considerations on job creation, or corporate decision making

These changes, which affect not only what people do during their leisure but, more importantly, the style in which they participate and the benefits sought, occur increasingly quickly. Thus, almost every zoo in the modern world is today considered obsolete by many of the visitors who now believe animals should be viewed in their natural habitat, not cages. A more highly educated visitor recognizes the pacing back and forth of many animals in the zoo as neurotic behavior, similar to the pacing of prisoners in a cell.

Other examples include the fact that many elderly users of conservation areas value convenience more and want indoor restrooms and showers. Gay and lesbian organizations field softball teams in the city league and teenage vegetarians ask if there is lard in the beans before they will order a burrito at the snack bar. The manager of the golf course may be questioned about use of fertilizers and chemical sprays by members of the club or the state environmental protection agency. Environmental issues can increasingly present a dilemma for park managing organizations which must sometimes choose between admitting increasing number of paying customers to make up for financial squeezes or better protecting the habitat of plants and animals which live in the park.

Against this backdrop of change, the following seems apparent:

**1. All leisure service organizations must become increasingly agile.**

As our mass culture is ending, as the rate of change increases, organizations which provide goods and services in the public, private, nonprofit and market sectors are being challenged in fundamental ways. In mass society, with mass production, providing "mass leisure" services was appropriate. The next step in this process was to individualize such services providing hundreds of individualized activities, programs and services which put the responsibility of finding out about all of them on the "customer." The agile organization, however, is one which enters a continuous dialogue with its customers to deal with their changing wants and needs.

> What customers will increasingly value in a company is its ability to create, and to continue creating, mutual beneficial relationships with them. (Goldman, Nagel and Preiss, 1995)

At the people level, the agile competition is characterized by the development of a skilled, knowledgeable and innovative work force. At the management level it represents a shift from the command and control philosophy of the modern industrial corporation to one of leadership, motivation, support and trust.

> An agile workforce is composed of people who are knowledgeable, informed, flexible and empowered. People who are expected to think about what they are doing, are authorized to display initiative, and are supported by management to become innovative about what they do and how they do it. (Goldman, Nagel and Preiss, 1995, p. 108)

For many leisure service organizations, this means a change in philosophy from continued learning as an afterthought to continued learning as an expectation of every employee which is planned for in job descriptions, assignments and in the reward system. It also means that: (1) expertise, initiative and authority are distributed as widely as possible within the organization; (2) decision-making is accelerated by replacing rigid, multilevel, functionally divided organizational structures with ones which have a flexible focus on routinely providing access to the information, skills and knowledge that are the ultimate organizational assets; (3) support of multiple, concurrent highly flexible organizational structures; and (4) leadership, motivation and trust replace the command and control model of organizations.

The agile organization is also different from others in that it actively seeks cooperation with other organizations which might previously have been thought of as competitors. Such cooperation may take the form of partnerships, joint ventures, and collaborations of every kind. Some of these efforts are aimed at establishing an economy of scale by merging capabilities in order to avoid the costs of adding capacity. An example might be a sport league managed by both a YMCA and a municipal recreation and park department. Other joint ventures are to produce win-win situations. A soft drink company sponsoring a program for at-risk youth organized by a Girls' Club, for instance, might serve the developmental needs of the youth involved while enhancing the image of the soft drink company. Such examples are becoming more commonplace. Less typical of leisure services are consortiums, whereby all organizations do some things in common, such as jointly sponsoring employee training or purchasing equipment. Such consortiums will likely become more common and may be organized around themes such as interest in a given leisure activity such as skiing, a given population such as people in wheelchairs, or a given objective such as increasing tourism in a geographic region. The future of leisure service organizations is wrapped up in such collaborative efforts.

As organizations which provide a wide variety of leisure services respond to the rapidly changing world, the secret of success for many will be to succeed in working with their clients or customers in ways which allow the client to help the organization help the client. Traditional professionalism sometimes gets in the way of this. Many medical doctors, for example, have not been sufficiently trained in how to question their patients in ways which provide the doctor with better quality information about the patient so that the patient, in turn, can be better helped by the doctor.

The critical question which those in a leisure organization must ask is what does the organization enable its clients or customers to do (Preiss,

Goldman and Nagel, 1996). As was discussed earlier, for some organizations which manage parks, one answer may be "reduce stress." When
that question has been answered, the employees may better understand
they are involved in a health service. This question is very much related
to the concept of benefits-based management, (Driver, Brown and
Peterson, 1991) which some recreation, park and leisure services are
seeking to implement. That is, the agile leisure service is delivering, first
and foremost, a benefit (which has value as identified by the client) rather
than a fixed set of services, products or information.

Organizations which provide leisure services must become dynamic
and dynamic systems behave in fundamentally different ways from static
ones. Management methods tend to be based on static behavior and as an
organization becomes more dynamic and interlinked, these static methods
don't apply to the new reality (Preiss, Goldman and Nagel, 1996).

### 2. All leisure services must increasingly cooperate with competitors.

There are more win-win situations than win-lose situations in the provision of leisure services. Kids may learn how to play tennis from a program sponsored by municipal recreation and parks with the support of an
athletic shoe company, move on to take advanced lessons at their country
club, play in tournaments sponsored by the U.S. Tennis Association and
eventually help coach a youth tennis team in a county-sponsored league.
The local museum may collaborate with an art gallery and the arboretum
to display paintings for sale while raising money for art lessons for prom-
ising inner-city artists. A ski resort may enter a lease agreement with a
state park department for long-term use of public land and then sublease
parts of that property to local restaurateurs. The number of consortiums
which can be developed in leisure services is almost infinite. What is important is imagination, communication and the will to do it.

### 3. Most leisure services will have to figure out what they are good at and "outsource" everything else.

An agency may not be good at maintaining buildings, working with the
elderly, or teaching people about arts and crafts. Most "leisure" service
agencies don't deal with all aspects of "leisure" or "recreation." How
could they? They must, therefore, figure out their core competencies and
outsource the rest. Should the organization be involved in league sports?

What is its special competency in managing league sports? Should a resort train its own lifeguards? Should a nursing home staff train its volunteers? Should U.S. Forest Service employees be doing "interpretation?" Trying to do what you don't do well is always a disadvantage. Identifying what an organization doesn't or can't do well and outsourcing it is of critical importance.

**4. Reconceptualizing government-sponsored leisure services will require a change in management strategy toward benefits-based management.**

Benefits-based management, as identified by Lee and Driver (1992):

> ...is based on the ideas that (1) the reason public recreation opportunities are provided is because people benefit from them, and (2) management will be most responsive, efficient and effective when it explicitly targets specific types of benefit opportunities that will be provided at designated locations. This is done by providing activity and associated setting opportunities defined in terms of the beneficial experiences and other responses that can be realized from using these opportunities. (p. 17)

This approach to management supplants activity-based management and experience-based management. Activity-based management was primarily supply-oriented with attention given to attributes of a recreation setting required to produce different types of activities. Management objectives were concerned with number of activity opportunities with little concern for quality. Experience-based management is "...the concept of product or management output is expanded to include not only the activity opportunity but also the specific types of experience opportunities produced" (Lee and Driver, 1992). Although experiences were not defined as beneficial, this was an advancement since managers could specify types of experience opportunities (e.g., solitude, fitness) to be targeted as a product of management. This approach is reflected in the Recreation Opportunity Spectrum system (Driver, 1987) where specifically targeted types of experience opportunities are provided with each spectrum-defined management zone designated on the ground.

> Benefits-based management focuses on what is obtained
> from amenity resource opportunities in terms of conse-
> quences that maintain or improve the lives of individuals
> and groups of individuals, and then designates and pro-
> vides opportunities to facilitate realization of these ben-
> efits. The basic purpose is to provide an array of benefit
> opportunities among which users can choose. (Lee and
> Driver, 1992)

Benefits-based management can facilitate an explicit attempt on the part
of a recreation and park agency to manage for increased wellness.

**5. Leisure services must become interprises.**

According to Preiss, Goldman and Nagel (1996), the organizations that
successfully adapt to the new dynamic environment may be called
"interprises."

> They can readily respond to the rapidly changing demands
> of their customers and the marketplace. They strive to un-
> derstand and meet the needs of their customers. They pro-
> vide more than 'good service.' They become part of their
> customers' businesses. They forge strong, enduring bonds
> with suppliers to enhance mutual goals. The internal orga-
> nization of these companies encourages an adaptive, entre-
> preneurial attitude among staff who recognize that the
> company's success is tied to their ability to support their
> clients. They are interactive and international as is the
> new culture of the internet. (p. 4)

Many of the characteristics of an interprise are appropriate for almost all
leisure services. This is, in fact, how some of the best leisure services
have historically operated. What has changed is the amount of information needed for an organization to behave this way, the mix and number
of other organizations with which it must interact, the speed with which it
must act and react, the technology which allows it to do so, and total
volume of communication necessary for it to master if it is to succeed.
These changes are of fundamental importance.

As mentioned previously, a constraint to many leisure service organizations becoming agile is the drive for professionalization, which is found among government employees at the municipal, county, state and federal level, among those in therapeutic recreation (who distinguish between clinical and community-based practice—an increasingly false dichotomy) among tourism agents, librarians, those who work in botanical gardens, museums, and other places where interpretation takes place.

While much good has come from such efforts, the professionalization of many leisure services rests on assumptions which are increasingly faulty. These faulty assumptions include:

- an exclusive and fixed body of knowledge which separates the professional from others who do not have access to it,

- a "career path" which can be identified for the next few decades,

- an assured clientele and funding source,

- a population with fixed values concerning leisure behavior,

- processes of certifying professional competence which have meaning over a professional's lifetime, and

- the idea that professional organizations should operate independently of other organizations.

These false assumptions, in combination, make much of the professionalization of leisure services obsolete (as they do many other services, such as medicine).

### 6. The successful leisure service will treat people appropriately, not equally.

In the agile organization, being trustworthy and behaving predictably is critical. Those in the organization are no longer merely offering a fixed opportunity; they are engaged in a continuous effort to solve the problems identified by their customers or clients. Trust is therefore all important and a significant factor in competitive capability. "Products and services are changed from being a goal in themselves to being a means to establish close, long-term interactive customer relationships" (Preiss, Goldman and Nagel, 1996).

The idea of trust does not mean, however, that "fair" treatment is equal treatment. To treat people fairly is to treat each one appropriately. Clients will have unique needs in a diverse, decentralizing society and leisure services will have multiple strategies to deal with the diverse problems identified by different subgroups of their clients. In a mass society, treating everyone equally might have been thought of as "fair," but today treating individuals appropriately is far different. It may be appropriate to have a brochure translated into Spanish for residents in one part of a community but not another. One individual may need to receive information about golf tournaments, daycare centers or historic tours of Russia. The food served in one snack bar may be quite different from another, based on the differing needs of the individuals who use it. Even airplane food is no longer the same for everyone. Someday soon, however, it may be different for each passenger.

One reason for treating all clients or customers the same is that the organization in question doesn't know much about them. Thus, many pharmaceutical companies manufacture medicines in the form of pills of standard size since the maker of the pill does not know if the customer weighs 75 pounds or 300 pounds. If they did, the appropriate dose of many medicines would be different. Restaurants serve salads with walnuts in them because they don't know that a given customer is allergic to nuts. If they did, they would not treat all salad customers the same; they would treat them appropriately.

### 7. The successful leisure service organization will customize services, information and products.

One of the most important qualities of an agile organization is its ability to customize products and services. Each client or customer can be treated as a unique individual (appropriately). For leisure services, where people vary greatly in the degree to which they are specialized in the activity or experience in question, and in which their motives and satisfactions for participation vary tremendously, customization is a critical variable. To a great extent, however, customization has been avoided. Thus, there is sometimes a "senior citizen" program for people 65 and over with no recognition of the great diversity among clients within that increasingly large age group. Brochures are sent to every resident of a community containing the same information by an urban recreation and park department rather than customizing the brochure to reflect the composition of the household it is being mailed to, the known leisure interests of the client based on previous interaction with the agency, the neighborhood in which the client lives, and other more personal information.

One factor that gets in the way of such customizing, in addition to lack of use of existing informational technology, is the recreation and park planning processes which assume that: (1) all clients must be treated "equally," (2) certain facilities, such as neighborhood parks, are "generic" entities whose characteristics and features can be prescribed in advance or are made up of component parts which are identical, or that (3) a leisure service, such as a tour of the Sydney Opera House, is a fixed commodity. While this way of thinking makes it easier for the organization to understand its mission, it is a way of thinking which dooms the organization to failure in a world in which "mass leisure" is disappearing, along with mass society.

One type of customizing may occur when a given leisure service or product has reached maturity. A product or service may go through a life cycle until it reaches maturity and then begin a process of decline. At the stage of maturity the product or service in question may fragment, or be fragmented, into many customized versions. Municipal summer playground programs, for instance, have been around since early this century. Many such programs have remained relatively standardized for decades and attendance in many such programs dropped off. At that stage in the life cycle of playground programs, the opportunity for "customizing" such programs existed. A playground program might be built around the expressed needs of individuals in an urban neighborhood who wanted a program which featured learning more about the English language or gardening or integrating adult daycare with the playground program or stressing competitive sport for girls and boys in sex-segregated situations. Much the same process happens or can happen with mature tourist destinations, sport leagues or nature centers. Some tourist sites, which have reached maturity, fragment into a number of secondary attractions.

Fragmenting mature leisure services, of course, is another example of treating clients or customers appropriately rather than equally. A fragmented leisure service may, itself, go through a life cycle and differentiate again at its maturity.

**8. The successful leisure service will rethink pricing, timing and platforms.**

Other important aspects of agility include the idea that the price for services should not be fixed but based on how much it enriches the individual customer, the idea that reducing time involved for the consumer is critical, and the idea that a given product or service can serve as a platform for interacting with the client over a long period of time to supply other services, information or maintenance of products.

The concept of a fixed price for a fixed service no longer makes sense. It is a parallel concept to treating everyone equally, but not appropriately. Pricing depends, increasingly, on how much it enriches the customer. Thus, an outdoor recreation "team building" program may be worth much more to members of a small company trying to develop a sense of cohesion than members of a stable, working class neighborhood. How much a given leisure service "enriches" a client or group of clients must be decided in their terms, not the sponsoring organization's. Getting from a resort hotel to the airport may be worth $50 to a busy group of business executives but only $10 to college students on spring break. Solitude in a park may be worth a lot to a hypertense working mother but little to a farmer.

One of the biggest issues in becoming more agile is the ability to reduce or eliminate the time involved in services which when such time spent by the client doesn't add value to the service. As we have seen previously, the extent to which people feel rushed has increased dramatically. A leisure service can add a competitive advantage to its services by reducing the time it takes to register, sign in, or wait in line. Time spent paying a parking fee, waiting to get on the golf course, or waiting for personal instruction from the scuba diving instructor add no value to the experience and, usually, but not always, detract value.

Finally, agility assumes that a given service or product supplied to customers or clients can serve as a "platform" from which the organization can possibly enter into a long-term relation with them. Doing this is aided by a modern system of order fulfillment or registration which allows the company to see every interaction it has had with the client or customer. In many leisure service organizations, this is not possible. A better understanding of how the client has used the services of the origination in the past may be used to recruit volunteers, send information for "frequent" or "preferred" users, or otherwise form a basis to find out more about the interests and problems of the individual.

The new service economy to which most leisure services belong will be increasingly based on communication and the use of information to add value to services. Work will be done by teams which come together for highly specific purposes and break up when the purpose is achieved. Advances in communication and informational technologies will play a key role in shaping how leisure services operate.

At the same time, many leisure services will have to find ways to balance the new technology with people's need for the familiar, sense of place, community, contact with nature and respect for the past. Many aspects of leisure services cannot be substituted for with technology. Many tourist experiences, more than anything else, are people watching people. Many successful therapeutic recreation interventions involve a demonstration of caring and acceptance which involves repeated personal interaction. The best part of a park experience may be listening to the wind in trees while walking on a forest trail. Putting paint on a canvas involves touch and smell as well as vision. Camping may involve cooking over an open fire or the sound of unknown animals after dark.

Some of the changes a leisure service makes in becoming more agile will uncomplicate the life of a client, getting rid of delays, paperwork, and provide more highly targeted information to him or her rather than reams of information and lots of waiting.

The challenge for those who manage leisure services will be to integrate the new technology into their services without changing what is magic about the leisure experience; to recognize the revolutionary changes going on in the world without uncritically giving in to them.

## *Personal Strategies*

What do these organizational strategies mean in terms of personal strategies for those who work, or want to work in leisure services? Obviously, there are lots of ways to interpret how organizational change may require the individual to react. The following, like everything else in this book, is presented for your consideration, not as unerring truth.

### 1. Seek continuous learning opportunities.

As the primary basis of our economy becomes knowledge, your chances of succeeding in leisure services will become more directly related to what you have learned—and are learning. It may make sense to seek an entry-level job based upon what you can learn from that job—or create one for the same reasons. Part of the negotiation process with any employer needs to be what kind of learning or training opportunities are available or can be developed. Informal opportunities must also be taken advantage of. What knowledgeable employees can you interview or otherwise learn from? How can you learn from your competitors and from other organizations with whom you could potentially cooperate?

In answering such questions, it may make sense to first develop some goals with regard to your own learning. Such goals may be highly specific or general. They may involve book learning or other forms of learning, e.g., "In the next twelve months I will find out the opinion of ten tour bus drivers concerning what sites interest their passengers in our county. Such learning may also be done in regard to a hypothetical situation, e.g., "During the next two months I will try to find out what happens if our department contracts out the maintenance of our parks."

Intellectual curiosity about the day-to-day operation of a leisure service organization is likely to be increasingly rewarded, particularly if it is combined with entrepreneurship.

### 2. Become more flexible.

In a world of rapid and continuing change, the ability to adapt and adjust to changing circumstances is critical. Actually, flexibility is a sign of intelligence. "Since intelligence means a flexible response to environmental stimuli, the more flexible its response capabilities, the more intelligent an organism is" (Shlain, 1991). Being flexible does not mean that one gives up one's goals. Rather it means that one comes to the understanding that there are many ways to attain a goal. Frequently, universities prepare students for occupations in such a narrow way and with such specific expectations that students lose flexibility. This is a great shame since in the rapidly changing world in which we live, the ability to adjust to change without giving up one's goals, or values, is critical.

One of the worst ways that students and professionals in leisure services sometimes lose flexibility is to assume that an issue doesn't concern them because it doesn't have "leisure" or "recreation" as a central theme. Leisure is among the more diverse and complex ideas in the world and, perhaps unfortunately, it relates to the myriad of issues that concern freedom, pleasure, human growth and understanding, health, nature, spirit, learning and other huge ideas. Becoming more flexible means the boundaries of what is relevant to you must become more flexible.

## 3. Become an entrepreneur.

As individuals take more responsibility for themselves, entrepreneurship will become more important. While there may be a tendency to think that entrepreneurship has to do with big corporations, many such corporations aren't interested in entrepreneurship, seeking instead to avoid competition and gain maximum government support or subsidies for their products or services. At its best, entrepreneurship means that a good idea may result in a good product or service which benefits both the developer of that product or service as well as society. To be an entrepreneur means that you are willing to take a chance to accomplish something worthwhile. (Being concerned only with making money does not mean one is an entrepreneur, only that one's imagination is limited.) It also means that, for some period of your life, you are likely not to have much leisure. Remember, however, that the flow state occurs in both work and leisure. Remember, also, that to be an entrepreneur means that you are willing to lead a simple life, materially, in pursuit of a dream. There are increasing opportunities for entrepreneurs to reshape the way many leisure services are provided in ways which increase our quality of life. The biggest division among individuals who provide leisure services may be those who care and those who don't.

## 4. Serve others.

What distinguishes successful people in leisure services and, in the public, private, nonprofit and commercial sectors, is an ethic of service. Your allegiance should not be to recreation, but to the people and environment you serve. Don't fall in love with a label. Many people have been convinced that their whole identity rests on being recognized as professionals in "recreation and park," "leisure service," "tourism," "exercise and sport science," "therapeutic recreation," "hospitality," "interpreter" or other labels. It doesn't. In the public sector, recreation, park and leisure services must always serve as the means to some increase in the well-being of the public, unless it is managed as a for-profit organization, paying its own costs. It is not recreation which is important; it is improving well-being. In the private, nonprofit sector, the missions are diverse and may include helping some specific group, promoting a certain activity, or dealing with a social problem. In the commercial sector, it is satisfying customers. In none of these missions is recreation or leisure the focus, rather it is the helping, the specific activity, or the social problem which is important. Leisure services are helping services in all sectors. It makes no difference if the individual is director of recreation for a commercial resort, a home for delinquent youth, or director of tourism promotion for the state of Hawaii. Leisure services are about helping, serving, hospitality, community, and belief in the ability of humans to find life meaningful. "Leisure" or "recreation" are only means to help people.

Somehow, people who work in recreation, park and leisure services and in the leisure and hospitality industries have gotten in the habit of defending recreation or leisure as if it is something which is automatically a good thing or the end result of what the profession is all about. To do so loses sight of the fact that recreation, in and of itself, was never thought of as important by the pioneers in our field. It was always a means to an end—a higher quality of life, increased learning, better health, improved physical fitness, more appreciation and understanding of nature, improved morale, and less crime are among the many benefits. Recreation, defended as an end in itself, is usually just defending an occupation or an aspiring profession. The worth of that profession, however, is not linked to recreation, but to the benefits recreation, under some conditions and in some circumstances, can provide.

### 5. Call attention to the importance of what you do.

Lots of leisure service professionals think the best thing they can do is avoid calling attention to themselves. Part of the reason for this may be lack of confidence that the public or their customers think they are important. As we have seen, the public thinks leisure is important and is willing to pay for leisure services which they think provide benefits to them. Therefore, it is critical to let your customers know what you are doing and how it benefits them. Individually, the ability to show that you add value to a leisure product or service may be critical in your occupational advancement. In the postmodern world, public relations and getting your message out are critical. Rather than an annual report, occasional newspaper piece or speech, communication about what you and your organization are doing is an ongoing process; there must be a continual dialogue with those you serve as well as with those who hold power.

### 6. Practice optimism.

The world is changing in ways which can make it better or can end it. None of us know what the outcome will be. Life is never assured and anyone who thinks it is doesn't understand much about history. Our response to what happens or will happen, however, is an important independent variable which can change the meaning of future events and how they affect us. To see the possibilities of the future, to appreciate the miracles of the present, to expect good things to happen and to help make them happen—all these attributes make a person more optimistic and increase one's health and happiness.

This is not to argue for a naive view of the world which ignores the fact that life is not fair or that we all die. It is rather the ability to marvel at the extent to which we have been blessed.

### 7. Stay out of debt and live below your means.

It is very easy to tell someone to stay out of debt, but difficult to do. Debt is built into our way of life. Nevertheless, in the coming era of unpredictable work situations and shifting wealth, to stay flexible and mobile seems related to owning less "stuff" and incurring less debt. As we have seen previously, what makes people happy is largely unrelated to large amounts of material goods (although poor people are made happier by receiving the basics of shelter, transportation, adequate food). The agile individual will own less but be more attached to what they do own.

Being flexible means some other things; among them staying out of debt. People who start businesses often live on almost nothing until the business gets established or, if the business fails, they are able to start another one. It's hard to adjust to change if you have a mountain of debt. Actually, getting into debt only makes sense if you can predict how the future will unfold or if change occurs very slowly. When the future is unpredictable and change occurs rapidly, staying out of debt makes lots of sense. Doing this often means lowering one's definition of what is necessary. Most of what you "have to have," in reality, are merely things you have been taught to want.

### 8. Follow your heart—After using your head.

Recreation and leisure are areas of life that involve love. In spite of the massive change taking place on our planet, leisure will likely continue to consist of finding a few things you love to do—and then doing them. What the world's greatly expanded population finds, or does not find, may determine our fate. Leisure service employees can help in this most critical of processes. This is a field of endeavor that deals with love— helping people find worthwhile activity that they love or can learn to love to do. As a leisure service professional you also must follow your heart—but only after using your head. The heart and the mind are, ultimately, one. A life of perpetual learning need not relegate the heart to obscurity. Leisure involves both learning and loving.

The Welsh poet Dylan Thomas, in the poem "In My Craft or Sullen Art," said he wrote all his poems for lovers: "Their arms round the griefs of the ages..." (Thomas, 1959, p. 142). To put one's arms around the griefs of this age must involve first learning what the griefs, and joys, really are.

The following poem is about change, which is the basis of our lives. The changes of one water drop could be followed forever. This book, however, will stop here; in the midst of change.

### Rain at Night

The single drop falls from a place
it cannot remember
and hurtles through the dark
with its numb song
and has no place in mind
just the falling

There are drops which
land in the salt sea

To join the restless
reaching of the tides

And drops which bounce
off the ground
becoming many smaller drops
each with memories

Which land again and
enter the dark earth
(as I hope I will)
with their longing
still whistling

                                        GCG

# References

Academy of Leisure Sciences. (1992). Issue Papers. Denton, TX: Academy of Leisure Sciences.

Alberta Centre for Well Being. (1989). Newsletter. Edmonton, AB: University of Alberta.

Anderson, W. T. (1990). *Reality isn't what it used to be.* San Francisco, CA: HarperCollins.

Antonovsky, A. (1987). *Unraveling the mystery of health: How people manage stress and stay well.* San Francisco, CA: Jossey-Bass.

Antonovsky, A. and Sagy, S. (1986). The development of a sense of coherence and its impact on responses to stress situations. *Journal of Social Psychology, 126,* 213–225.

Ashford, L. (1995, March). New perspectives on population: Lessons from Cairo. *Population Bulletin, 50*(1), 30.

Attali, J. (1991). *Millennium—Winners and losers in the new world order.* New York, NY: Random House.

Austin, D. (1996). *Learning technology—Roots and webs.* Bloomington, IN: SPRE Teaching Institute.

Ausubel, J. and Grubler, A. (1994). Working less and living longer: Long-term trends in working time and time budgets, Working Paper 94–99. Laxenburg, Austria: International Institute for Applied Systems Analysis.

Ausubel, J., Marchetti, C. and Meyer, P. S. (1997). Toward green mobility: The evolution of transport submitted for publication. Available from the Program for the Human Environment, The Rockefeller University.

Ayres, E. (1996, July/August). The expanding shadow economy. *World Watch*, pp. 11–16.

Balmer, K. and Harper, J. (1989, Spring). The perceived benefits of public leisure services: An exploratory investigation. *Loisir et Société/ Society and Leisure,* pp. 171–188.

Baltes, P. (1987). Theoretical propositions of life-span developmental psychology: On the dynamics between growth and decline. *Developmental Psychology, 23*(5), 611–626.

Batty, R. (1994). Of leisure, religion, and place. Unpublished paper. Penn State University: University Park, PA.

Bennett, G. (1987). *Crimewarps, The future of crime in America* (1st ed.). New York, NY: W. W. Norton.

Berlyne, D. E. (1960). *Conflict, arousal and curiosity.* New York, NY: MacGraw-Hill.

Berlyne, D. E. (1966). Curiosity and exploration. *Science, 153,* 25–33.

Berlyne, D. E. (1971). *Psychobiology and aesthetics.* New York, NY: Appleton-Century-Crofts.

Bloom, A. (1987). *The closing of the American mind.* New York, NY: Simon and Schuster.

Boyer, P. (1978). *Urban masses and moral order in America: 1820–1920.* Cambridge, MA: Yale University Press.

Brightbill, C. (1960). *The challenge of leisure.* Englewood Cliffs, NJ: Prentice Hall.

Brown, L. (1990–1997). *Vital signs: The trends that are shaping our future.* New York, NY: W. W. Norton.

Brown, L. (1991–1997). *State of the world.* New York, NY: W. W. Norton.

Brown, L. (1995). *Who will feed China? Wake-up call for a small planet.* New York, NY: W. W. Norton.

Butler, G. (1965). *Pioneers in public recreation.* Minneapolis, MN: Burgess.

Cappo, J. (1990). *Future scope—Success strategies for the 1990s and beyond.* New York, NY: Longmans.

Capra, F. (1988). *Uncommon wisdom—Conversations with remarkable people.* New York, NY: Simon and Schuster.

Celente, G. (1990). *Trend tracking—The system to profit from today's trends.* New York, NY: Wiley.

Chesnais, J-C. (1997). The demographic sunset of the west. *Population Today, 25*(1), 4–5.

Clawson, M. and Knetsch, J. (1966). *Economics of outdoor recreation.* Baltimore, MD: Johns Hopkins University.

Cohen, E. (1972). Toward a sociology of international tourism. *Social Research, 39*(1).

Commonwealth Fund of New York. (1993, November 27). In *The Centre Daily Times,* p. A5.

Coontz, S. (1992). *The way we never were—American families and the nostalgia trap.* New York, NY: HarperCollins.

Crawford, D. and Godbey, G. (1987). Reconceptualizing barriers to family leisure. *Leisure Sciences, 9*(1).

Crompton, J. and McGregor, B. (1994). Trends in the financing and staffing of local government park and recreation services: 1964/5 to 1990/91. *Journal of Park and Recreation Administration, 12*(3), 19–37.

Cross, G. (1993). *Time and money—The making of consumer culture.* London, UK: Routledge.

Csikszentmihalyi, M. (1975). *Beyond boredom and anxiety.* San Franciso, CA: Jossey-Bass.

Csikszentmihalyi, M. (1991a). *Activity, experience and personal growth.* Ottawa, ON: Fitness Canada.

Csikszentmihalyi, M. (1991b). *Flow—The psychology of optimal experience.* New York, NY: Harper Collins.

Csikszentmihalyi, M. (1993). *The evolving self—A psychology for the third millennium.* New York, NY: HarperCollins.

de Beauvior, S. (1952). *The second sex.* New York, NY: Vintage Books.

de Grazia, S. (1962). *Of time, work and leisure.* New York, NY: The Free Press.

Driver, B. L. (1987). The ROS planning system: Evolution, basic concepts, and research needed. *Leisure Sciences 9*(3), 201–212.

Driver, B. L., Brown, P. and Peterson, G. (1991). *The benefits of leisure.* State College, PA: Venture Publishing, Inc.

Drucker, P. (1997, March 10). Seeing things as they really are. *Forbes Magazine,* pp. 122–128.

Drucker, P. (1993). *Post-capitalist society.* New York, NY: Harper Business.

Dublin, M. (1989). *Futurehype—The tyranny of prophecy.* Toronto, ON: Viking.

Dwyer, J. (1994, August). Customer diversity and the future demand for outdoor recreation. *USDA Forest Service General Technical Report RM-252.*

Dychtwald, K. (1990). *Agewave—How the most important trend of our time will change your future.* New York, NY: Bantam.

Erlich, P. and Erlich, A. (1991). *Healing the planet—Strategies for resolving the environmental crisis.* Reading, MA: Addison-Wesley.

Faderman, L. (1985). *Surpassing the love of men—Romantic friendship and love between women from the Renaissance to the present.* London, UK: The Women's Press.

Falenmark, M. and Widstrand, C. (1992). Population and water resources: A delicate balance. *Population Bulletin, 47*(3). Washington, DC: Population Reference Bureau.

Feather, F. (1989). *G-forces: The 35 global forces restructuring our future.* Toronto, ON: Summerhill Press.

*Financial Times.* (1994, November 23). Chinese roads paved with gold. In L. Brown (1995), *Who will feed China? Wake-up call for a small planet.* New York, NY: W. W. Norton.

Fitness Canada. (1992). *Active living: Looking ahead.* Ottawa, ON: Government of Canada.

Flavin, C. and Lenssen, N. (1994, June). Powering the future: Blueprint for a sustainable electricity industry. *Worldwatch Paper, 119,* 32.

Flavin, C. and Tunali, O. (1996). Climate of hope: New strategies for stabilizing the world's atmosphere. *Worldwatch Paper, 130.*

Food and Agricultural Organization. (1994). *Production yearbook.* Rome, Italy: FAO.

Fraser, S. (Ed.). (1995). *The bell curve wars: Race, intelligence and the future of America.* New York, NY: Basic Books.

Gehl J. and Douglas, S. (1997, July 7). When the information age finally arrives. *Innovation—A NewsScan Service.* [On-line serial]. Available: http://www.newsscan.com [Note: Archives available only to subscribers; Six-week trial subscriptions available E-mail: innovation-trial@newsscan.com Message: Subscribe]

Gelbspan, R. (1995, December). The heat is on. *Harpers,* pp. 31–37.

Gerber, J., Wolff, J., Klores, W., and Brown, G.. (1989). *Life trends— Your future for the next 30 years.* New York, NY: Avon Books.

Gergen, K. (1991). *The saturated self—Dilemmas of identity in contemporary life.* New York, NY: Basic Books.

Gershuny, J. (1992). Are we running out of time? *Futures,* January/February, 1–18.

Gilder, G. (1994). *Life after television—The coming transformation of media in American life.* New York, NY: W. W. Norton.

Godbey, G. C. (1997, March 5). Memo. Center for Agile Pennsylvania Education.

Godbey, G. C. (1995, December 13). Memo. Center for Agile Pennsylvania Education.

Godbey, G. and Blazey, M. (1983). Older people in urban parks: An exploratory investigation. *Journal of Leisure Research, 15*(3).

Godbey, G. and Graefe, A. (1993, April). Rushin Americans. *American Demographics.*

Godbey, G., Graefe, A. and James, S. (1993, January). Reality and perception—Where do we fit in. *Parks and Recreation.*

Godbey, G., Graefe, A. and James, S. (1992, July). *The benefits of local recreation and park services: A nationwide study of the perceptions of the American public.* Arlington, VA: National Recreation and Park Association.

Goldman, S., Nagel, R. and Preiss, K. (1995). *Agile competitors and virtual organizations.* New York, NY: Van Nostrand Reinhold.

Hagestad, G. (1987). Able elderly in the family context: Changes, chances, and challenges. *The Gerontologist, 27*(4), 417–422.

Handy, C. (1990). *The age of unreason*. London, UK: Arrow Books.

Handy, C. (1994). *The age of paradox*. Boston, MA: Harvard Business School Press.

Harper, D., Neider, D. and Godbey, G. (1996). *The use and benefits of local government recreation and park services in Canada*. Winnipeg, MB: University of Winnipeg.

Hawking, S. (1988). *A brief history of time*. New York, NY: Bantam.

Heilbroner, R. (1995). *Visions of the future—The distant past, yesterday, today and tomorrow*. New York, NY: Oxford University Press.

Henderson, K, Bialeschki, M. D., Shaw, S. M. and Freysinger, V. (1989). *A leisure of one's own: A feminist perspective on women's leisure*. State College, PA: Venture Publishing, Inc.

Herrnstein, R. and Murphy, C. (1994). *Intelligence and class structure in American life*. New York, NY: The Free Press.

Heywood, L. (1993, Fall). Revisiting the future leisure lifestyles of Canada's older adults. *Journal of Leisurability, 20*(4), 12–21.

Hill, D. (1985). Implications of home production and inventory adjustment processes for time-of-day demand for electricity. In F. T. Juster and F. Stafford (Eds.), *Time, goods, and well-being*. Ann Arbor, MI: Institute for Social Research.

Hilton Time Values Survey. (1991). In J. Robinson and G. Godbey (1997), *Time for life—The surprising ways Americans use their time*. University Park, PA: Penn State Press.

Hochschild, A. (1989). *The second shift—Working parents and the revolution at home*. New York, NY: Viking.

Holloway, C. (1983). *The business of tourism* (2nd ed.). Plymouth, UK: MacDonald and Evans

Hood, L. (1989, October 31). Decoding the book of life. *Nova*, transcript pages 12–13. Boston: WGBH-TV.

House, J. et al. (1988). Social Relationships and Health. *Science, 241*, 540–545.

Howard, P. (1994). *The death of common sense—How law is suffocating America.* New York, NY: Random House.

Howe, N. and Strauss, B. (1993). *13 gen—Abort, retry, ignore, fail?* New York: Random House.

Huizinga, J. (1950). *Homo ludens—A study of the play element in culture.* London, UK: Paladin.

Hunnicutt, B. (Ed.) (1995, Winter). *Society for the Reduction of Human Labor Newsletter.*

Ishihara, S. (1989). *The Japan that can say no—Why Japan will be first among equals.* New York, NY: Simon and Shuster.

Ivanko, J. (1995). *Trends in leisure service professions.* Unpublished manuscript. University Park, PA: Penn State University.

James, J. (1996). *Thinking in the future tense.* New York, NY: Simon and Schuster.

Janeway, E. (1989). *The economics of chaos—On revitalizing the American economy.* New York, NY: Dutton.

Jones, S. (1993). *The language of the genes.* London, UK: Flamingo.

Kaplan, R. (1996). *The ends of the Earth—A journey to the frontiers of anarchy.* New York, NY: Vintage.

Kapuscinski, R. (1982). *Shah of shahs.* New York, NY: Harcourt, Brace, Jovanovich.

Kennedy, P. (1987). *The rise and fall of great powers.* New York, NY: Random House.

Kennedy, P. (1992). *Preparing for the 21st century.* New York, NY: Random House.

Kelly, J. (1992). *Leisure.* New York, NY: Macmillan.

Kiplinger, Austin and Knight. (1989). *America in the global '90s.* Washington, DC: Kiplinger Books.

Kotkin, J. and Kishimoto, Y. (1988). *The third century—America's resurgence in the Asian era.* New York, NY: Crown Books

Kunstler, J. (1993). *The geography of nowhere—The rise and fall of America's man-made landscape.* New York, NY: Simon and Schuster.

Lane, R. (1997). The information age is not yet here. In J. Gehl and S. Douglas (1997, July 7), *Innovation—A NewsScan Service.* [On-line serial] Available: http://www.newsscan.com [Note: Archives available only to subscribers; Six-week trial subscriptions available E-mail: innovation-trial@newsscan.com Message: Subscribe]

Lapham, L. H. (1996, August). Lights, camera, democracy! *Harper's Magazine,* pp. 33-38.

Larson, R. W., Mannell, R. C. and Zuzanek, J. (1986). Daily well-being of older adults with friends and family. *Journal of Psychology and Aging, 1,* 117–126.

Lee, M. and Driver, B. L. (1992). Benefits-based management: A new paradigm for managing amenity resources. Paper presented at The Second Canada/U.S. Workshop on Visitor Management in Parks, Forests, and Protected Areas. May 13–16, 1992. Madison, WI.

Lefkowitz, B. (1979). *Breaktime—Living without work in a nine to five world.* New York, NY: Hawthorn

Lasch, C. (1979). *The culture of narcissism.* New York, NY: Warner Books.

Light, P. (1988). *Baby boomers.* New York, NY: Norton.

Linder, S. (1969). *The harried leisure class.* New York, NY: Columbia University Press.

Little, C. (1995). *The dying of the trees: The pandemic in America's forests.* New York, NY: Viking Penguin.

Lutz, W. (1994). The future of world population. *Population Bulletin, 49*(1), 28.

MacCannell, D. (1976). *The tourist: A new theory of the leisure class.* New York, NY: Schocken Books.

Maddision, A. (1991). *Dynamic forces in capitalistic development: A long-run comparitive view.* Oxford, UK: Oxford Unversity Press.

Maddox, G. (1987). Aging differently. *The Gerontologist, 27*(5), 557–564.

Mathews, J. (1996, January 21). Greenhouse warming underway. *The Louisville Courier Journal*, p. D5.

McGinnis, J. and Lee, P. (1995). Healthy people 2000 at mid decade. *Journal of the American Medical Association, 273*(14), 1123–1128.

Merwin, W. S. (1967). *The moving target.* New York, NY: Antheneum.

Montague, P. (Ed.) (1997, May 15). Crimes of Shell. *Rachel's Environmental and Health Weekly* [On-line serial], *546.* Available FTP: ftp://ftp.std.com/periodicals/rachel File: r454: rehw 546: Crimes of Shell

Montague, P. (Ed.) (1996, January 11). The dying of the trees. *Rachel's Environmental and Health Weekly* [On-line serial], *476.* Available FTP: ftp://ftp.std.com/periodicals/rachel File: r527: rehw476: The dying of the trees

Montague, P. (Ed.) (1995, December 21). The fourth horseman: Nuclear. *Rachel's Environmental and Health Weekly* [On-line serial], *473.* Available FTP: ftp://ftp.std.com/periodicals/rachel File: r527: rehw 473: The Fourth Horseman: Nuclear Tec...

Moyers, B. (1989). *A world of ideas—Conversation with thoughtful men and women about American life today and the ideas shaping our future.* New York, NY: Doubleday.

Naisbett, J. and Aburdene, P. (1990). *Megatrends 2000—Ten new directions for the 1990s.* New York, NY: Morrow.

Naisbett, J. and Aburdene, P. (1985). *Re-inventing the corporation.* New York, NY: Warner Books.

Nash, J. B. (1953). *Philosophy of recreation and leisure.* Dubuque, IA: William C. Brown Company.

National Recreation and Park Association. (1997). Agenda. Active Living, Health Lifestyles—1997 Agenda.

Ofreuil, J. and Salomon, I. (1993). Travel Patterns of the Europeans in Everyday Life. In I. Salamon, P. Bovy, and J. Ofreuil (Eds.), *A billion trips a day—Tradition and transition in European travel patterns.* Amsterdam, Netherlands: Kluwer Academic.

Oliver, R. (1991). *The African experience.* New York, NY: HarperCollins.

Organization for Economic Cooperation and Development. (1994). *Environmental indicators.* Paris, France: OECD.

Organization for Economic Cooperation and Development. (1991). *Environmental indicators.* Paris, France: OECD.

Ornstein, R. and Erlich, P. (1989). *New world—New mind: Moving toward conscious evolution.* New York, NY: Doubleday.

Ornstein, R. and Sobel, D. (1987). *The healing brain—Breakthrough discoveries about how the brain keeps us healthy.* New York, NY: Simon and Schuster.

Osborne, D. and Gaebler, T. (1992). *Reinventing government—How the entrepreneurial spirit is transforming the public sector.* New York, NY: Penguin Books.

Oster, P. (1990). *The Mexicans—A personal portrait of a people.* New York, NY: Harper and Row.

Paepke, C. O. (1993). *The evolution of progress—The end of economic growth and the beginning of human transformation.* New York, NY: Random House.

Peele, S. (1989). *The diseasing of America: Addictions treatment out of control.* New York, NY: Lexington Books.

Perlstein, R. (1997, January). Blind alley? Field notes. *Lingua Franca,* 12–13.

Peters, T. (1988). *Thriving on chaos—A handbook for a management revolution.* New York, NY: Knopf.

Peters, T. (1994). *The Tom Peters seminar—Crazy times call for crazy organizations.* New York, NY: Vintage.

Plummer, J. (1989, Jan/Feb). Changing values: The new emphasis on self-actualization. *The Futurist.*

Pollock, L. (1987). *A lasting relationship—Parents and children over three centuries.* London, UK: Fourth Estate.

Population Reference Bureau. (1990). *Infrastructure needs: America in the 21st century.* Washington, DC: Government Printing Office, pp. 3–4.

Preiss, K., Goldman, S. and Nagel, R. (1996). *Cooperate to compete—Building agile business relationships.* New York, NY: Van Nostrand Reinhold.

Public Agenda. (1997, April 6). Many unprepared for retirement. *Centre Daily Times,* p. A7.

Putnam, R. (1995, January). Bowling alone: America's declining social capital. *Journal of Democracy, 6*(1), 65–78.

*Random House College Dictionary* (rev. ed.). (1988). New York, NY: Random House.

*Randon House Thesaurus—College Edition.* (1989). New York, NY: Random House.

Reinhold, H. (1993). *The virtual community: Homesteading on the electronic frontier.* New York, NY: HarperCollins.

Research Alert. (1992). *Future vision: The 189 most important trends of the 1990s.* Naperville, IL: Sourcebooks Trade.

Rifkin, J. (1987). *Time wars—The primary conflict in human history.* New York, NY: Henry Holt.

Rifkin, J. (1992). *Beyond beef—The rise and fall of the cattle culture.* New York, NY: Dutton.

Rifkin, J. (1995). *The end of work.* New York, NY: Tarcher-Putnam.

Riley, N. (1997, May). Gender, power and the population change. *Population Bulletin, 52*(1), 53.

Robinson, J. and Godbey, G. (1997). *Time for life—The surprising ways Americans use their time.* Univertsity Park, PA: Penn State Press.

Robinson, J. and Godbey, G. (1993). Sport fitness and the gender gap. *Leisure Sciences, 15*(4), 291–308.

Rockefeller-Growald, E. and Luks, A. (1988, March). The immunity of samaritans—Beyond self. *American Health,* pp. 51-55.

Roper Poll. (1992). In J. Robinson and G. Godbey. The great American slowdown. *American Demographics.*

Roper Poll. (1991). *Roper reports, 91-10.* New York, NY: Roper Starch Worldwide.

Roper Organization. (1990). *Roper reports, 90-10.* New York, NY: Roper Startch Worldwide.

Ryan, J. C. (1992). Life Support: Conserving Biological Diversity. *Worldwatch Paper 108.* Washington, DC: Worldwatch Institute.

Rybczynski, W. (1991). *Waiting for the weekend.* New York, NY: Viking.

Sacks, P. (1996). *Generation X goes to college: An eye opening account of teaching in postmodern America.* LaSalle, IL: Open Court.

Sagoff, M. (1997, June). Do we consume too much? *Atlantic Monthly,* 80–96.

Saltzman, A. (1991). *Downshifting—Reinventing success on a slower track.* New York, NY: HarperCollins.

Samuelson, P. (1995). *The good life and its discontents: The American dream in an age of entitlement: 1945–1995.* New York, NY: Times Books.

Samuelson, P. (1997, April 29). Living well? *U.S. News and World Reports,* p. 79.

Schneider, W. (1992, July). The suburban century begins. *The Atlantic,* 33–44.

Schor, J. (1991). *The overworked American—The unexpected decline of leisure.* New York, NY: Basic Books.

Sessoms, D. (1993). *Eight decades of leadership development—A history of programs of professional preparation in parks and recreation 1909–1989.* Arlington, VA: National Recreation and Park Association.

Shlain, L. (1991). *Art and physics—Parallel visions in space, time and light.* New York, NY: William Morrow.

Simons, G. (1985). *Silicone shock: The menace of the computer invasion.* New York, NY: Blackwell.

Skinner, B. F. (1971). *Beyond freedom and dignity.* New York, NY: Bantom Books.

Smith, R. (1995, May). Trends in therapeutic recreation. *Parks and Recreation,* pp. 67–71.

Sobel, J. and Ornstein, R. (1987). *Healthy pleasures.* Reading, MA: Addison Wesley.

Soldo, B. J. (1980). America's elderly in the 1980s. *Population Bulletin, 35*(4), 1–47.

Spannuth, J. (1989, February) Water—The new fitness center. *Parks and Recreation.*

Stallones, R. A. (1996). *Public health monograph 76.* Washington, DC: Government Printing Office.

Stanford Research International. (1997). In J. Gehl and S. Douglas (Eds.) (1997, January 23), *Innovation—A NewsScan Service,* p. 4. [On-line serial] Available: http://www.newsscan.com [Note: Archives available only to subscribers; Six-week trial subscriptions available E-mail: innovation-trial@newsscan.com Message: Subscribe]

Stengel, R. (1996, July 22). Bowling together. *Time,* p. 35.

Stienstra, T. (1997, June 29). Big changes afoot at the forest service, *San Francisco Examiner,* p. C-16.

Sykes, C. (1992). *A nation of victims—The decay of the American character.* New York, NY: St. Martins Press.

Szwak, L. (1989). The nonprofit sector as recreation suppliers. *Trends 26*(2), 36.

Troll, L., Miller, S. and Atchley, R. (1979). *Families in later life.* Belmont, CA: Wadsworth Publishing Co.

Proceedings of the 4th International Outdoor Recreation and Tourism Trends Symposium (1995). Compiled by J. D. Thompson, B. Lime, B. Gartner and W. Sames. Minneapolis, MN: University of Minnesota.

The Republic of China Yearbook. (1994). Taipei, Taiwan: Government Information Office.

Thomas, D. (1959). *Collected poems.* New York, NY: New Directions.

Thomas, M. and Godbey, G. (1993) Value shifts and social trends: Implications for recreation. *Journal of Leisurability—Futures Issue, 20*(4), 28–38

Trussell, G. (1996). Selected impacts of international visitation on domestic resources. In J. Thompson, D. Lime, B. Gartner and W. Sames (Eds.), Proceedings of the 4th International Outdoor Recreation & Tourism Trends Symposium. Minneapolis, University of Minnesota.

*UNDP Human Development Report.* (1994). New York, NY: Oxford University Press.

UNICEF. (1995). *The state of the world's children.* New York, NY: Oxford University Press.

United Nations. (1994). *World population prospects: The 1994 revision.* New York, NY: United Nations.

United Nations. (1993). *World urbanization prospects: The 1992 revision.* New York, NY: United Nations.

U.S. Bureau of the Census. (1975). *Historical statistics of the United States: Colonial times to 1970.* Washington, DC: Government Printing Office.

U.S. Bureau of the Census. (1993a). *Current population reports P25–1104.* Washington, DC: Government Printing Office.

U.S. Bureau of the Census. (1993b). *Population reports 1092.* Washington, DC: Government Printing Office.

U.S. Bureau of the Census. (1995). *Current population reports PLS–1104; middle series projections.* Washington, DC: Government Printing Office.

U.S. Bureau of the Census. (1997). In *The Centre Daily Times* (1997, January 26), p. A5.

U.S. Department of Education. (1993, November 24). Quoted by Pat Carr and Jeff Dionise, Knight-Ridder Tribune, cited in *Centre Daily Times,* p. 7A.

U.S. Department of Health and Human Services. (1990). Public Health Service. *Healthy People 2000.* Washington, DC: Government Printing Office.

Van Crevald, M. (1991). *The transformation of war.* New York, NY: The Free Press.

Visaria, L. and Visaria, P. (1995, October). India's population in transition. *Population Bulletin, 50*(3).

Waggoner, P., Ausubel, J. H., and Wernick, I. K. (1996). Lightening the tread of population on the land: American examples. *Population and Development Review 22*(3): 531–545.

Walker, E. L. (1980). *Psychological complexity and preference: A hedgehog theory of behavior.* Monterey, CA: Brooks-Cole.

Weiner, J. (1990). *The next one hundred years—Shaping the fate of our living planet.* New York, NY: Bantam.

Wernick, I., Herman, R., Govind, S. and Ausubel, J. (1996, Summer). Materialization and dematerialization: Measures and trends. *Daedalus, 125*(3).

Whyte, D. (1992, Fall). Key trends and issues impacting local government recreation and park administration in the 1990s: A focus for strategic management and research. *Journal of Park and Recreation Administration, 10*(3), 89–107.

World Future Society. (1991). *The art of forecasting: A brief introduction to thinking about the future.* Washington, DC: World Future Society.

World Tourism Organization. (1994). In Ivanko, J. (1995). *Trends in leisure service professions.* Unpublished manuscript. University Park, PA: Penn State University.

Zeldin, T. (1994). *An intimate history of humanity.* London, UK: Harper.

# Authors Index

## A

Academy of Leisure Sciences 173-174, *190–191*
Alberta Centre for Well Being 139
Anderson, W. T. 77–78
Antonovsky, A. 138, 141
Attali, J. 89
Austin, D. *117*
Ausubel, J. 42, 43, 51, 64, 65, 66, 166
Ayres, E. 130

## B

Baltes, P. 97–98
Bandura, A. 141
Batty, R. 90
Berlyne, D. E. 141
Blazey, M. 99, 144–145
Brightbill, C. 152
Brown, L. 4, 41
Brown, P. 218
Butler, G. 13

## C

Capra, F. 137, 159
Chesnais, J-C. 18
Clawson, M. 99
Cohen, E. 131
Commonwealth Fund of New York 105
Coontz, S. 148
Crawford, D. 143
Crompton, J. 191–192
Csikszentmihalyi, M. 88, 101, 141, 142–143, 209

## D

De Laquil, P. *37*
Demographic and Health Surveys *21*

Driver, B. L. 218, 219–220
Drucker, P. 116, 148, 166, 178, 179, 180, 189–190, 194, 197, 198–199
Dwyer, J. *102*, 103

## E

Environmental Research Foundation 68
Erlich, P. 124–125, 137

## F

Faderman, L. 83
Falkenmark, M. 49
Fitness Canada 143–144
Flavin, C. 38
*Financial Times* 65
Food and Agricultural Organization (FAO) *44*

## G

Gaebler, T. 188–189
Gelbspan, R. 29
Gergen, K. 78–79
Gershuny, J. 167, 173
Gilder, G. 5, 60, 142
Goldman, S. 211, 213, 216–218, 220, 222
Godbey, Galen 117–118
Godbey, Geoffrey 58, 59, 64, 99, 110, 143, 144–145, 148, *150*, 152, 153, 158–159, 163, 168–169, *171*, 199–200, *201*, 203
Govind, S. 42, 43
Graefe, A. 144, 148, 153, 158–159, 163, 199–200, *201*, 203
Grubler, A. 166

# Subject Index

# ❋ Other Books From Venture Publishing ❋

The A•B•Cs of Behavior Change: Skills for Working with Behavior Problems in Nursing Homes
    by Margaret D. Cohn, Michael A. Smyer and Ann L. Horgas
Activity Experiences and Programming Within Long-Term Care
    by Ted Tedrick and Elaine R. Green
The Activity Gourmet
    by Peggy Powers
Advanced Concepts for Geriatric Nursing Assistants
    by Carolyn A. McDonald
Adventure Education
    edited by John C. Miles and Simon Priest
Aerobics of the Mind: Keeping the Mind Active in Aging—A New Perspective on Programming for Older Adults
    by Marge Engleman
Assessment: The Cornerstone of Activity Programs
    by Ruth Perschbacher
At-Risk Youth and Gangs—A Resource Manual for the Parks and Recreation Professional—Expanded and Updated
    by The California Park and Recreation Society
Behavior Modification in Therapeutic Recreation: An Introductory Learning Manual
    by John Dattilo and William D. Murphy
Benefits of Leisure
    edited by B. L. Driver, Perry J. Brown and George L. Peterson
Benefits of Recreation Research Update
    by Judy M. Sefton and W. Kerry Mummery
Beyond Bingo: Innovative Programs for the New Senior
    by Sal Arrigo, Jr., Ann Lewis and Hank Mattimore
Both Gains and Gaps: Feminist Perspectives on Women's Leisure
    by Karla Henderson, M. Deborah Bialeschki, Susan M. Shaw and Valeria J. Freysinger
The Community Tourism Industry Imperative—The Necessity, The Opportunities, Its Potential
    by Uel Blank
Dimensions of Choice: A Qualitative Approach to Recreation, Parks, and Leisure Research
    by Karla A. Henderson
Effective Management in Therapeutic Recreation Service
    by Gerald S. O'Morrow and Marcia Jean Carter
Evaluating Leisure Services: Making Enlightened Decisions
    by Karla A. Henderson with M. Deborah Bialeschki
The Evolution of Leisure: Historical and Philosophical Perspectives (Second Printing)
    by Thomas Goodale and Geoffrey Godbey
File O' Fun: A Recreation Planner for Games and Activities, Third Edition
    by Jane Harris Ericson and Diane Ruth Albright
The Game Finder—A Leader's Guide to Great Activities
    by Annette C. Moore
Getting People Involved in Life and Activities: Effective Motivating Techniques
    by Jeanne Adams
Great Special Events and Activities
    by Annie Morton, Angie Prosser and Sue Spangler

*Inclusive Leisure Services: Responding to the Rights of People with Disabilities*
  by John Dattilo
*Internships in Recreation and Leisure Services: A Practical Guide for Students, Second Edition*
  by Edward E. Seagle, Jr., Ralph W. Smith and Lola M. Dalton
*Interpretation of Cultural and Natural Resources*
  by Douglas M. Knudson, Ted T. Cable and Larry Beck
*Introduction to Leisure Services—7th Edition*
  by H. Douglas Sessoms and Karla A. Henderson
*Leadership and Administration of Outdoor Pursuits, Second Edition*
  by Phyllis Ford and James Blanchard
*Leadership in Leisure Services: Making a Difference*
  by Debra J. Jordan
*Leisure And Family Fun (LAFF)*
  by Mary Atteberry-Rogers
*The Leisure Diagnostic Battery: Users Manual and Sample Forms*
  by Peter A. Witt and Gary Ellis
*Leisure Diagnostic Battery Computer Software*
  by Gary Ellis and Peter A. Witt
*Leisure Education: A Manual of Activities and Resources*
  by Norma J. Stumbo and Steven R. Thompson
*Leisure Education II: More Activities and Resources*
  by Norma J. Stumbo
*Leisure Education III: More Goal-Oriented Activities*
  by Norma J. Stumbo
*Leisure Education Program Planning: A Systematic Approach*
  by John Dattilo and William D. Murphy
*Leisure in Your Life: An Exploration, Fourth Edition*
  by Geoffrey Godbey
*Leisure Services in Canada: An Introduction*
  by Mark S. Searle and Russell E. Brayley
*Leveraging the Benefits of Parks and Recreation: The Pheonix Project*
  by The California Park and Recreation Society
*The Life Story Re-Play Circle*
  by Rosilyn Wilder
*Marketing for Parks, Recreation, and Leisure*
  by Ellen L. O'Sullivan
*Models of Change in Municipal Parks and Recreation: A Book of Innovative Case Studies*
  edited by Mark E. Havitz
*Nature and the Human Spirit: Toward an Expanded Land Management Ethic*
  edited by B. L. Driver, Daniel Dustin, Tony Baltic, Gary Elsner and George Peterson
*Outdoor Recreation Management: Theory and Application, Third Edition*
  by Alan Jubenville and Ben Twight
*Planning Parks for People*
  by John Hultsman, Richard L. Cottrell and Wendy Zales Hultsman
*Private and Commercial Recreation*
  edited by Arlin Epperson
*The Process of Recreation Programming Theory and Technique, Third Edition*
  by Patricia Farrell and Herberta M. Lundegren

# ❊ Other Books From Venture Publishing ❊

*Protocols for Recreation Therapy Programs*
    edited by Jill Kelland, along with the Recreation Therapy Staff at Alberta
    Hospital Edmonton
*Quality Management: Applications for Therapeutic Recreation*
    edited by Bob Riley
*Recreation and Leisure: Issues in an Era of Change, Third Edition*
    edited by Thomas Goodale and Peter A. Witt
*The Recreation Connection to Self-Esteem—A Resource Manual for the Park, Recreation
    and Community Services Professional*
    by The California Park and Recreation Society
*Recreation Economic Decisions: Comparing Benefits and Costs, Second Edition*
    by John B. Loomis and Richard G. Walsh
*Recreation Programming and Activities for Older Adults*
    by Jerold E. Elliott and Judith A. Sorg-Elliott
*Recreation Programs that Work for At-Risk Youth: The Challenge of Shaping the Future*
    edited by Peter A. Witt and John L. Crompton
*Reference Manual for Writing Rehabilitation Therapy Treatment Plans*
    by Penny Hogberg and Mary Johnson
*Research in Therapeutic Recreation: Concepts and Methods*
    edited by Marjorie J. Malkin and Christine Z. Howe
*A Social History of Leisure Since 1600*
    by Gary Cross
*A Social Psychology of Leisure*
    by Roger C. Mannell and Douglas A. Kleiber
*The Sociology of Leisure*
    by John R. Kelly and Geoffrey Godbey
*Therapeutic Activity Intervention with the Elderly: Foundations and Practices*
    by Barbara A. Hawkins, Marti E. May and Nancy Brattain Rogers
*Therapeutic Recreation: Cases and Exercises*
    by Barbara C. Wilhite and M. Jean Keller
*Therapeutic Recreation in the Nursing Home*
    by Linda Buettner and Shelley L. Martin
*Therapeutic Recreation Protocol for Treatment of Substance Addictions*
    by Rozanne W. Faulkner
*Time for Life—The Surprising Ways Americans Use Their Time*
    by John Robinson and Geoffrey Godbey
*A Training Manual for Americans With Disabilities Act Compliance in Parks and Recre-
    ation Settings*
    by Carol Stensrud
*Understanding Leisure and Recreation: Mapping the Past, Charting the Future*
    edited by Edgar L. Jackson and Thomas L. Burton

Venture Publishing, Inc.
1999 Cato Avenue
State College, PA 16801

Phone: (814) 234-4561; FAX: (814) 234-1651